Democracy, Social Justice and The Role of Trade Unions

Advance Praise for *Democracy, Social Justice and the Role of Trade Unions*

"In an era when democratic institutions are under great strain, this important volume brings together leading scholars to examine the central constitutional role of trade unions as guarantors of democracy and social justice. The chapters consider the multiple challenges presented by climate change, migration, the erosion of secure employment, the global pandemic, and international trade. The need for strong and democratic trade unions has never been so urgent. This book is a vital scholarly contribution to these debates." —Alan Bogg, Professor of Labour Law, Bristol University, UK

"After decades of being decimated by hostile and repressive politics, this important book considers whether trade unions can emerge once more to cement their place as a formidable democratic institution; to give workers a proper voice at work and on the political stage . I commend it to you." —Josh Bornstein, Principal Lawyer, Maurice Blackburn Lawyers, Australia

"This collection of essays by eminent experts provides a timely analysis of the vital role that trade unions can, and must, play in meeting the existential challenges facing contemporary industrial democracies. It is essential reading for anyone concerned about the impact of disruptive technologies, climate change, and neoliberal ideology on labour markets." —Joellen Riley Munton, Professor of Law, The University of Technology Sydney, Australia

"*Democracy, Social Justice and The Role of Trade Unions* is a timely co-edited volume examining the democratic role of trade unions in the context of increasing precariousness in labour markets and capital mobility coupled with decline of worker representation in an era of pandemic capitalism. Advancing novel theoretical and empirical approaches and claims, contributors explore the role of trade unions in struggles for social justice in the form of decommodification of labour and economic democracy." —Leah Vosko, Professor of Political Science and Canada Research Chair in The Political Economy of Gender & Work, York University, Canada

"This edited collection makes a significant and timely contribution to labour law and industrial relations, especially given the ongoing impact of the COVID-19 pandemic. It brings a strong scholarly focus to the often fraught role of trade unions as social partners, particularly in face of the fragmentation of employment relationships. A particular innovation is the attention paid to the democratising role of unions, both within nation states and transnationally."—Sara Charlesworth, Professor of Gender, Work & Regulation, RMIT University, Australia

"This book provides a clear-sighted vision for the remedial role of trade unions and social democratic governance in an age of atomising and precarious work relationships and climate crisis. It is a 'must read' for labour policy-makers and trade union leaders alike." —Dr Eugene Schofield-Georgeson, Senior Lecturer in Law, The University of Technology Sydney, Australia

Democracy, Social Justice and The Role of Trade Unions

We the Working People

Edited by
Caroline Kelly and Joo-Cheong Tham

ANTHEM PRESS

Anthem Press
An imprint of Wimbledon Publishing Company
www.anthempress.com

This edition first published in UK and USA 2021
by ANTHEM PRESS
75–76 Blackfriars Road, London SE1 8HA, UK
or PO Box 9779, London SW19 7ZG, UK
and
244 Madison Ave #116, New York, NY 10016, USA

British Library Cataloguing-in-Publication Data
A catalogue record for this book is available from the British Library.

Library of Congress Control Number: 2021942257

ISBN-13: 978-1-78527-780-1 (Hbk)
ISBN-10: 1-78527-780-4 (Hbk)

Cover image: Craig Abraham, The Age

This title is also available as an e-book.

CONTENTS

FOREWORD

Sally McManus

It has always been true that working people have had to fight to improve their lot in life. Fighting for what is right is in our DNA.

In 2020, though, workers were fighting a very different battle – saving Australia from the ravages of a devastating pandemic that threatened to plunge millions of people into economic distress and a cataclysmic health crisis.

Australian Unions met that crisis in the only way it knows how. Through collective action, a commitment to community and the well-being of others, and a conviction that science and solidarity would be the equal of any challenge we had to face.

And so, while the pandemic is exacting a terrible toll on countless countries, Australia has so far been saved from the very worst that COVID-19 can exact. The resolve to commit to each other and prioritise the needs of the community from this country's essential workers helped us to hold the line.

2020 in Australia was the year of the worker.

These are the everyday heroes working in our shops, our early education and health systems, cleaning our workspaces and keeping them COVID free, running public transport, teaching our children and in countless other sectors. They are what saw Australia through its worst crisis in living memory.

The values that have underpinned this enduring Australian social contract are union values. They also reside in the long and proud history of international trade union movement and institutions like the International Labour Organization.

This book is testament to the vital role the labour movement plays as a powerful civic force for good – underpinning democracy and winning social justice.

Despite years of vilification by its political opponents, misrepresentation by self-interested media oligarchs and attempts to pass hostile legislation to weaken the union movement, here we stand, resilient, focused and determined to continue to do what is right for working people.

There is still plenty to be done.

The pandemic exposed the Australian economy's dependence on insecure work. A virus will exploit a willing host, and COVID-19 found the perfect partner in insecure work: workers on those arrangements faced the invidious choice of working on regardless of their health or not working at all and not getting paid.

This addiction to insecure work needs to end.

Wage growth has stalled for nearly a decade while the profits of big companies continue to grow.

The attacks on the retirement plans of millions of Australians by those who spread false choices between a healthy superannuation balance and decent pay need to be stared down and defeated.

The growing gender income and savings gap must be closed if we believe that everyone should share in the wealth of this country.

To help meet these challenges, I welcome the contributions in this book. They demonstrate that when working people come together to change the world, they can indeed be the change the world needs.

ACKNOWLEDGEMENTS

We would like to thank the team at Anthem Press for its support, professionalism and care in the editing and publication process. Megan Grieving, in particular, was wonderfully supportive of the book and also understanding of the challenges we faced in bringing the book together in a pandemic. We would also like to acknowledge those who made the Symposium on the Centenary of the International Labour Organization: Democracy, Labour Law and the Role of Trade Unions held at the Melbourne Law School between 18 and 19 July 2019 possible. This book is an outcome of this symposium which was organised under the auspices of the Centre for Employment and Labour Relations Law and in partnership with the Australian Council of Trade Unions. The symposium was also generously supported by Gordon Legal and Maurice Blackburn Lawyers; in addition, the evening panel was supported by the Fair Work Commission. We also thank Julian A. Sempill for his efforts as one of the organisers of the symposium. Last but not least, we would like to recognise the support of the Centre for Employment and Labour Relations Law and its members.

Chapter 1

DEMOCRACY AND SOCIAL JUSTICE AS ORGANISING PRINCIPLES

Joo-Cheong Tham and Caroline Kelly

Trade unions are central to organised social life. They are among the largest voluntary organisations in society. They represent hundreds of millions of workers[1] and, as workplace organisations, they are often the only effective vehicle to give voice to working people. They are often too a significant presence in politics. For instance, the peak international trade union body the International Trade Union Confederation represents 200 million workers in 163 countries and regularly participates in key policy-making forums such as G20, the International Monetary Fund, the World Bank and the International Labour Organization (ILO).[2]

There is equally no doubt that the role of trade unions globally and in Australia is under serious challenge. The ILO Global Commission on the Future of Work observed that 'changes in legal frameworks, together with changes in the organization of work and the persistence of informal employment, make it harder for workers to organize and represent their collective interests'.[3] A publication arising from an ILO symposium on the future of trade unions similarly commented that 'it has become harder for trade unions in both developed and emerging countries to protect the rights of workers and working conditions, as shown not only in the reduction of unionization, but also the fall in the labour share of income in most countries'.[4] Among the key challenges it nominated were 'technology, climate change and the increasing complexity of globalization',[5] sentiments that clearly correspond with the recognition in the *ILO Centenary Declaration for the Future of Work* that the present is 'a time of transformative change in the world of work, driven by technological innovations, demographic shifts, environmental and climate change, and globalization, as well as a time of persistent inequalities, which have profound impacts on the nature and future of work, and on the place and dignity of people in it'.[6]

These global tendencies are evident in Australia. Union membership is declining as a proportion of the labour force. Low and declining union density (around 15 per cent) and shrinking coverage of collective bargaining mean that many workplaces, especially in the private sector, are union-free and/or union-hostile zones.[7] Controversies surrounding a number of union officials have called into the question the legitimacy of trade unions. And for some governments, trade unions are not social partners but rather targets of restrictive legislation. Alongside these are the challenges stemming from precarious work, digitisation of work (including the rise of the gig economy), migration, trade liberalisation and the climate crisis.

The COVID-19 pandemic is likely to deepen the difficulties faced by trade unions. Whilst in many countries, including Australia, trade unions were enlisted by governments to assist in the immediate management of the pandemic, their continued role as social partners is moot.[8] High levels of unemployment and underemployment[9] will inevitably weaken the bargaining power of unions, most of whom will be forced into concessional bargaining with the extensive industry and workplace restructuring underway.

Two connected threads run through these challenges to trade unions. The first is the ascendancy of capital over labour, specifically the growing power of employers. This is due in part to the failure of trade unions to effectively organise large parts of the workforce, particularly those in precarious work, calling into question the legitimacy of trade unions as representatives of working people. As consequential, if not more so, are other structural factors. The increased mobility of capital has expanded the range of exit options for employers with the prospect (or threat) of transferring work to overseas jurisdictions with lower wages and less labour protection lurking in many industries, particularly those exposed to global competition. Reconfiguration of the firm has also tended to undermine the ability of trade unions to organise. Vertical disintegration of the firm has meant less reliance on labour being supplied through stable employment relationships, an institutional feature supportive of trade unions, and more so through contracting arrangements.[10] The transnationalisation of production through mega-transnational firms and global supply chains not only challenges the trade union movement through massive agglomeration of capital but also puts in doubt the locus of their (traditional) activity, the nation-state.

The second thread is the ideological climate of the past four decades which goes by the shorthand of ‘neoliberalism’. Notwithstanding neoliberalism’s messy contradictions especially between rhetoric and policy,[11] its general effect has been to undermine trade unionism in principle and in practice. Key principles of trade unionism are delegitimised under neoliberalism. It adopts a quantitative understanding of economic prosperity anchored in economic growth (as measured by GDP), job growth (as measured by the number of jobs) and control of inflation. In this framework, concerns regarding the quality of working conditions and jobs – which go to the heart of trade unionism – become of lesser, even marginal, importance.

Relatedly, democracy and social justice take on a narrow meaning under neoliberalism. Democracy is equated with electoral democracy with workplaces carved out from the sphere of democracy. Even then there is a shrunken notion of electoral democracy, what some have characterised as 'post-democracy', with popular participation confined to voting every few years and public decision making principally determined by elite bargaining, a process that naturally lends itself to the dominance of commercial interests.[12] The scope of social justice (what goods should be subject to distributive principles)[13] is also constricted to opportunities to compete for a job through 'human capital' and the ability to engage in consumer spending. Outside scope are the quality of working conditions and, importantly, the power relations at work.[14]

Features of the institutional context supportive of trade unions have also been undercut. Of salience here is the abandonment of 'full employment' as a central goal of public policy. Indeed, unemployment (at some level) is not only accepted but welcomed as an antidote to wage inflation. Predictably, the bargaining power of labour as a class and also of organised labour have been weakened through the 'reserve army of labour'. Bound up with all this is the delegitimisation of trade unions as institutions vital to economic prosperity. A neoliberal perspective portrays trade unions as anticompetitive organisations that are not only anathema to economic freedom (understood as freedom of contract) but also enemies of job and productivity growth, barriers to workplace innovation and adaptability as well as a persistent cause of inflation.

How trade unions can revitalise themselves to address these challenges, in what David Peetz has aptly characterised as a 'contrary world',[15] is the most pressing question for the labour movement. Clearly a complex range of considerations bear upon this question, including the strategic directions taken by trade unions, employer strategies and the extent to which the political-economy is supportive or hostile to trade unionism. What is clear, however, and a key premise of this book, is that these challenges will not be effectively met without a clear and abiding sense of the central principles of labour movement, without a forthright grasp of its vocation.

Democracy, Social Justice and Trade Unions

This book examines the contemporary role of trade unions in society through the principles of democracy and social justice.

Democracy – the essence of which is well captured by the proclamation of the *Universal Declaration of Human Rights* that 'the will of the people shall be the basis of authority of government'[16] – is constitutive of trade unions in four ways.[17] First, as representative organisations, democracy is central to the internal regulation of trade unions. Second, trade unions give voice to the concerns of their members and other workers in the political process including governmental and electoral processes. Third, trade unions contribute to democratising the workplace, particularly through collective bargaining, a form of social dialogue as recognised by the ILO.[18] As a counter to the 'private government' of the workplace by employers,[19] this democratic function of trade unions is premised upon the legitimacy and importance of economic democracy.[20]

The fourth way in which democracy is constitutive of trade unions is powerfully recognised by the *ILO Declaration of Philadelphia*, a landmark document that endures in its relevance.[21] The declaration lays down the core principle that 'the representatives of workers and employers, enjoying equal status with those of governments, join with them in free discussion and democratic decision with a view to the promotion of the common welfare'.[22] In a more recent affirmation, the ILO Global Commission on the Future of Work stated that 'collective representation of workers and employers through social dialogue is a public good that lies at the heart of democracy'.[23] Hugh Sinzheimer, one of the founders of the discipline of labour law, advocated this mode of government as the 'economic constitution' of nation-states.[24]

It is significant that democracy has been selected as a key theme. The democratic role of trade unions has been relatively neglected, with emphasis predominantly being given to their social justice role (in the workplace). A broad understanding of democracy is adopted in this book with democratic principles applying to all spheres where there is government, where there is systematic power exerted – not just a space conventionally, and, we say, arbitrarily marked out as 'public' or 'political'.[25]

Social justice is the other principle underlying this book. A cogent understanding of this principle is found in the *ILO Declaration of Philadelphia* which affirms that:

> all human beings, irrespective of race, creed or sex, have the right to pursue both their material well-being and their spiritual development in conditions of freedom and dignity, of economic security and equal opportunity.[26]

This is a goal that the declaration unequivocally posits as 'the central aim of national and international policy'.[27]

The principle of social justice is central to trade unions. It underpins their efforts to set labour standards, including through collective agreements, in order to secure for workers a fair share of income vis-à-vis employers, what the *ILO Declaration of Philadelphia* eloquently characterises as 'a just share of the fruits of progress to all'.[28] This social justice function is related to another: trade unions protecting workers from overbearing employer power. They provide a countervailing force to the superior bargaining power employers would enjoy when markets are not regulated by labour standards. As Justice Henry Bournes Higgins vividly put it:

> The power of the employer to withhold bread is a much more effective weapon than the power of the employee to refuse labour. Freedom of contract under such circumstances is surely misnamed; it should rather be called despotism in contract [...] the worker is in the same position as [...] a traveller, when he had to give up his money to a highway man for the privilege of life.[29]

And it is not just the unequal power employers have over workplace bargains but also the exercise of power generally at the workplace that is tamed by the countervailing power of trade unions – they provide a curb to managerial prerogative.

These social justice functions connect deeply with the decommodification function of trade unions. They are institutions that seek to insulate – to some extent – workers from the pressures and vagaries of labour markets. Effective trade unions can breathe life into a fundamental principle of the ILO, the principle that labour is not a commodity.[30] In doing so, they contribute to the conditions of security, freedom and dignity central to the goal of social justice laid out in the *ILO Declaration of Philadelphia.*

This goal further reminds us that the principle of social justice as it relates to trade unions pertains not only to equalising the position of labour vis-à-vis capital but to equality among workers. The universalism and egalitarianism of this goal is patent: it speaks of 'all human beings irrespective of race, creed or sex' and the condition of 'equal opportunity'. These principles are affirmed by the *ILO Declaration on Fundamental Principles and Rights at Work* which identifies as a fundamental principle, the elimination of discrimination in respect of employment and occupation.[31] The *ILO Centenary Declaration for the Future of Work* moreover commits the ILO to 'achieving gender equality at work through a transformative agenda'.[32]

The principle of social justice, it should be emphasised, does not become otiose with globalisation. On the contrary, the social justice goal of the *ILO Declaration of Philadelphia* seeks, as is the raison d'être of the ILO, to deal with the social impact of globalisation,[33] in particular, the downward pressure on decent working conditions that tends to accompany global competition.[34] It is the 'universal aspiration for social justice' that the *ILO Declaration on Social Justice for a Fair Globalization* affirms in the 'the present context of globalization'.[35]

Trade unionism brings together the principles of democracy and social justice. This can be clearly seen with freedom of association. As affirmed by the *International Covenant on Civil and Political Rights*, the ability to form and act through trade unions is an incident of freedom of association, a basic human right.[36] This same freedom together with the effective recognition of the right to collective bargaining are fundamental rights at work (as recognised by the ILO).[37] These are rights integral to the democratic effectiveness of trade unions, to their ability to give voice to the concerns, grievances and aspirations of working people. Not only that, freedom of association is essential for the pursuit of the social justice goal of trade unions. T. H. Marshall, for instance, placed this freedom at the centre of 'industrial citizenship' where freedom of association, a civil right in Marshall's view, is extended through the right to collective bargaining which, in turn, aims to secure social rights, particularly, the right to a living wage.[38] Indeed, the *ILO Declaration of Philadelphia* states more generally that 'freedom of expression and of association are essential to sustained progress'.[39]

Democracy and social justice are also united in the principle of solidarity. Solidarity is etched deep into the psyche of trade unions. It arises from the essential fact that acting in concert, acting through trade unions, is solidarity in action. It also stems from a recognition of workers as a class in capitalist societies and that in an economic system based on competition among workers (labour *markets*), the fates of workers are intertwined and interdependent – that an injury to one is an injury to all. This is a recognition reflected in the *ILO Declaration of Philadelphia* which stresses that 'poverty anywhere constitutes a danger to prosperity everywhere'.[40] The necessity of solidarity through trade unions also arises from a further recognition that workers as a class are in a grossly unequal relationship to employers as a class; that acting individually for the overwhelming majority of workers is, as Justice Higgins concluded, a formula for 'despotism in contract'.[41] It is this that allows us to appreciate the truth of the trade union slogan 'united we bargain, divided we beg'.

Solidarity through trade unions, we should add, is not necessarily confined to the boundaries of particular unions, workplaces, industries or even nation-states. Indeed, the trade union movement is strongly informed by the sentiments of international solidarity. The *ILO Declaration of Philadelphia* is again instructive, speaking of 'the war against want [being] carried on with unrelenting vigour within each nation, and by continuous and concerted international effort'.[42]

That international solidarity is not a naïve aspiration but rather a practical imperative is brought home by the COVID-19 pandemic. The *Joint Statement on COVID-19 by International Organisation of Employers and International Trade Union Confederation* emphasises that solidarity is 'key to prevent the spread and protect lives and livelihoods'.[43] The World Health Organization director general has said that international solidarity is foremost in overcoming the pandemic: that 'either we get through this pandemic together, or we fail', that 'either we stand together, or we fall apart'.[44] Trade unions are strongly positioned to positively contribute here: as Sharan Burrow, general secretary of the International Trade Union Confederation, observed, 'the antidote to this crisis is in the solidarity that is the lifeblood of trade unions, throughout history and today'.[45]

Outline of the Book

The book treats democracy and social justice as organising principles. By this, we mean to refer to several things. Democracy and social justice found the concerns and issues addressed in this book. More than this, the book is based on the recognition that democracy and social justice matter greatly to trade unions and their members. This recognition, however, does not imply a sanguine acceptance that trade unions invariably work towards these goals. On the contrary, these principles provide critical stand points for evaluating the aims, strategies and activities of trade unions. These principles, then, occupy a liminal space between 'what is' and 'what ought to be'.

There is also a further sense that the principles of democracy and social justice themselves need to be organised, to be given structure and meaning, and that this process of elaboration should be anchored in particular contexts, specifically the contemporary challenges faced by trade unions. In this way, the book seeks to combine theory, context and practice.

The first four chapters of the book address the relationship between democracy and trade unions. The chapter by David Peetz deals with the theme of economic democracy and trade unions. It, first, compares democratic and shareholder decision-making models. It then discusses three paths to enhancing economic democracy: first, leave formal decision-making power with those who hold it but, through countervailing force, require owners to take account of other interests in decision making; second, change the decision-making process; and third, change the owners of capital themselves. Unions, Peetz argues, are most relevant to the first of these paths, but can also facilitate the achievement of the other two. The implications of this analysis are further explored by Peetz in relation to the climate crisis with his chapter specifically considering the democratic role that can be played by workers' funds.

Julian A. Sempill in his chapter continues on the subject of economic democracy and the role of trade unions. The impulse to economic democracy, Sempill argues, is in urgent need of revival and trade unions ought to contribute to its resurgence. In order to persuade people that democratic principles are relevant to economic life, his chapter contends that the orthodoxy of the liberal-democratic-capitalist regime must be challenged especially in the context of climate change and the COVID-19 pandemic in order to avoid a Hobson's choice between saving lives and saving livelihoods.

The chapter by Caroline Kelly shifts the focus to regulation of the internal affairs of trade unions. Her analysis of the shifting regulatory approaches in Australia leads her to argue that the traditional goal of ensuring 'democratic control' of trade unions by the rank-and-file membership – achieved in part through the application of principles and techniques associated with administrative law – has in recent years become a subsidiary concern to that of the 'accountability' of trade unions and their officials, achieved by applying to trade unions the duties and liabilities typically applied to corporations and their officers. This, Kelly argues, raises serious issues relating to the organisational security of collective institutions, the corporatisation of labour law and the democratic mandate of trade unions.

The focus turns to electoral democracy in the chapter by Joo-Cheong Tham on the regulation of election funding and trade unions. Given that laissez-faire regulation of money in federal elections has led to the corrosion of Australian democracy, how should trade unions respond to the call for increased regulation? Tham's chapter considers two normative perspectives on this question: a libertarian and an egalitarian approach. He argues that an egalitarian approach would enable trade unions to respond to the issues around election funding in a way that is consistent with the social justice and democratic rationales of the union movement, as well as addressing the legitimate concerns Australian trade unions have with caps on contributions and expenditure.

The next three chapters by Campbell, Forsyth and Howe address the challenges to trade unions from the fragmentation of the workforce, challenges relevant both to their social justice and democratic functions. Iain Campbell in his chapter addresses precarious work and trade unions. His chapter affirms the value and necessity of trade union strategies to address precarious work. After considering strategies pursued by European trade unions, including a number of 'levers' for action, Campbell argues that the response of the Australian union movement has been disappointing due to structural barriers and barriers at the level of union agency, particularly with respect to the objective of regulation.

Anthony Forsyth in his chapter addresses the challenge of the gig economy and trade unions. Forsyth argues that the delivery of services and organisation of work through technology raises pressing questions about freedom of association. His chapter examines these questions through a study of two significant recent aspects of gig work regulation: the debate over legislation in California which challenges the platform economy's contracting model, and second, the COVID-19 pandemic. The implications of these developments for Australian unions are analysed, emphasising the preconditions to ensuring genuine expression of collective worker power in the world of platform work.

Joanna Howe in her chapter explores the complex relationship between temporary migrant workers and trade unions in Australia. She argues that trade unions must adapt to represent the interests of the migrant workforce. Migrant workers face greater barriers in joining and accessing trade unions, but, paradoxically, have a pronounced need for unions due to the peculiar vulnerabilities they face. Howe's chapter argues that Australian unions have been largely unsuccessful in recruiting and representing temporary migrant workers and need new strategies to meet this challenge, an argument she concretises through a case study of the Australian horticulture industry.

The last three chapters by Moss, Ranald and Ewing address the overlapping global crises facing trade unions. Jeremy Moss in his chapter focuses squarely on a crisis picked up by Sempill and Peetz: the climate crisis. He specifically considers the concept of a just climate transition and the role of trade unions. Questions of justice, he argues, must be central to a climate transition so that the benefits and burdens of such a transition can be paid for and shared within society. The role of the union movement in this is crucial but not always straightforward – while unions have the potential to play a key role in arguing for a climate transition, they might have to make decisions that involve short-term disadvantage for some members and some unions as a whole. Moss examines these complexities through the example of the fossil fuel industry and argues that unions ought to focus upon broader justice goals rather than the interests of some sectors.

Patricia Ranald in her chapter deals with the question of economic globalisation by addressing trade agreements, labour rights, democracy and the role of trade unions. Ranald's chapter explores the progressive critique of the impact of neoliberal trade policies through four key issues: the impact on global labour rights; the influence of transnational corporations in achieving self-serving international trade rules such as monopolies on medicines; the inclusion in trade agreements of additional legal rights for transnational investors; and the secrecy and lack of democratic process in trade negotiations themselves. Ranald argues that in each of these areas unions have played a key role as consistent critics of neoliberal trade policies and as advocates for change.

The final chapter is by K. D. Ewing who addresses the COVID-19 crisis and the future of labour law in the context of the United Kingdom. He argues that decades of neoliberalism and austerity measures have laid the groundwork for the abject failure of the UK system of labour law to cope with the crisis caused by the pandemic. As a result, many workers have been left precarious and without resilient capacity, exposed further by the lockdown in early 2020 and the way in which the country was later instructed to emerge. Ewing argues that trade unions are critical in any countervailing proposal on how to replace neoliberalism and rebuild: they are essential as intermediate organisations between the citizen and the state and as levers for the delivery of change. A 'Post-COVID-19 Manifesto' is appended to Ewing's chapter.

Notes

1 A total of 514 million all together and 214 million (not including China, Cuba and Belarus: Jelle Visser, *Trade Unions in the Balance: ILO ACTRAV Working Paper* (Geneva: ILO, 2019), 14, https://www.ilo.org/wcmsp5/groups/public/—ed_dialogue/—actrav/documents/publication/wcms_722482.pdf.

2 International Trade Union Confederation, https://www.ituc-csi.org/.

3 ILO Global Commission on the Future of Work, *Work for a Brighter Future* (Geneva: International Labour Organization, 2019), 41.

4 Maria Helena Andre, 'Preface', *The Future of Work: Trade Unions in Transformation: International Journal of Labour Research* 9, nos 1–2 (2019): 7, 8.

5 'The Future of Work We Want: A Brief Summary of the ACTRAV Symposium, Geneva, 7–8 October 2019', *The Future of Work: Trade Unions in Transformation: International Journal of Labour Research* 9, nos 1–2 (2019): 254–56.

6 *ILO Centenary Declaration for the Future of Work* (21 June 2019), art. IA.

7 Tess Hardy and Andrew Stewart, 'What's Causing the Wages Slowdown?', in *The Wages Crisis in Australia: What It Is and What to Do About It*, ed. Andrew Stewart, Jim Stanford and Tess Hardy (Adelaide: University of Adelaide Press, 2018), 57–60.

8 For Australia, see Anthony Forsyth, 'Conflict or Cooperation? Australian Union Responses to COVID-19', *Labour Law Down Under*, 8 October 2020, https://labourlawdownunder.com.au/?p=949.

9 ILO, *ILO Monitor: COVID-19 and the World of Work*, 6th ed. (Geneva: International Labour Organization, 23 September 2020).

10 Hugh Collins, 'Independent Contractors and the Challenge of Vertical Disintegration', *Oxford Journal of Legal Studies* 10, no. 3 (1990): 353; Karl Klare, 'Countervailing Workers' Power as a Regulatory Strategy', in *Legal Regulation of the Employment Relation*, ed. Hugh Collins, Paul Davies and Roger Rideout (London: Kluwer Law International, 2000), 63–82.

11 David Harvey, *A Brief History of Neoliberalism* (Oxford: Oxford University Press, 2005); Jamie Peck, *Constructions of Neoliberal Reason* (Oxford: Oxford University Press, 2010).

12 Colin Crouch, *Post-Democracy* (Oxford: Polity Press, 2004).
13 See David Miller, *Principles of Social Justice* (Cambridge: Harvard University Press, 1999), chapter 1.
14 Elizabeth Anderson, 'What Is the Point of Equality?', *Ethics* 109, no. 2 (1999): 287.
15 David Peetz, *Unions in a Contrary World* (Cambridge: Cambridge University Press, 1998).
16 *Universal Declaration of Human Rights*, GA Res 217A (III), UN Doc A/810 (10 December 1948), art. 21(3).
17 See, generally, Alan Bogg, *The Democratic Aspects of Trade Union Recognition* (Oxford: Hart Publishing, 2009).
18 ILO *Centenary Declaration*, art. IIB.
19 Elizabeth Anderson, *Private Government: How Employers Rule Our Lives (and Why We Don't Talk about It)* (New Jersey: Princeton University Press, 2017).
20 Robert A. Dahl, *A Preface to Economic Democracy* (Berkeley: University of California Quantum Books, 1986).
21 Alain Supiot, *The Spirit of Philadelphia: Social Justice vs. the Total Market* (London: Verso, 2012).
22 *Constitution of the International Labour Organization*, annex 'Declaration Concerning the Aims and Purposes of the International Labour Organization (Declaration of Philadelphia)' (1944), part I(d).
23 ILO Global Commission on the Future of Work, *Work for a Brighter Future* (2019), 41.
24 See Ruth Dukes, *The Labour Constitution: The Enduring Idea of Labour Law* (Oxford: Oxford University Press, 2014), chapter 2.
25 Dahl, *A Preface to Economic Democracy*.
26 *ILO Declaration of Philadelphia*, part II(a)
27 Ibid., part II(a)–(b).
28 Ibid., part III(d).
29 *Federated Engine Drivers' and Firemen's Association of Australasia v Broken Hill Pty Co Ltd* (1911), 5 CAR 9, 27 per Higgins J.
30 *ILO Declaration of Philadelphia*, part I(a).
31 ILO *Declaration on Fundamental Principles and Rights at Work and Its Follow Up* (18 June 1998), art. 2(d).
32 ILO *Centenary Declaration*, art. IIA(vii).
33 Francis Maupain, *The Future of the International Labour Organization in the Global Economy* (Oxford: Hart Publishing, 2013).
34 As the Preamble to the ILO Constitution states, 'the failure of any nation to adopt humane conditions of labour is an obstacle in the way of other nations which desire to improve the conditions in their own countries'.
35 *ILO Declaration on Social Justice for a Fair Globalization* (10 June 2008), 5–6.
36 *International Covenant on Civil and Political Rights*, 999 U.N.T.S. 171 (23 March 1976), art. 22(1).
37 ILO *Declaration on Fundamental Principles and Rights at Work and Its Follow Up* (18 June 1998), art. 2(a).
38 T. H. Marshall, *Class, Citizenship, and Social Development* (Westport, CT: Greenwood Press, [1950] 1973), 94–103. For discussion, see Guy Mundlak, 'Industrial Citizenship, Social Citizenship, Corporate Citizenship: I Just Want My Wages', *Theoretical Inquiries in Law* 8, no. 2 (2007): 719–48.
39 *ILO Declaration of Philadelphia*, art. I(b). Others have similarly argued that freedom of association through trade unions contributes to human flourishing: Alan Bogg,

'Labour Law and the Trade Unions: Autonomy and Betrayal', in *The Autonomy of Labour Law*, ed. Alan Bogg, Cathryn Costello, A. C. L. Davies and Jeremias Prassl (Oxford: Hart Publishing, 2015), chapter 3.

40 *ILO Declaration of Philadelphia*, part I(c).

41 *Federated Engine Drivers' and Firemen's Association*, per Higgins J.

42 *ILO Declaration of Philadelphia*, part I(d).

43 Joint Statement on COVID-19 by International Organisation of Employers and International Trade Union Confederation (2020), https://www.ituc-csi.org/IMG/pdf/20200323_joint_ioe-ituc_statement_on_covid-19.pdf.

44 'UN Chief Renews Call for COVID-19 Solidarity as WHO Warns "Majority" of World Still at Risk', *UN News*, 18 May 2020, https://news.un.org/en/story/2020/05/1064252.

45 'COVID-19 and Workers' Organisations: Interview with Sharan Burrow', ILO Bureau for Workers' Activities (4 May 2020), https://www.ilo.org/actrav/media-center/news/WCMS_743439/lang—en/index.htm.

Chapter 2

ECONOMIC DEMOCRACY, WORKERS AND UNIONS

David Peetz

This chapter compares democratic and shareholder decision-making models and looks at the role of unions in those. It discusses three ways of enhancing economic democracy at the point of production: to leave the formal decision-making power with those who hold it, but through countervailing force, require owners to take account of other interests in decision making; to change the formal decision-making process – that is, who makes the decisions; and to change the owners themselves – that is, by mobilising greater ownership by employees, or ownership by employees' collectively owned funds. Unions are relevant, in varying ways, to all of these. The first corresponds to increasing workers' associational power; the second to increasing their institutional power. Both of these are well-established concepts in the power resources literature regarding trade unions.[1] The third concept is about increasing workers' financial power. This is not so heavily discussed in the power resources literature, as it focuses on trade unions and so the concept of finance is typically tied to either the financial strength of a union or the effects of financialisation on unions. Here we are talking about a form of financial power that might be of the members rather than the unions themselves. However, unions are in reality closely linked to whether and how employees can have financial power. The chapter concludes with discussion of economic democracy, the future of the planet and the role of unions in that, including through active use of workers' pension funds.

Types of Decision-Making Models

We can speak of two types of decision-making models: (1) the democratic model, in which everybody has a say of equal value, and (2) the shareholder model, in which people have influence in proportion to the resources they hold (and at times, those with low resources have zero say, while those with the most resources have all the say).[2] Corporations are run on the shareholder model. A union meeting is closer to the democratic model. Elections are formally based on the democratic model. They are important, but most other aspects of politics reflect the shareholder model – that is, those with the most resources have the most say.[3]

When we refer to economic democracy, we mean that the control of the resources that determine the form and effects of economic activity is distributed along democratic lines. That is, people's ability to shape economic decisions is determined not by their wealth or income but by their existence.

The economy presently distributes benefits according to a shareholder model, but most people want benefits distributed more like a democratic model. Most think we do need some level of inequality, to make the economy function. Those who already have resources and power seize on this idea. But it turns out, from several studies, that most people think the current distribution of income is much more unequal than what they think would be appropriate, and the *actual* level of inequality is much higher than the level people think exists.[4] So the actual level of inequality is much worse than what most people want. Centuries ago, Plato even suggested a useful benchmark – that no one should accumulate more than five times the income of the lowest paid.[5]

Trade unions are an important part of reducing that disparity. On balance, there appear to be positive correlations between union density and equality. As union density and hence power has declined in most industrialised countries, the impact unions have in reducing inequality has declined.[6]

Capitalism is defined by the ownership of the means of production, and so I turn to the level at which production takes place – the workplace or the enterprise. Elizabeth Anderson, in *Private Government: How Employers Rule Our Lives (and Why We Don't Talk About It)*,[7] said that a quarter of American employees describe their workplace as being a dictatorship. She added that most of the next 55 per cent are only one step away from finding that out the hard way. To her, the old ideals of democracy from markets based on small firms and happy entrepreneurs, evident she says in the work of Adam Smith and the like, have been usurped by the power of modern corporations. She sees unions as *one* of the ways that this dictatorship can be battled.

That is a way to see unions' role. Broadly speaking, at the workplace there are three paths to go down to enhance economic democracy at the point of production. The first approach is to leave the formal decision-making power with those who hold it, that is the owners of capital, but have some countervailing force that forces owners to take account of other interests in decision making. The second is to try to change the formal decision-making process, that is change who makes the decisions. The third is to try to change the owners themselves.

Associational Power and the Constraints on Capital

Unions are integral to that first approach, of providing a countervailing force to capital, as discussed in the opening chapter. It is not possible to have more democratic workplaces unless there are more powerful unions (unless one of the other, more fundamental approaches discussed later on is taken up). As unions have become weaker, real wages have decoupled from productivity, so the gains from new technology have mainly gone to capital.[8]

Trade unions are not the only form of worker voice. In recent years, there have been several innovative ways in which workers have sought to express their voice. These include

- many non-government organisations in the global South;
- the Google Walk Out of late 2018, which has partly morphed into a movement called 'End Forced Arbitration';[9]
- OUR Walmart, a body established by a union that sought to connect and mobilise workers in an organisation that had until recently been impossible to unionise in the United States;[10] and
- the spread of 'workers centres' providing advice, mostly without representation, to non-union workers.

In the end, though, if other forms of worker voice are going to do something meaningful, they are going to create power for the workers; and if they do that, they should probably be called a union because that is likely what they end up being.

This is not to deny that it is sometimes strategically useful to call them something else – some body for independent representation – at least for a while, because the term trade union has been itself so heavily contested and demonised that workers sometimes do not recognise that what they want is what we call a trade union. For example, there are American data showing that people are more likely to say they would join an independent body that represented the interests of workers than saying they would join a trade union.[11] Some observers might say 'that's America', but historically unions have had a more negative place in public opinion in Australia than in just about any other industrialised country.[12] Density is so low in the United States relative to elsewhere, not because workers do not want unions, but because institutions are lined up so effectively against them. The issue to fight over is the representation, not the word 'union'.

This is not to deny that words matter. Control of language is important. Labour need not give away the word to the other side; rather, it can defend the word, but pick its fights.

At the national level, unions can also use their workplace power to influence political outcomes. Union movements vary in the extent to which they do this: the Australian movement's sometimes heavy reliance on this was termed 'labourism'.[13] Probably their peak of influence was during the 'Accord' years of the 1980s. Unions' ability to exercise political power, however, ultimately depends on how much workplace power it can demonstrate. It also depends on the ideology of the party in government. So, when the Liberal Party was in government in Australia, union political influence was commonly zero in the twenty-first century – except, perhaps, during the COVID-19 pandemic, when unions were critical in successfully pressuring the government to introduce a wage subsidy scheme.[14]

Institutional Power and the Identity of Decision Makers

The second approach to economic democracy is changing *who makes* the decisions. Here people sometimes talk about various schemes for employee participation in decision making, ranging from quality circles, through joint consultative committees and the like. Sometimes this gets called 'industrial democracy'. The problem is that its continued existence is determined by the employer. Democracy is not something that is at the whim of the king. So, I do not consider those schemes for employee participation in decision making here. The issue is not whether they are worthwhile, it is that they are not economic democracy. Likewise, I do not consider financial participation schemes, like profit sharing, productivity sharing, employee share ownership schemes and the like. It is true they grant an economic entitlement, but only for as long as management lets them last, and they do not inherently promote democracy. When combined with employee participation, they do better, but they are still at the whim of the king.[15]

However, a form of employee participation in decision making that is worth mentioning is the system known in Germany as *Mitbestimmung*; in English, it is codetermination. It is a formal mechanism covered by several laws. The governance of larger firms is almost jointly decided by shareholders and workers – almost, because in the key body, the supervisory board, which has equal representation of worker and shareholder representatives, an independent chair who, in reality, would rarely vote against management's interests, has the balance of power.

In fact, the worker representatives themselves, having far fewer resources than management, rarely challenge the management agenda. For a broader perspective, they are sometimes dependent on their own external board member – one of the worker representatives cannot be an employee or union official, they must be someone else external, but sympathetic to, the workers. The choice of personnel director in larger firms must be jointly agreed between both factions in the supervisory board. Works Councils, dealing with more work specific issues like training and work allocation, contain worker representatives. Where unions exist, their members tend to dominate employee representation on supervisory boards and works councils. In non-union firms, it is just the employees.

Mitbestimmung originated in the immediate post-war era, when: philosophers, politicians and theologians wanted a system or governance that was more democratic; the British occupiers wanted to ensure the German steel cartels would not re-emerge; the unions wanted socialisation of the means of production; and the employers wanted something that they could offer the unions, who had demonstrated their power in earlier decades, without losing ownership of the means of production.

There was also a proposal at the time, coming from the Catholic church, that the interests of the *public* be covered, through some representatives chosen for that purpose by mutual consent of employees and management – but not the state. It did not end up as being part of the system.[16]

Another model for changing the decision makers comes from Belgian academic Isabelle Ferreras, in her recent book *Firms as Political Entities: Saving Democracy through Economic Bicameralism.*[17] She argues for the creation of the bicameral firm. Just like our Parliament has two houses, so too the firm would have two governing bodies, one representing shareholders, and the other representing workers. Each would have a power of veto.

If this model came about, it would be much more effective than trade unionism, as a countervailing force, in advancing workers' interests – though it does not follow that unions would disappear. It would greatly strengthen worker power at the workplace. The people involved would mostly be those we now see as workplace delegates, or at least as works councillors in Germany. We would also expect that the people from the workers' side would still want to associate with their equivalents in other firms, to form organisations. What we now see as unions outside the workplace would become those bodies, possibly still called unions. Those bodies would be a critically important force for economic democracy in society as a whole, representing the interests genuinely of all workers in a way that unions cannot claim to do at present.

That approach, like all I have mentioned, does still leave open the question as to the role for the community in governance of the corporation, and how community interests are represented. That goes to the objectives of the corporation, its license to operate and its interaction with state regulation.[18] It is for another day.

Financial Power and the Question of Ownership

The third approach to economic democracy is about changing who the owners are. Here I focus initially on worker cooperatives. Would a world of worker ownership be a world of economic democracy?

If each worker owned one share in their company, there was no sham contracting, and nobody else creamed off surplus value, then economic democracy would exist. We would not need unions at that workplace level. Workers would own the means of production. There are examples of this, throughout the Mondragon region of Spain, and in individual firms dotted around the world.

The studies suggest it *is* economically efficient, perhaps more so than the conventional corporation.[19] The economic benefits of worker cooperative arrangements appear more consistent than those of employee share ownership, probably because the research suggests that it is not ownership, in itself, that improves productivity but rather the opportunity to combine greater worker say in decision making with greater employee ownership or some other form of employee financial participation.[20] Mondragon workers in Spain are usually keen to introduce new technology, to maintain competitiveness. A job is always found for displaced workers. The surplus generated by labour does not get wasted on jets and exclusive golf club memberships, the role of which in the market for executive remuneration is to signify the status and power of a CEO and their corporation.[21]

Not all cooperatives go well. Some are bad concerns to begin with (if workers buy up failing companies) but on average they are at least as productive as traditional capitalist firms, and the Argentine ‘worker-recuperated enterprises’ show high rates of innovation.[22] Still, few have grown to dominate their industries, because they lack the capitalist urge to grow through merger and acquisition, and they lack the discipline that finance capital imposes on capitalist firms in share markets, which is to maximise short-term returns, often through cost cutting, at threat of a cut in share price that could see a well-heeled CEO out the door. The logic of capitalism, not of efficiency, prevents the dominance of non-capitalist, democratic firms.

Suppose, though, that the way to think about this issue of ownership is not by considering workers as individual shareholders but by considering workers as collective owners? The cooperative perspective involves talking about employees as individuals, owning a share of the company because they are producing profit for the company through their labour. But of course, that is not how ownership works in modern capitalism. Ownership is not related to labour and instead arises from the possession of 'shares'. These days, the shareholders in most corporations, especially in the centre of global capitalism, the United States, are finance capital: banks, insurance companies, fund managers and pension funds. This appears to be also the case, though probably to a lesser degree, in other Anglophone liberal market economies such as Australia and Canada, and less so in a coordinated market economy such as Germany, where finance capital is of growing importance but old, traditional family shareholdings are still important.[23] Overall, mainly because the United States dominates global capitalism, finance capital owns the greatest part, and a growing part, of the shares of the 300 largest corporations in the world.[24]

Corporations are, technically, just collective formations of the capital owned by shareholders, who are wealthy or (less commonly) not-so-wealthy individuals. (Unions are collective formations of labour, established largely to counter the power of these collective formations of capital to exploit those reliant on the sale of their labour power.) An employee's savings are, individually, minuscule compared to the wealth of a corporation. But aggregations of employees' savings can be substantial. In Australia, these take the form of superannuation funds, known in other countries as pension funds. The notable aspect of Australian superannuation funds is that many of them ('industry funds') were established through industrial agreements at the local or national level, and they have union representation on the governing boards of these funds – usually comprising half the board members but without the power to control the chair.

As these funds purchase shares of corporations, they have the capacity to genuinely shape the decisions of firms. Yet few take an active involvement in individual corporate affairs or shape the decisions of firms. Indeed, hedge fund managers and private equity aside (and these are only a small portion of finance capital on share registries), finance capitalists in general play a less active direct role in corporate management than the individuals and families that owned the dominant portions of most corporations in the past. This is despite the fact that the shareholdings of most firms are dominated by finance capital.[25] Few finance capitalists even take seats on boards. Similarly, pension funds rarely take an activist position in relation to corporations. They do not move dissenting shareholder motions at annual general meetings, they do not usually take seats on boards and they do not get on the phone and tell a CEO 'you do this, or else!'

Instead, the influence of finance capital is mostly indirect: implicitly threatening on a daily basis to force downwards the share price of a firm that fails to generate high enough returns, implicitly threatening to have the CEO or senior management removed if that share price fails to perform; and, in doing so, refocusing corporate management to the short term, and away from such longer-term considerations as training, employee development, relations with workers and sustainability. If concern with these issues is lessened, and concern with employee affairs is lessened, then the democratic influence of employees is lessened.

Industry superannuation funds are, in the end, worker owned. They exist to provide secure income for workers in retirement. The board members are literally trustees for the workers whose funds they control. The union officials on those boards are there to protect the interests of the workers. They are there to ensure some level of democracy in the running of these funds. Without that representation, financiers cream off surplus for their own benefit – for example, through excessive executive salaries or related-party outsourcing.[26] Hence 'retail' superannuation funds (generally owned by banks or other conventional financial institutions) consistently produce lower returns for members than the industry funds that have union representation on boards.[27] At a cross-national level, pension funds in nations where unions have a significant role perform better than those where they do not.[28] Despite rhetoric to the contrary, economic democracy in superannuation funds increases returns to members.

This idea that economic democracy relates to funds held in trust for workers is not all that new. In some ways it harks back to the Meidner ideas of 1960s and 1970s Sweden, which planned that economic surpluses could be amassed to make investments for workers' interests.[29] Meidner faltered but, as we see below, the stakes now are much higher. There are now some bodies that attempt to make workers' capital work – such as the Committee on Workers' Capital – in which representatives of many union-related funds meet once a year.

Economic Democracy and the Planet

The damage to worker interests from the lack of economic democracy arises not just from the impact on training, development and industrial relations. It also arises from the impact on the longer-term prospects for employees' survival. Atomised workers, each acting out of self-interest, are likely to ignore the negative externalities their actions might create. Acting solidaristically, however, they are much more likely to overcome those externalities.[30]

The problems facing the planet, however, are much greater than just those of insufficient solidarity between workers. The logic of capitalism, because of how it encourages negative externalities, threatens the planet – an issue discussed in this volume in Chapters 9 and 3 by Jeremy Moss and Julian A. Sempill, respectively . Hence in this final part, I shift the perspective on economic democracy upwards, from the workplace level, to the planetary. Doing so immediately throws two big things into the equation. We need to take account of the economic interests of workers in the global South. We need to take account of the sustainability of the system. For space reasons, I focus on the second.

Can a grand compromise be found between the presently envisioned interests of environmental and labour groups – between the planet and jobs? *Negative* economic growth will not achieve the aims of environmental sustainability. The outcome of negative growth would be major unemployment and another depression. Negative economic growth would not suddenly lead to machines being replaced by people in large enough numbers as to enable continued job creation. (Certainly, if wages eventually fall, some labour replacement investment would not occur, but this would not be enough to stop job losses.) Indeed, firms would still try to increase their share of (declining) markets, searching for ways to increase productivity, through better machines. With declining output, the incomes of those in employment would fall, whether by a drop in hourly wages, or in hours worked, or both.

Unions could never support this outcome. Nor would most citizens. If a progressive government tried deliberately to induce negative growth, it would very likely be followed by the political response of fascism. That would be the antithesis of democracy. Fascist governments, apart from suppressing books like this, would also ensure that capital was able to continue producing lots of carbon emissions. Negative economic growth would also doom workers from the global South to permanent poverty and unremitting imperialism.

Yet present trends in carbon emissions cannot continue. We need a very large increase in carbon productivity – the amount of GDP that can be generated by a unit of emissions.[31] Recycling, enforced by regulation, is a step towards that, but just a small one. Large state investments, and large changes in relative prices are central to achieving a major change in carbon intensity.[32]

In this context, of the search for a grand compromise, the union phrase 'a just transition' recurs, for good reason. It is to do with things like: environmental remediation; energy 'democracy'; 'green' jobs; worker retraining; revitalisation or diversification of energy sources for local communities; and community agency.[33] But the 'just' has another angle. If we continue along the present path, a small group of people will make a lot of money, and the planet will become uninhabitable to most people – but not to all. We should never assume that the ultra-rich cannot find a way to survive comfortably – be it in a bunker in the Waikato, or a gated or better still a floating community on the Pacific rim, with its own private, heavily armed security. We are not *all* going to die. If the climate becomes so extreme, then it is again plausible that, under the influences of the ultra-wealthy, political processes would lead to some sort of fascist governments to rule society and protect those with great wealth and power. Again, that would be the opposite of democracy. For those among the wealthy, thinking of building bunkers or floating cities, the knowledge that they have a way out gives them little incentive to do anything to prevent the rest of us roasting.

There is a major political question about how to garner the political constituency necessary to respond to the global environmental crisis. Part of it is about making use of the potential for common interests between unions, many environmental groups as well as parts of industrial and finance capital. That may seem bizarre, as this chapter had opened by commenting on the undemocratic nature of driving decisions by access to money. Yet some of the critical money is *workers'* money – superannuation from Australia, pension funds from Europe or North America. Economic democracy is not just about workers' current incomes; it is about their future incomes as well. The state of the planet will shape *how much* that future income will be, and the *use* to which workers' capital is put will shape that planet.

The workers' pension funds are not the only parts of finance capital that can take a progressive line on climate matters. Others include the reinsurance companies, and a range of fund managers or asset owners linked to such entities as the International Investor Group on Climate Change. It may seem odd to talk about insurance companies as agents of change or allies in the fight for a fairer, sustainable society. But this is actually about the possibility of having a democratic future. Not all parts of finance capital might look at longer-term structural issues – some will likely remain motivated by short-termism, not least the hedge fund managers and private equity who presently feature as intervenors in the affairs of industrial corporations. Finance capital is no more homogeneous than industrial capital or labour. Even the workers' pension funds will face a tension between the long-term interests of their members and the perceived short-term fiduciary responsibilities of the board. So it is that, up until now, workers' pension funds have often behaved very similarly to the rest of finance capital.[34] Part of the problem lies in the education of pension fund trustees themselves, and part in the persistence of outdated notions of fiduciary duties.[35] However, just as financial markets will inevitably, and probably soon, price into their calculations the likely policy response to climate change,[36] so too pension funds, insurance firms and many other parts of finance capital will increasingly orient their pricing behaviour towards a long-term horizon. This increases opportunities for engagement with a broader constituency for action on climate change, including trade unions.

The alternatives are grim. If greenhouse emissions continue on present trajectories, humanity will not kill the whole planet, and not all the humans on earth will be killed. The greatest casualty may be democracy itself. In its place may come a system worse than any readers have personally experienced. There is no shortage of wealthy people who are only too happy to see that happen. However, there is also no shortage of wealthy people who are keen to avoid that. In the past, when democracy has been introduced, or saved, it has often involved many strange coalitions or alliances of groups acting together, but those alliances have worked.

So, to summarise the situation:

- a grand compromise must be found between the need for jobs and for sustainable incomes, and the environmental needs of the planet;
- this requires a massive increase in carbon productivity, partly through changing price signals but also through intervention in the decisions and allocation of resources that shape economic activity;
- achieving worker voice in the financial decisions that allocate those resources is critical;
- workers' pension funds have a crucial role to play in shaping those financial decisions, both through their direct actions and through what may be done in concert with other interested parts of finance capital and civil society;
- unions are the only organised part of civil society that can influence the behaviour of these funds, most directly, where it happens, through their role as trustees for their members' funds.

In the end, we need economic and political democracy, and we need strong unions to play a key role in enabling those things to happen and to prevent a descent into fascism. We need them to do that through a more active use of workers' pension funds to achieve democratic purposes, rather than the undemocratic logic of finance, and with recognition of the legitimate interests of workers as requiring a democratic voice in the workplace, whether as a stronger countervailing force to capital, or as facilitating an institutionalised workers' say in the decisions that affect them. Unions are not the only way to achieve those means, but at the moment they are the best that is on offer. Economic democracy is enhanced when the associational power and the institutional power of workers is enhanced, and trade unions are typically closely tied to these. Economic democracy is most evident, however, when workers have financial power, and the resultant ability to make decisions as owners – not just of shares in capital, but of shares in the planet.

Notes

1 Stefan Schmalz, Carmen Ludwig and Edward Webster, 'The Power Resources Approach: Developments and Challenges', *Global Labour Journal* 9, no. 2 (2018): 113–34.

2 In the United States, this would be referred to as a 'stockholder' model.

3 Cameron Murray and Paul Frijters, *Game of Mates: How Favours Bleed the Nation* (Brisbane: Cameron Murray, 2017).

4 See, for example, Michael I. Norton and Dan Ariely, 'Building a Better America – One Wealth Quintile at a Time', *Perspectives on Psychological Science* 6, no. 1 (2011): 9–12, cited in G. William Donhoff, 'Wealth, Income, and Power', Who Rules America, https://whorulesamerica.ucsc.edu/power/wealth.html.

5 Glenn Raymond Morrow, *Plato's Cretan City* (Princeton, NJ: Princeton University Press, 1993), 131.

6 David Card, Thomas Lemieux and W. Craig Riddell, 'Unionization and Wage Inequality: A Comparative Study of the U.S., the U.K., and Canada' (NBER Working Paper No. 9473, National Bureau of Economic Research, Cambridge, MA, 2003), http://www.nber.org/papers/w9473; Bevery Gage, 'Should You Care About the Fate of Unions?', *Slate*, 30 June 2014, http://www.slate.com/articles/news_and_politics/history/2014/06/supreme_court_harris_decision_if_you_care_about_income_inequality_you_should.html; Jonas Pontusson, 'Unionization, Inequality and Redistribution', *British Journal of Industrial Relations* 51, no. 4 (2013): 797–825; Engelbert Stockhammer, *Why Have Wage Shares Fallen? A Panel Analysis of the Determinants of Functional Income Distribution*, Conditions of Work and Employment Series No. 35 (Geneva: International Labour Office, 2013); Ünal Töngür and Adem Yavuz Elveren, 'Deunionization and Pay Inequality in OECD Countries: A Panel Granger Causality Approach', *Economic Modelling* 38 (2014): 417–25; Bruce Western and Jake Rosenfeld, 'Unions, Norms, and the Rise in U.S. Wage Inequality', *American Sociological Review* 76, no. 4 (2011): 513–37; Georgina Murray and David Peetz, 'Plutonomy and the One Per Cent', in *Challenging the Orthodoxy: Reflections on Frank Stilwell's Contribution to Political Economy*, ed. Susan Schroeder and Lynne Chester (Sydney: Springer, 2013), 129–48.

7 Elizabeth Anderson, *Private Government: How Employers Rule Our Lives (and Why We Don't Talk About It)* (Princeton, NJ: Princeton University Press, 2017), 63.

8 Matt Cowgill, *A Shrinking Slice of the Pie* (Melbourne: Australian Council of Trade Unions, March 2013).

9 Shirin Ghaffary and Eric Johnson, 'After 20,000 Workers Walked out, Google Said It Got the Message. The Workers Disagree', *Recode*, 21 November 2018, https://www.recode.net/2018/11/21/18105719/google-walkout-real-change-organizers-protest-discrimination-kara-swisher-recode-decode-podcast; Noam Scheiber, 'Google Workers Reject Silicon Valley Individualism in Walkout', *New York Times*, 6 November 2018, https://www.nytimes.com/2018/11/06/business/google-employee-walkout-labor.html?smid=nytcore-ios-share.

10 Andy Kroll, 'Walmart Workers Get Organized – Just Don't Say the U-Word', Mother Jones, March/April 2016, http://www.motherjones.com/politics/2013/02/our-walmart-black-friday-union/; Eduardo Munoz, 'Walmart Warns Workers Not to Use App Helping Them Understand Company's Labor Rules', *RT*, 17 November 2016, https://www.rt.com/usa/367062-walmart-worker-app-workit/.

11 Richard B. Freeman, 'Do Workers Still Want Unions? More Than Ever!', (Briefing Paper 182, Economics Policy Institute, Washington, DC, 2007), http://www.sharedprosperity.org/bp182/bp182.pdf.

12 David Peetz, 'Sympathy for the Devil? Attitudes to Australian Unions', *Australian Journal of Political Science* 37, no. 1 (2002): 57–80.

13 Gwynneth Singleton, 'Corporatism or Labourism?: The Australian Labour Movement in Accord', *Journal of Commonwealth and Comparative Politics* 28, no. 2 (1990): 162–82.

14 Jacqueline Maley, 'Turns Out Politicians Can Drop the Ideology and Fix Things. Never Let "Em Forget It"', *Sydney Morning Herald*, 5 April 2020, https://www.smh.com.au/politics/federal/turns-out-politicians-can-drop-the-ideology-and-fix-things-never-let-em-forget-it-20200403-p54gu7.html.

15 General Accounting Office, *Employee Stock Ownership Plans: Little Evidence of Effects on Corporate Performance* (Washington, DC: GAO, March 1987); Bjørne Grimsrud and Torunn Kvinge, 'Productivity Puzzles – Should Employee Participation Be an Issue?', *Nordic Journal of Political Economy* 32, no. 2 (2006): 139–67; Douglas Kruse, *Employee Ownership and Employee Attitudes: Two Case Studies* (Pennsylvania: Norwood Editions, 1984); Derek C. Jones, 'British Producer Co-Operatives 1948–1968: Productivity and Organisational Structure', in *Participatory and Self-Managed Firms*, ed. Derek C. Jones and Jan Svejnar (Lexington, MA: Lexington Books, 1982); Michael Quarrey, 'Employee Ownership and Corporate Performance' (Research Paper in Employee Ownership, National Center for Employee Ownership, Oakland, October 1986).

16 My thanks to Professor Dr Werner Nienhüser for assistance on the issues in these four paragraphs. See also Herbert J. Spiro, 'Codetermination and German Politics', *Relations Industrielles* 11, no. 2 (1956): 66–86; Matt Mazewski, 'Bringing the Workers on Board', *Commonweal Magazine* 146, no. 6 (2019): 17–21.

17 Isabelle Ferreras, *Firms as Political Entities. Saving Democracy through Economic Bicameralism* (Cambridge, UK: Cambridge University Press, 2017).

18 For a beginning of this discussion, see Joel Bakan, *The Corporation: The Pathological Pursuit of Profit and Power* (London: Constable & Robertson, 2004).

19 Avner Ben-Ner and Saul Estrin, 'What Happens When Unions Run Firms?' (Centre for Labour Economics Discussion Paper No. 217, London School of Economics, London, April 1986); Jones, 'British Producer Co-Operatives'; Derek C. Jones and Jan Svejnar, 'The Economic Performance of Participatory and Self-Managed Firms: A Historical Perspective and a Review', in Jones and Svejnar, *Participatory and Self-Managed Firms*, 3–16; Tom Webb and George Cheney, 'Worker-Owned and -Governed Co-Operatives and the Wider Co-Operative Movement', in *The Routledge Companion to Alternative Organization*, ed. Martin Parker, George Cheney, Valérie Fournier and Chris Land (London: Routledge, 2014), 64–88; Virginie Pérotin, 'What Do We Really Know About Workers' Cooperatives?', in *Co-Operation: A Business Model for the 21st Century*, ed. Tony Webster, Linda Shaw and Rachael Vorberg-Rugh (Manchester: Manchester University Press, 2016), 239–260.

20 Jones, 'British Producer Co-Operatives'; Quarrey, *Employee Ownership and Corporate Performance*; General Accounting Office, *Employee Stock Ownership Plans*.

21 David Yernack, 'Flights of Fancy: Corporate Jets, CEO Perquisites and Inferior Shareholder Returns', *Journal of Financial Economics* 80 (2005): 211–42.

22 Maurizio Atzeni and Marcelo Vieta, 'Between Class and the Market: Self-Management in Theory and in the Practice of Worker-Recuperated Enterprises in Argentina', in Parker et al., *The Routledge Companion to Alternative Organization*, 47–63.

23 David Peetz, Georgina Murray and Werner Nienhüser, 'Wem Gehören Die Großen Unternehmen? Restrukturierung Des Eigentums Während Der Finanzkrise in Deutschland Und Den USA', *WSI-Mitteilungen* 8 (2016): 584–94; Georgina Murray and David Peetz, 'Restructuring of Corporate Ownership in Australia through the Global Financial Crisis', *Journal of Australian Political Economy* 71 (2013): 76–105.

24 David Peetz and Georgina Murray, 'The Financialisation of Global Corporate Ownership', in *Financial Elites and Transnational Business: Who Rules the World?*, ed. Georgina Murray and John Scott (Cheltenham: Edward Elgar, 2012).

25 See note 23 and note 24.

26 Kevin Liu and Elizabeth Ooi, 'The Impact of Related-Party Outsourcing and Trustee Director Affiliation on Investment Performance of Superannuation Funds' (unpublished paper, Industry Super Australia and UNSW Business School, Sydney, 2017); William D. Cohan, 'On Wall Street: All Reward, No Risk', *New York Times*, 28 October 2010.

27 Australian Prudential Regulation Authority, *Annual Superannuation Bulletin, June 2011* (Sydney: APRA, 2012); Trish Power, 'Industry Funds Outperform Retail Funds for 2017/2018 Year, and Longer Term', *SuperGuide*, 21 August 2018. https://www.superguide.com.au/boost-your-superannuation/industry-funds-retail-funds-performance-comparison; Productivity Commission, *Superannuation: Assessing Efficiency and Competitiveness*, Productivity Commission Draft Report (Canberra: Productivity Commission, 2018); Kenneth Hayne, *Royal Commission into Misconduct in the Banking, Superannuation and Financial Services Industry, Volume 1* (Canberra: Commonwealth of Australia 2019), https://www.royalcommission.gov.au/sites/default/files/2019-02/fsrc-volume-1-final-report.pdf.

28 David Peetz, *The Relationship between Collective Representation and National Pension Fund Outcomes* (Melbourne: Industry Super, January 2019).

29 Rudolf Meidner, *Employee Investment Funds: An Approach to Collective Capital Formation* (London: George Allen & Unwin, 1978).

30 See the introductory chapter for discussion of solidarity.

31 David Peetz, 'What If We Measured the Thing That Matters Most: "Carbon Productivity"', *The Conversation*, 25 October 2019, https://theconversation.com/what-if-we-measured-the-thing-that-matters-most-carbon-productivity-124902.

32 David Peetz, 'Why It Would Be Wrong to Ignore a Carbon Price', *Arena*, 24 September 2020, https://arena.org.au/why-it-would-be-wrong-to-ignore-a-carbon-price/.

33 The concept of 'just transition' is discussed further in the chapter by Moss.

34 Johanna Weststar and Anil Verma, 'Protector or Activist? Consistency and Contradiction in Labor's Voice on Pension Boards', in *The Contradictions of Pension Fund Capitalism*, ed. Kevin Skerrett et al. (Ithaca: Cornell University Press, 2017); Dick Bryan and Mike Rafferty, 'The Financial Responsibilities of Our Grandparents – Towards a Political Economy of Pension Restructuring', Skerrett et al., *The Contradictions of Pension Fund Capitalism.*

35 Johanna Weststar, 'Critical Perspectives from the Field of Pension Fund Education', in Skerrett et al., *The Contradictions of Pension Fund Capitalism*; Baker and McKenzie, *Pension and Superannuation Trustees and Climate Change Report* (Sydney: Baker and McKenzie, 2012); Freshfields Bruckhaus Deringer, *A Legal Framework for the Integration of Environmental, Social and Governance Issues into Investment Management* (Geneva: Asset Management Working Group, United Nations Environment Programme Finance Initiative, 2005).

36 Principles for Responsible Investment, *The Inevitable Policy Response: Preparing Financial Markets for Climate Related Policy/Regulatory Risks* (London: Principles for Responsible Investment, with Vivid Economics, Energy Transition Advisers, 21 Investing Initiative, Carbon Tracker & Grantham Research Institute, 2019).

Chapter 3

NOBODY OWNS THE FUTURE

Julian A. Sempill

Reviving the Impulse to Economic Democracy

The subject of this chapter is economic democracy. It is an old topic, and one that has generated a rich history of fertile thought and mostly frustrated action.

The impetus to economic democracy stems, in part, from a simple intuition: under capitalism, economic life tends to be autocratic, and, yet, we condemn autocracy and praise democracy; therefore, for the sake of consistency, we ought to demand the transformation of the economy along more democratic lines; this is the basic impulse that animates economic democracy. As the nineteenth century writer Henry Demarest Lloyd put it, 'there is to be a people in industry, as in government'.[1] That demand has always represented an important moral challenge to orthodox beliefs about our society. Defenders of the orthodoxy have never convincingly seen off the challenge, at least not at the level of principle. As a matter of political practice, however, economic democracy has been a marginal phenomenon.

In this chapter, I want to suggest that the impulse to economic democracy is in urgent need of revival and that trade unionists ought to contribute to its resurgence: see also, Chapter 2 by David Peetz in this volume. I refer to the 'impulse' to economic democracy because I want to focus on its underlying moral impetus and its general implications. So, I will not consider any particular institutional forms or structures that have been, or might be, imagined for it. Developing an institutional blueprint for economic democracy is not the most urgent thing.

What is needed right now, I will argue, is something more basic – namely, a concerted effort to challenge concentrated, private economic power, and to do so in a way that gives voice to the democratic spirit. We need to begin to encroach upon plutocracy – economic autocracy – in the name of democracy. The initial aim would be simple, yet nonetheless fairly ambitious: to persuade people that democratic principles are relevant to the basic organisation and running of economic life, and not only at the level of the particular firm or industry – which is the traditional terrain of 'industrial democracy' – but in relation to the economy as a whole. That aim challenges the orthodoxy of the capitalist-democratic regime, according to which democratic principles belong exclusively in the so-called 'political sphere', and therefore have no place in the 'private' 'economic sphere'.

Under that regime, to be sure, democratically elected governments do play a role in economic life. However, governments normally understand that they must respect, and must be seen to respect, defining features of capitalism, especially the predominance of private ownership of economic resources as well as the deployment of such resources for the enrichment, and at the direction, of resource owners. According to this orthodox understanding, the role properly played by democratically elected governments in economic life constitutes respectful 'intervention' in another domain – one that belongs, morally, legally and practically, to resource owners above all others. Whatever powers the legal constitution might technically afford them – say to replace the profit-oriented economy – democratically elected officials know that they would imperil not only their own reign, but perhaps also democracy, if they dared to seriously question, let alone to repudiate, the orthodoxy; this in the rare cases where they might be inclined, in their hearts, to do so. A spectrum of well-known cases, such as those of Salvador Allende and François Mitterrand, demonstrate the potency of the unwritten capitalist-democratic constitution: when it comes to economic life, the democratic spirit must be strictly contained.

The case in favour of enlarging democracy, which I advance here, rests on the following proposition, one that underpins not only economic democracy, but democracy as such: that members of a community should be entitled to democratically determine matters that significantly affect the community. If that idea's relevance to economic life were accepted, it would be at the expense of the plutocratic principle that currently holds sway – that is, the normally unquestioned idea that those who own the economy ought largely to control it. And the displacement of that principle would be an important gain, especially today, when so much is at stake for the community.

In the midst of the climate emergency, these questions have taken on renewed – and, indeed, unprecedented – importance. The nature of economic life today will significantly affect not only the members of today's community, but also the future of human community as such. Sir Robert Watson, former chair of the International Governmental Panel on Climate Change, has declared that the climate crisis demands nothing less than 'transformative change', meaning 'a fundamental, system-wide reorganization across technological, economic and social factors, including paradigms, goals and values'.[2]

Thankfully, given the urgency of our situation, much progress has been made in developing progressive options for a just and green 'system-wide reorganization'; Green New Deal proposals and proposals for selective de-growth are among the most prominent examples. Yet, however viable and plausible these models might be – in moral, logistical, scientific and technical terms – they confront daunting ideological and political obstacles. Further, it is widely acknowledged that, for those obstacles to be overcome, and for 'transformative change' to be realised, the weight of a formidable social movement would need to be brought to bear.[3]

In the discussion below, I outline some of the ideological and political obstacles, as well as certain aspects of their structural, systemic and historical roots. I also sketch what I hope is a promising counter-hegemonic rhetorical strategy which might be adopted by progressive forces, irrespective of whether they are proponents of a Green New Deal, selective de-growth or other such ambitious programmes; trade unionists and trade unions – because of their organisational resources and their strategic location within the supply-side of the economy – are particularly well placed to play a key role in the prosecution of that strategy.

The strategy is simple in theory, though of course easier to describe than to execute: the idea would be to open up a new democratic front, one that begins inside the economy and seeks to undermine plutocracy and the limitation of democracy to the so-called political sphere. That aim is particularly pertinent in connection with climate change: the relative insulation of basic economic questions from democratic deliberation and decision is a fundamental, structural cause of the virtual paralysis in the face of climate change – as discussed below. The climate emergency means that our paralysis, and therefore its structural underpinnings, must urgently be addressed.

By basing our advocacy on democratic principles, trade unionists might increase the prospects of surmounting some of the rhetorical and political obstacles that stand in the way of those who want to argue for a just transition to a green economy. Whether one supports a Green New Deal, selective de-growth or an alternative vision of such a transition, progress depends to a very great extent on challenging the normally unquestioned power of the economy's owners to decide – by and for themselves – basic matters about its organisation and running. In other words, we must argue for the realisation of greater economic democracy, and, in particular, for the democratic determination of those aspects of economic life that bear crucially on the survival of human civilisation in the face of the climate crisis. The question of how we might go about mounting that challenge provides the impetus for this chapter. The suggested response is no more than a preliminary outline for one possible strand of argument in what must be a broader set of arguments. The discussion below sets out the ideological and political context in which are forced to make our arguments, as well as some of the threats and opportunities embedded within that context.

So, that's where this chapter is going. But, in order to get there, I'm going to take a fairly roundabout journey. In the first section, I consider how liberal-democratic-capitalism emerged from the Cold War in a seemingly unassailable position of ideological pre-eminence, which is now threatened by the climate crisis. In the second section, I outline how certain defenders of capitalists' privilege and power have sought to meet that threat by advancing what I label the 'New Denialism'. In the third and fourth sections, respectively, I explain how (1) the traditional social democratic compact – with its emphasis on unlimited economic growth – and (2) so-called economic freedom represent significant rhetorical and political hurdles which must be overcome by trade unionists who want to agitate for a just transition to a green economy. In the fifth section, I sketch a rhetorical strategy which might be adopted by progressive forces in seeking to put in question the normally unquestioned power of the economy's owners to determine its basic organisation and running. In the sixth section, I argue that the role played by defenders of capitalist power and privilege in the COVID-19 crisis is a microcosm of their role in the climate crisis; in each case, capitalist imperatives distort our ability to respond to human needs.

The Zenith of Liberal-Democratic-Capitalism

The collapse of the Soviet system was the catalyst for widespread reflection on the merits of capitalism. Where I was at the time, at high school and university, reflection sometimes took the form of vigorous debates. The critics of capitalism naturally had a hard time of it, tilting gamely against the tide of the times. For the most part, the defenders of capitalism secured more support from the waverers. Apart from the pro-capitalist mood of the moment, which might have played a subliminal, emotional part, one or more of the following beliefs usually appeared to weigh heavily in capitalism's favour:

1. Capitalism, thanks to its efficiency at wealth generation, has immensely improved the material standard of living of vast numbers of people.
2. Liberal-democratic-capitalism has demonstrated that it has the wherewithal to weather challenges and crises; it is more solid, stable and sustainable than its rivals, which have mostly collapsed or been defeated.
3. Even if one thought there were reasons in favour of replacing liberal-democratic-capitalism, such a large change is best avoided because of

(i) the daunting uncertainty about whether any other system would be better or worse; and
(ii) the very real risk that implementation would lead to chaos and authoritarianism, as seen in the Soviet experience.

Faced with those considerations, against the backdrop of the collapse of what was widely portrayed as the only plausible alternative to capitalism, debaters often reached the conclusion – sometimes gleefully, sometimes ruefully – that 'the historical debate is over. The answer is free-market capitalism.'[4] That was how Thomas Friedman put it, gleefully. The course of the classroom debates mirrored wider public discussions. Those discussions tended to nurture the beliefs just outlined, urging us to treat them as common sense and therefore beyond question.

Various social forces began to adjust. Establishment liberals, like Friedman, worked to fortify the impression that their views marked the outer-left-limit of the political spectrum. Social democratic parties took heed, and they grew more resolute in their use of neoliberal vocabulary and their espousal of neoliberal values, thereby doing their bit to erode the hard-won civic culture of communal, rather than atomised, aspiration upon which the flourishing of social democracy, and trade unionism, depends.

Largely unopposed in the field of culture and ideas, the neoliberal vanguard pressed home its advantage. Their objective – achieved, today, to a very great extent – was not only to dismantle social democratic policies and institutions, but to ensure that they would stay dismantled. Having understood – better than their social democratic opponents – the world shaping power of culture and ideas – the neoliberals sought to bury the socialist-tinged values that animate social democracy; to destroy the civic culture that is nurtured by those values; and to discredit and disperse the communities and institutions that give voice to those impulses and sustain that culture – including, especially, trade unions.

In sum, to many sincere people – not only to neoliberal propagandists – it seemed incontestable that capitalism was a successful system, especially because of three features attributed to it, which I described earlier:

1. Capitalist growth credibly promised a better material life.
2. Liberal-democratic-capitalism seemed adept at overcoming internal and external challenges.
3. Seemingly viable alternatives had shown themselves to be engines of fanaticism, chaos and authoritarianism, unlike liberal-democratic-capitalism, which seemed moderate and stable.

In the years following the Soviet system's collapse, those simple propositions appeared to serve – more widely than ever – as knockdown arguments in favour of liberal-democratic-capitalism's pre-eminent legitimacy. But, over the same period, capitalism was busy generating a state of affairs that has drastically undermined these and other redemptive claims made on its behalf. Today, each proposition is in the process of being progressively and profoundly negated, right before our eyes. What happened? And what does it mean for trade unions and trade unionists?

Capitalism First! and the New Denialism

In the 30-year period that began in 1992, with the founding of the UN's climate change initiative, we emitted more than 50 per cent of the carbon ever emitted by the burning of fossil fuel: for further discussion of the challenges presented by the fossil fuel industry in the context of a climate transition, see Chapter 9 by Jeremy Moss in this volume.[5] So, as David Wallace-Wells puts it, during that period, we 'engineered as much ruin knowingly as we ever managed in ignorance'.[6] And we also radically altered the economic and political implications of addressing climate change. Wallace-Wells sums up the problem:

> If we had started global decarbonization in 2000 […], we would have had to cut emissions by only about 3 percent per year to stay safely under two degrees of warming. If we start today, when global emissions are still growing, the necessary rate is 10 percent. If we delay another decade, it will require us to cut emissions by 30 percent each year.[7]

According to a 2018 study, if we maintain our current trajectory, we will fall far short of the energy transformation needed to reach 'net zero' by 2050 – so far short that it will take us an additional 380 years.[8] According to Kevin Anderson of the Tyndall Centre for Climate Change Research, the upshot is that we have 'squandered any opportunity for the "evolutionary change" afforded by our earlier (and larger) 2°C carbon budget'.[9] Sir Robert Watson, former chair of the International Governmental Panel on Climate Change, has said, 'Let's be quite candid'; 'we're not on the pathway to 2°C. We're on a pathway to 3, 3.5°C.'[10] A UN report released in 2019 estimates that over one million species are at risk of extinction. Watson was the chair of the intergovernmental body that produced that report, and he commented on its findings thus:

> Through 'transformative change', nature can still be conserved, restored and used sustainably – this is also key to meeting most other global goals. By transformative change, we mean a fundamental, system-wide reorganization across technological, economic and social factors, including paradigms, goals and values […] [But] transformative change can expect opposition from those with interests vested in the status quo, but also that such opposition can be overcome for the broader public good.[11]

And yet, many political and economic leaders talk, and act, as though the changes could be piecemeal, gradual and perhaps even imperceptible to most of us. Some politicians promise to take serious action on climate change. But, at the same time, they promise to maximise economic growth, as in the past – usually without acknowledging that doing both might not be feasible. Enlightened seeming business leaders talk about carbon-neutrality, which they enthusiastically welcome – so long as 'greening' is compatible with growing profits; that goes without saying.

This upbeat posture represents a new form of climate denialism. Its proponents accept that climate change is real. But they tacitly refuse to accept that we have squandered the opportunity for evolutionary change. This New Denialism is less crude than its anti-science predecessor. However, its relative sophistication hardly makes it less dangerous or less reactionary. It is dangerous simply because it is causing us to waste more time. And it is reactionary, like the old denialism, because its function is to prioritise the imperatives of capitalism over the imperative to safeguard nature and civilised human life. I will call this order of priorities 'Capitalism First!'.

A symptom of the New Denialism, and a corollary of Capitalism First, is the marginalisation of mitigation options that do not create some sort of 'incentive compatibility' – by which I mean an incentive structure that promises to align the profit maximisation principle with our ecological security. There is nothing new about this. Public policy making often entails, more or less explicitly, the search for happy coincidences between profit maximisation and some human good. However, although the notion was always a twisted one, its consequences were never as destructive as they are now.

The New Denialism effectively proceeds according to the following logic. It is assumed, first of all, that climate security and an economy based on profit maximisation are both goods worth promoting. Many would agree with that assumption. But it also seems to be taken for granted that, in the event of any serious conflict between climate security and the profit maximisation principle, the profit maximisation principle should prevail. The evidence for the stranglehold of this logic is clear: it is the absence of sustained and meaningful mainstream discussion of plausible mitigation options that would seriously conflict with Capitalism First. Once we look behind the recent upsurge of responsible sounding political rhetoric, we are confronted with denialism in a new guise – a public policy outlook that remains, in effect, both fanatical and reckless.

Naomi Klein argues persuasively that, in general, elite denialism is not based on ignorance of, or hostility to, the reality of climate change: on the contrary, it is based on a sober and farsighted assessment of the probable implications of free, democratic deliberation about mitigation. By way of illustration, consider the not-really-optional option of drastic decarbonisation and how the president of the US Chamber of Commerce responded to it:

> There is no way this can be done without fundamentally changing the American way of life, choking off economic development, and putting large segments of our economy out of business.[12]

If an open-minded discussion were to be undertaken, with a view to democratic, public spirited consideration of *all options* for effective and just mitigation, some of the sensible options might seriously challenge – and they do in fact challenge – the existing capitalist economy and power structure. By 'capitalist economy and power structure' I mean an economy that is very substantially under the undemocratic control of large private owners and which is aimed at unlimited profits, unlimited capital accumulation and unlimited economic growth.

Frederic Jameson has suggested that 'it is easier to imagine the end of the world than to imagine the end of capitalism'.[13] This formulation captures some of the darkness at the heart of the elite response to climate change. However, Jameson's choice of words – 'it is easier to imagine' – obscures a greater darkness. It obscures the responsibility of the powerful flesh-and-blood actors whose interests are chiefly served by Capitalism First. It would be more telling to say that 'the beneficiaries of Capitalism First would prefer to imagine the extinguishment of millions of lives and countless species than to imagine the diminution of their privilege and power'.[14]

'But, surely' – it might be said – 'when it comes to climate change, we are all in it together: even the beneficiaries of Capitalism First stand to lose from pathological climate change, and this means that they have an incentive to mitigate such change.' That sentiment is, by now, a leitmotif of the Panglossian climate change genre. To be sure, there is much that all humans would lose – including biodiversity, climatic stability and more – and some beneficiaries of Capitalism First are, and might still be, moved by these considerations.

But it is not self-evident, or even likely, that climate change would lead to the loss of privilege and power, or even of luxurious lifestyles. Some parts of the planet are likely to remain relatively hospitable, and some of the powerful and privileged could be expected to retain those places – or to colonise them, formally or informally – and to fortify their lifestyles by the heavy militarisation of land and sea borders, keeping out those who would flee worse conditions elsewhere.

At first, that scenario might seem far-fetched, until it is realised that, in various ways, privileged individuals and nations already adopt such measures and have done so, in various ways, throughout history. In Australia, both major political parties already extol the callous fortification of our borders, pandering to an allegedly widespread fear that good fortune shared with refugees is good fortune lost. The chief beneficiaries of Capitalism First could reasonably expect the augmentation and adaptation of these and similar measures to protect their power and privilege. So, some beneficiaries of Capitalism First are likely to have made the calculation that, despite climate change, they, and their descendants, can probably avoid the loss of their power and privilege for at least several generations.[15] It is implausible, then, to maintain that, when it comes to climate change, we are all in it together: if the chief beneficiaries of Capitalism First have often inflicted, or accepted, suffering where it merely promotes their power and privilege, why wouldn't they do the same in the case of climate change, in order to avoid losing those prizes altogether?

Another aspect of the New Denialism is a sanguine response to that question, a response which imagines either: that, if sacrifices are to be made, we would all, willingly, shoulder them together, or that the maintenance of existing privilege and power can be reconciled with ecological security. The New Denialism denies that *just* mitigation and *just* adaptation are likely to require a confrontation with those who would prefer to risk a deadly catastrophe for others than to contemplate the removal or diminution of their own privilege and power. In sum, both the old and new denialism obscure one of the most important questions that humanity must now confront: can a capitalist economy and power structure be maintained without destroying the conditions needed for human civilisation and without extinguishing millions of lives and at least one million species?

Pathological climate change is, in very large part, a function of capitalist economic life as we know it. Mitigation measures must affect the nature of the economy, as must the now inevitable adaptation measures, and, in each case, very substantially. Will mitigation and adaptation be just? Or will they entrench, or perhaps even enlarge, concentrated power, privilege and injustice at the expense of workers and the community generally? These are open questions. How they are resolved will depend to a great extent on whether concentrated economic power and privilege are displaced by powerful countervailing forces that stand for democracy and justice. How can trade unionists act as a countervailing force?

The well-known difficulty is that workers have only an indirect influence over the shape of economic life. Workers make the economy run, but they do not run the economy: see, further, Chapter 2 by David Peetz in this volume. According to the liberal-democratic version of democracy, workers have to resort to electoral politics to try to exert some influence over the economy. Even then, such influence can only be very circumscribed, so long as private ownership of the economy is to be respected. The owners of the economy have a much more direct say, by virtue of the legal prerogatives they enjoy as owners.

There are reasons why it would be unwise for trade unionists, or for the community generally, to put all of our eggs in the liberal-democratic basket. In the fifth section, I explain how we might open up another democratic front, one that begins inside the economy. The ultimate aim would be to transcend the separation of so-called economic and political spheres, which is a hallmark of liberal-democratic-capitalism. A more immediate aim would be to begin to erode plutocracy and the confinement of democracy to the so-called political sphere. That goal is especially apt in connection with climate change: the arbitrary and substantial insulation of the economic sphere from democratic government is a deep, structural cause of the paralysis in the face of climate change – for reasons that will be underscored in a moment. That paralysis, and therefore that structural problem, must be addressed. Moreover, by grounding our arguments in democratic principles, we might improve our chances of overcoming some of the rhetorical and political hurdles that stand in the way of trade unionists who want to argue for a just transition to a green economy.

In order to consider how to overcome those hurdles, it makes sense to begin by taking stock of them. All of the things I am about to say are widely understood. But, nonetheless, they are rarely articulated. Perhaps that is not surprising: the animating logic of a profit-centred economy – its priorities and its values – are not, in themselves, humane values. And the redemptive idea that private vice yields public benefit is not easy to accept. That is a problem which has tested its defenders' intellectual ingenuity, from Bernard Mandeville to Ayn Rand, up to the present. And so, it is understandable that defenders of capitalism would try to associate it with more noble notions such as 'freedom'. But, once we peel away such branding devices, what we see is a system of concentrated power and privilege, which, in its essentials, is not unlike those that preceded it, such as feudalism. They too were shrouded in high-sounding principles. We tend to see those systems starkly, for what they were, and we describe their logic baldly, in an unalloyed way. That is what I think we should do more often in the case of capitalism. We should say: 'The chief beneficiaries of capitalism proceed on the basis that the principle of profit-maximisation should prevail at all costs, even at the cost of jeopardising human civilisation; and that is a fanatical and reckless logic, which cannot continue.' Speaking like that, in my view, would complement the approach that I want to recommend.

So, what are the hurdles in the way of trade unionists who want to argue for a just transition to a green economy?

Untrammelled Economic Growth and the Social Democratic Compact

One of the greatest hurdles is the special cultural and structural status of the goal of maximum economic growth. According to many who have carefully considered the problem, the mitigation of climate change is either going to require some form of selective, though far-reaching, de-growth, or it is going to require a much more restrained and discriminating attitude to ongoing economic growth; this latter attitude is embodied in Green New Deal proposals.[16] However, despite promising signs that proposals for a Green New Deal are beginning to gain traction, and save for limited and ad hoc 'green initiatives' by some businesses, the long-standing public and private goal of unlimited and indiscriminate economic growth continues, at least tacitly, to guide much public and private economic management. The difficulty of displacing that goal stems at least partly from the fact that even mild forms of growth scepticism – for example, calls for a more restrained or discriminating attitude to growth – are anathema (1) to Capitalism First and 'economic freedom' (see the fourth section below) as well as (2) to the traditional social democratic model.

Social democracy, at least since the New Deal, has been based on the idea of a social contract between labour and capital. Under that contract, labour agrees to participate in promoting capital accumulation. Labour's reward for 'adding to the nation's economic pie' comes in the forms of a state-orchestrated redistributive social wage and tolerance for strictly bounded union brokered income gains. All capitalist economics is, in a sense, 'trickle-down economics', whether the prevailing regime is neoliberal or social democratic. The key difference between the two, in this respect, is that under neoliberalism there are weaker and fewer pumping mechanisms by which wealth can be made to flow from capital to the rest of society. The 1983 Prices and Incomes Accord is a good example of an explicit articulation of the social democratic compact's architecture and the design of pumping mechanisms.

The joint commitment to enlarging the economic pie rests on the prospect that capitalist enterprise can be a positive sum, rather than zero sum, game for labour and capital. Maximal economic growth has been central to the viability of social democracy as we have known it. It has also been central to trade unionism, at least since Federation. Trade unions' demands for material improvements have a better chance of being regarded as tolerable by capitalists insofar as those demands do not lead to declining profits. So, the efficacy of the social democratic compact depends upon, among other things, labour's commitment to capital accumulation. Trade unions have been willing to make that commitment, in part, because of the reasonable expectation that higher living standards for union members can only be regularly obtained as a side effect of sustained, successful capital accumulation.

But, if it is the case that unlimited and indiscriminate economic growth is incompatible with climate change mitigation, then this centrepiece of social democracy, and of trade unionism, must at least be revised; hence the various Green New Deal proposals, which envisage growth, but not unlimited and indiscriminate growth. Alternatively, if a policy of systematic no-growth or selective de-growth were deemed necessary, the positive sum promise would evaporate, diminishing the possibilities for cooperation and compact: unions would either have to give up on increasing wages or capital would have to give up on increasing profits – unless the need for a social compact were transcended by the replacement of capitalism, the prospects for which are presently remote. However, even if unions decide to commit themselves to a revised social compact – say, along the lines of a Green New Deal – a new, greener, attitude to growth would not automatically become the economic order of the day: capitalists would need to be persuaded to agree to that new compact. And that would require them to jettison the doctrine of Capitalism First and to give up a large measure their so-called economic freedom. Persuading them to do so represents a further, formidable hurdle in the way of trade unionists who want to argue for a just transition to a green economy.

Economic Freedom as a Public Health Risk

The notion of economic freedom is an ideological corollary of the liberal-democratic-capitalist separation of economic and political spheres: economic freedom is what 'we' are supposed to enjoy in our 'private' non-political-sphere lives. Put bluntly, it is largely a propagandist's term, masquerading as a lofty moral principle. Among other things, the idea of economic freedom extols the prerogative of private property owners to do what they will with their property, so long as it isn't unlawful. Warren Buffett vividly describes the kingly prerogative that allows him to deploy his wealth according to his whim:

> If I wanted to, I could hire 10,000 people to do nothing but paint my picture every day for the rest of my life. And the [GDP] would go up. But the utility of the product would be zilch and I would be keeping those 10,000 people from doing AIDS research or teaching, or nursing.[17]

Defenders of economic freedom say that one of its positive side effects is aggregate wealth generation: the freedom to seek maximum profits – or to rent 10,000 portrait painters – is supposed to promote efficient resource allocation. On this view, we should let investors offer the goods or services they want to offer – assuming they in fact do anything so useful – without making judgements about the overall consequences, subject only to very capacious legal limits.

So long as the private ownership of concentrated wealth is a fact of life, community welfare is dependent upon what is done with so-called economic freedom. In particular, welfare depends upon whether those who control concentrated wealth are willing to invest it in activities that are employment and tax generating and otherwise promote human welfare. Normally, the willingness of owners to invest depends upon their assessment of whether the investment will yield not just profits, but profit growth. The implications are simple: lack of sufficient prospects for expanding profits leads to lack of investment, which in turn diminishes the community's welfare. Therefore, all other things being equal, workers, unions and the community have an interest in promoting profitable investment.

However, there is a very serious question as to whether capitalist style economic freedom as we have known it is compatible with climate security. Is investment in certain kinds of economic activity – perhaps many kinds – incompatible with optimal climate change mitigation? Is seeking indiscriminately to maximise growth a public health risk? In other words, should economic freedom, as we know it, be regarded as dangerous, or at least highly suspect? If the answer to each question is 'yes', then trade unionism is in a difficult bind. So long as workers remain economically dependent on the profit-seeking decisions of investors, unions – and governments – will often face a Hobson's choice between promoting economic security, on the one hand, or climate security, on the other. There are signs that the pressures generated by this dilemma are already very real and that the champions of Capitalism First are exploiting those pressures with a view to driving a wedge between the trade union movement and the environmental movement.

The pressures imposed by the Hobson's choice do not merely assist particular industries, such as the fossil fuel industry. They serve the wider cause of Capitalism First. That is, they help to ensure that economic power and privilege are maintained no matter what else happens to the world as a result of climate change. One way to promote that cause is to encourage progressive forces to fight among themselves over the Hobson's choice, a choice and a fight that is artificially shaped by capitalism. This all helps Capitalism First, because if progressive forces are fighting one another, then they are not forging a countermovement that would refuse to be forced into a choice between economic security and climate security.

A union-led or -backed demand for a *just transition to a green economy* represents one way to reject the Hobson's choice; Green New Deal proposals aim to do just that. However, if a Green New Deal, or any similar venture, is to represent a genuinely green transition, it will require greater circumscription of 'economic freedom' – or, put differently, a diminution in plutocrats' power over the basic organisation and running of the economy. And the historical record provides ample evidence that the forces backing Capitalism First are not only awesomely powerful, but also capable of great brutality in their efforts to defend and extend the power and privilege of the economy's owners. So, we should not expect them to yield easily.

To summarise the second, third and fourth sections: climate change negates the notion that capitalist growth as we have known it promises a better life; if we continue to pursue untrammelled and indiscriminate economic growth, if we continue to respect economic freedom, it is almost certain that we will destroy the conditions required for civilised life and also extinguish millions of lives and countless species. One difficulty that confronts trade unions in responding to climate change is that there are limited prospects for a just and green labour-capital compromise. Capital would have to concede more than it ever has. And the Capitalism First vanguard seems to know that: in holding the line against a no-options-barred public discussion of mitigation, the vanguard reveals its fear that some of the realistic options would challenge the capitalist economy and power structure.

As I said, much of this is well understood. But it is often left unsaid. If we baldly describe the conflict between capitalism and climate security, we can starkly reveal the fanaticism that drives proponents of Capitalism First and the cravenness of the New Denialists.

Nobody Owns the Future

There are good reasons to encourage open, democratic discussion of the credible doubts about the compatibility of climate security, on the one hand, and untrammelled economic growth and economic freedom, on the other. However, due to the Hobson's choice I've just outlined, and the political bind it creates, capital has a natural, rhetorical and political advantage in any such discussion, which could only be meaningfully challenged by a very strong movement that is willing to set itself against the capitalist economy and power structure. To recall, capital's natural advantage stems from the relations of dependence described above: the economy must be run on capital's terms, to a very great extent, or else disinvestment follows, and, in turn, economic hardship for workers and vulnerable people generally. The implied threat of such hardship is already being used to undermine the formation of a movement for a just transition to a green economy, even before that movement has really gotten off the ground.

Moreover, it is important to recall that defenders of capitalist power and privilege fought methodically and relentlessly to prosecute the neoliberal project. One of the chief aims of that project was to fundamentally reshape culture, and to do so in ways that tend to promote capitalist power and privilege. For ambitious green transition measures to be adopted and implemented, there would need to be a similarly profound reshaping of our culture – if only to discredit and marginalise neoliberalism, which has travelled hand in hand with Capitalism First. Defenders of capitalist power and privilege are unlikely to see such a cultural transformation as anything but a grab for cultural and social power – and, perhaps, as a slippery slope to socialism; no matter how much Green New Deal proposals trumpet their compatibility with capitalism and profits, it is possible that certain capitalist forces will see them as a Trojan Horse. The examples of Allende and Mitterrand are telling: they remind us how vigorous – and, in the former case, how violent – can be the response when social democratic measures seem to represent, in the eyes of some, an augury of something 'worse'.

For that reason, we need to work on multiple fronts. Much work has already been done to establish the viability of a green macroeconomic and public policy agenda, and the availability of such an agenda is crucial to the task of persuading well-intentioned people to support a just transition to a green economy. We must also think about how to build the kind of political movement that is conscious of the need to overcome both (1) the Capitalism First countermovement, and also (2) the susceptibility of social democratic politicians to the accusation that they are overriding the prerogatives of private property, trampling 'private enterprise', and denying 'economic freedom', and therefore behaving as 'communists'. This second problem calls to mind the story about Franklin D. Roosevelt who, upon hearing the pleadings of a group of labour and civil rights activists, is reported to have told them: 'You've convinced me. Now go out and make me do it.'[18]

One approach would be to take aim at the very fact of capitalist domination of basic decisions about the organisation and running of the economy – and to do so on democratic grounds. The goal would be to begin to encroach upon plutocracy – at first culturally – by persuading people that democratic principles are relevant to the basic organisation and running of economic life, especially given the threat of catastrophic climate change.

The argument would be a simple one, if made along the following lines:

- The decisions that businesses make now will substantially determine whether our children and grandchildren have a chance of enjoying a civilised existence. Millions of human, and other, lives hang in the balance, together with the fate of at least one million species.
- Until now, our society has taken it for granted that core economic decisions – decisions about what goods and services to offer and how to generate them – are primarily 'private' decisions to be made by the people who own businesses.
- We have of course introduced various consumer and environmental protection laws that have imposed constraints, but those have still left substantial discretion to business owners.
- Now, scientists tell us that, for the sake of climate change mitigation, we need rapid 'transformative change', meaning 'a fundamental, system-wide reorganisation'.[19] So, we must think again about what we used to take for granted, including private domination of the economy.
- Whether transformative economic change happens, when it happens, and how it happens are matters that affect all of us.
- Decisions about matters so crucial to the future of humanity should be subject to democratic determination, not the private preferences of a tiny group of wealthy individuals and large corporations. But, currently, our political-economic arrangements leave many such decisions to be made by and for the owners of great wealth, and that is neither democratic nor conducive to addressing the climate crisis. We therefore should begin to think, talk and act in a democratic spirit with respect to the 'transformative change' that our economy must undergo, so that it might proceed democratically.
- That means that all of us should be involved in open debate and deliberation about how our community as a whole, and the smaller communities to which we belong, should implement transformative economic change.
- We will begin to establish for ourselves mechanisms for debate and deliberation because we have a right to be informed and to have an ongoing, effective say.
- That moral right is stronger than, and should trump, the rights that come with private ownership.
- Nobody owns the future.
- And so business owners should not be able to rely upon their ownership rights to determine all of our futures.

- Instead, the people must take democratic ownership of the question of how transformative change happens.
- In doing so, we will be doing nothing more than demanding that democratic principles be upheld when so much is at stake: matters that affect the whole community must be determined by the community, not by individuals using their privileged, private power.

Trade unionists could make this argument and also make it real by beginning to facilitate ground level, open, democratic debate and deliberation about how to implement transformative change. Workers, as unionists, could establish an ongoing, self-governing voice within the economy: see also Chapter 2 by David Peetz in this volume. This line of argument also serves to combat another danger, which was long ago presaged by André Gorz:

> The recognition of humanity's ecological interests does not necessarily take the form – desirable from the individual's point of view – of a defence or, better still, a reconquest of the life-world. On the contrary, it may well take a technocratic form, leading to tightening of the constraints and manipulations exercised by the administrative subsystem. It is impossible to base politics on a necessity or a science without by the same token denying its specific autonomy, and establishing a 'necessary' or 'scientific' dictatorship, no less totalitarian when it refers to the needs of the ecosystem than when it refers (as 'diamat' did) to the 'laws of dialectical materialism'. The problem that faces political ecology, then, is the problem of defining practical modalities enabling the needs of the ecosystem to be taken into account by the personal judgement of autonomous individuals in pursuit of their own ends within their own known world. It is the problem of retroactive coupling of necessity with normativeness or, if you prefer, the transformation of objective necessities into normative behaviour corresponding to needs that have been experienced, and that influence the form in which the objective necessities are perceived. This is none other than the problem of democracy.[20]

If the economy does not become much more democratic, there seems little chance that it will become just and green. The case in favour of an enlarged notion of democracy challenges the normally unquestioned idea that those who own the economy ought to control it. Today, the reasons for renewing that challenge are far greater than ever.

The COVID-19 Microcosm

The COVID-19 catastrophe demonstrates vividly how capitalist imperatives distort our ability to respond to human needs, even, or perhaps especially, when they are particularly pressing and weighty. A central component of the COVID-19 disaster – in societies where capitalist imperatives are not sufficiently restrained – is a tragic predicament: the tragedy is that people are obliged to choose between saving lives and saving livelihoods. To be sure, under any conceivable economic arrangements, a pandemic of this magnitude could be expected to generate tension between material well-being and the avoidance of infection. However, under capitalism, what might otherwise be a manageable tension becomes a potentially overwhelming crisis. Capitalism makes our bad situation even worse – and in many of the same ways that it aggravates the climate crisis. How so?

Capitalism adds perverse, tortuous and avoidable complexities to the problem of meeting human needs, not only under COVID-19, but also in its 'normal' mode. Insofar as the imperatives of profit maximisation and of the market determine whether human needs are met, then whether or not they are in fact met does not depend upon how urgent or important those needs are in human terms. Rather, it depends upon whether or not there is a happy coincidence between satisfying capitalist imperatives and meeting human needs. Sometimes that happy coincidence occurs; more often, it occurs with much 'interventionist' underwriting, facilitating, coaxing or manipulation; and sometimes it simply does not occur, and more or less extreme deprivation ensues, unless a non-market mechanism steps in. Those are the scenarios that typically obtain when the market system is able to function 'normally'.

However, under certain circumstances, such as the present pandemic, the operations of the market are suspended, partly by government fiat and partly as a result of capitalist and consumer withdrawal. When markets break down in such drastic ways, a crisis of apparent scarcity erupts, threatening a state of prolonged and widespread want – but not because there are insufficient resources to meet human needs. There is increased want because capitalist societies depend, by and large, on the capacity of the market to meet human needs, and the market is stalling. Thus, today, the problem is not the sheer unavailability, for the foreseeable future, of food, or clothing, or medicine, or energy, or shelter for everyone in the community. The problem is that the market mechanisms by which workers would earn the funds needed to purchase those necessaries, and the mechanisms by which supplies are made available for purchase, have broken down or are at risk of doing so.

The government possesses the formal constitutional authority to systematically appropriate the needed resources from private sources and to ensure their just distribution. But, despite that – and although, for a truly democratic government, *salus populi suprema lex* – capitalist-democratic governments cannot take such steps on a widespread and *open-ended* basis on pain of breaching the unwritten capitalist-democratic constitution, which I described in the first section.[21] The capitalist-democratic constitution elevates the hoarding of private wealth to the level of a supreme law, needlessly exacerbating any difficulties in meeting human needs that might be an unavoidable consequence of the pandemic; and needlessly aggravating the tension between material well-being and the avoidance of infection.

So, it is said that, beyond an initial emergency period, there are insufficient resources to supply the community with the funds to obtain essential goods and services, if we insist on maintaining wide-ranging restrictions on non-essential economic interaction in order to save lives. (Put aside the telling, jarring reasoning involved in saying that the distribution of *non-essential* goods and services must resume in order to ensure the distribution of *essential* goods and services.) Australia's treasurer has repeatedly stated that 'there is no money tree',[22] which, though literally true, is misleading. What is not acknowledged is that this problem could be relieved substantially if the extremely wealthy were forced to make sacrifices for the common good. Capitalism, by its sanctification of resource hoarding by the wealthy, puts such matters beyond the bounds of mainstream discussion. It is striking that there is not even discussion of moderate measures such as increased taxation of the extremely wealthy.

Hence the immense pressure we have seen to resume ordinary market operations, and, from some quarters, pressure to 're-open' even if that would risk a high cost in terms of human health: unless economic activity resumes on terms that are conducive to 'economic freedom', which, pre-widespread and effective vaccination, entails substantial health risks, those who must work for a wage are liable to suffer economic deprivation. The Hobson's choice is at once a real dilemma and an artificial one:

- It is a real dilemma so long as we live under a regime in which the interests of capitalists are allowed to trump community welfare. Trade unionists, and indeed everyone who must work for a wage, find themselves at the mercy of capitalist imperatives which must be satisfied if widespread poverty is to be avoided.[23] Workers are thus coerced into pleading and praying for a rapid return to profit maximising economic activity. And workers are thereby potentially conscripted as soldiers of Capitalism First, pressured to support the capitalist recipe for economic security over measures that would promote public health during COVID-19 as well as ecological security into the future.
- It is a largely artificial dilemma because it is substantially the product of human agency, rather than natural forces. This is illustrated by the parody of civic mindedness involved in the condemnation of toilet paper hoarders and the silence about the extremely wealthy; a small fraction of their hoarded wealth could greatly assist in meeting the community's needs, including its

needs for food, or clothing, or medicine, or energy, or shelter, until the virus can be conclusively eliminated.

The response of many defenders of capitalist power and privilege to the COVID-19 catastrophe involves the same order of priorities that is at work in the Capitalism First approach to climate change.

Beyond Fanaticism

Perhaps it was once plausible to maintain that liberal-democratic-capitalism stands for pragmatism and moderation. But, even if it was once the case, it is no longer. Supporters of liberal-democratic-capitalism across the spectrum – from the neoliberal vanguard to many, though not all, social democrats – have so far refused to systematically, openly and democratically address all credible options for tackling climate change. They have strained to avoid any option that would be incompatible, or even in tension, with maintaining the power and privilege of the economy's owners. They are insisting, in effect, that we make the preservation of human civilisation conditional upon the preservation of the capitalist economy and power structure. Urging faith in the capacity of the existing political and economic culture to overcome climate change – despite the mounting evidence to the contrary – is more utopian than pragmatic and more fanatical than moderate. Campaigners for capitalist power and privilege tell that us the existing order will save us, when there are good reasons to think that it will bury us. We must reject that faith by insisting that our future be determined by us, democratically. Trade unionists can take the lead in showing everyone what that demand means.

Notes

1 Henry Demarest Lloyd, *Wealth against Commonwealth* (New Jersey: Prentice Hall, 1963, first published 1894), 183.
2 Quoted in Meehan Crist, 'A Strange Blight', *London Review of Books* 41, no. 11 (2019): 7.
3 After this piece was substantially completed, but prior to its publication, two important books on the Green New Deal were published. They offer, among much more, accounts of ideological and political obstacles, and opportunities, that are very similar to the accounts advanced here. Noam Chomsky and Robert Pollin with C. J. Polychroniou, *Climate Crisis and the Global Green New Deal* (London: Verso, 2020). See, in particular: 20 (on economic freedom); 46–47, 49 (on the attitudes of some capitalists and their supporters to collaboration and compromise); 51, 53, 56, 145 (on the inherent anti-ecological tendency of capitalism); 58, 75, 96 (on the relationship between a progressive movement to combat climate change and further-reaching social change); 67, 75 on the need for very 'forceful government intervention', including (68) 'substantial levels of public investment, public ownership, and hard-cap regulations'; 69 on how

'if profit-making remains the driving force, then we are doomed'; and (86) 'the entire socioeconomic system based on production for profit, with its inherent imperative for growth whatever the consequences, cannot be sustained'. Naomi Klein, *On Fire: The Burning Case for a Green New Deal* (New York: Allen Lane, 2019). See, in particular: 70 (on the perception among some proponents of Capitalism First that environmentalism is a Trojan horse for socialism); 78–80, 84 (on the well-founded capitalist fear that substantial changes to 'our economic and political systems' would be required); 87 (on the need to curb 'the corporate sector, with its structural demand for increased sales and profits'); 91, 98 (on the need to confront 'a belief system that vilifies collective action and venerates total market freedom'); 96 (on the belief among some 'wealthy people in industrialized countries' that they can insulate themselves from climate change, and the willingness to 'write off huge swaths of humanity in the developing world'); 97 (on the possibility that wealthy nations will 'build ever more high-tech fortresses and adopt ever more draconian anti-immigration laws'); 99 (on how 'many of the biggest green groups have avoided, with phobic precision, any serious debate on the blindingly obvious roots of the climate crisis' including 'contemporary capitalism's quest for perpetual growth'); 101–3 (on the need to confront plutocracy, 'to change the culture so that this small but disproportionately influential minority, and the reckless worldview it represents, wields significantly less power'); 261–63 (on the Green New Deal's success depending on 'powerful social movements both backing' up a government 'and pushing them to do more').

4 Thomas L. Friedman, *The Lexus and the Olive Tree: Understanding Globalization* (New York: Farrar, Straus & Giroux, 1999).

5 About 85 per cent of emissions have occurred since the Second World War. David Wallace-Wells, *The Uninhabitable Earth: A Story of the Future* (London: Allen Lane, 2019), 4–5.

6 Wallace-Wells, *The Uninhabitable Earth.*

7 Ibid., 179–80; see also: 28; 263; 11.

8 Ibid., 181.

9 According to Kevin Anderson, the deputy director of the Tyndall Centre for Climate Change Research, quoted in Naomi Klein, *This Changes Everything* (London: Penguin, 2015), 56.

10 Quoted in Crist, 'A Strange Blight', 7.

11 Ibid.

12 Klein, *This Changes Everything*, 31.

13 Frederic Jameson attributes this thought to 'someone': quoted in Wallace-Wells, *The Uninhabitable Earth*, 161.

14 See, for example, Chomsky et al., *Climate Crisis*, 20, 53, on fossil fuel companies' burying of their findings, made around 40 years ago, positing a link between fossil fuels and climate change, and their subsequent campaigns of disinformation, which, in the main text, is described as the 'old denialism'; see also 140 on the outlook of those who are 'relentless in their pursuit of power and profit, whatever the human consequences'.

15 See, for example, Evan Osnos, 'Survival of the Richest', *New Yorker*, 30 January 2017. Consider also the apparent exodus of wealthy New Yorkers during the COVID-19 pandemic. 'Even though there's a strong rhetoric of "We're all in it together," that's not really the case', said Kim Phillips-Fein in response to a report that 'hundreds of thousands of New York City residents, in particular those from the city's wealthiest

neighborhoods, left as the coronavirus pandemic hit, an analysis of multiple sources of aggregated smartphone location data has found […] In the city's very wealthiest blocks, in neighborhoods like the Upper East Side, the West Village, SoHo and Brooklyn Heights, residential population decreased by 40 percent or more, while the rest of the city saw comparably modest changes.' Kevin Quealy, 'The Richest Neighbourhoods Emptied Out Most as Coronavirus Hit New York City', *New York Times*, 15 May 2020, https://www.nytimes.com/interactive/2020/05/15/upshot/who-left-new-york-coronavirus.html.

16 See the debate in *New Left Review*: Robert Pollin, 'De-Growth Versus a Green New Deal', *New Left Review*, 112 (July/August 2018): 5–25 (5); Mark Burton and Peter Somerville, 'Degrowth: A Defence', *New Left Review*, 115 (January/February 2019): 95–104 (95). See also: Jason Hickel, 'Is Green Growth Possible?', *New Political Economy* 25, no. 4 (2020): 469–86.

17 Quoted in Harry J. Glasbeek, *Class Privilege: How Law Shelters Shareholders and Coddles Capitalism* (Toronto: Between the Lines, 2017), 209.

18 Quoted in Seth Klein, *A Good War: Mobilizing Canada for the Climate Emergency* (Toronto: ECW Press, 2020), chapter 10.

19 Crist, 'A Strange Blight', 7.

20 Andre Gorz, 'Political Ecology: Expertocracy Versus Self-Limitation', *New Left Review* 1, no. 202 (November/December 1993): 55–67 (59).

21 Consider how and why the *United States' Defense Production Act 1950* is used: Zolan Kanno-Youngs and Ana Swanson, 'Wartime Production Law Has Been Used Routinely, but Not with Coronavirus', *New York Times*, 31 March 2020, https://www.nytimes.com/2020/03/31/us/politics/coronavirus-defense-production-act.html; James E. Baker, 'It's High Time We Fought This Virus the American Way', *New York Times*, 3 April 2020, https://www.nytimes.com/2020/04/03/opinion/defense-protection-act-covid.html.

22 Quoted in Phillip Coorey, ' "Australians know There Is No Money Tree": Treasurer', *Australian Financial Review*, 11 March 2020, https://www.afr.com/politics/federal/australians-know-there-is-no-money-tree-treasurer-20200511-p54rou.

23 And, so long as the virus remains a potent force, many workers are coerced into running an even higher risk of serious illness or death than usual, merely in order to earn a living.

Chapter 4

REGULATORY APPROACHES TO THE INTERNAL AFFAIRS OF TRADE UNIONS IN AUSTRALIA: FROM DEMOCRATIC CONTROL TO CORPORATE ACCOUNTABILITY

Caroline Kelly

The internal affairs of Australian trade unions have long been the subject of detailed statutory regulation. The early federal conciliation and arbitration system, which was premised upon the recognition and facilitation of trade unions, laid the groundwork for the introduction of a range of legislative provisions concerned with internal union governance. By the late 1970s, there was an extensive legislative regime in place to ensure that the collective institutions supported by the industrial relations framework were themselves regulated and, in particular, controlled democratically by the rank-and-file membership. To this end there were, for example, provisions that imposed upon trade unions electoral controls, controls on the content of union rules and a mechanism to require the performance of those rules. Those provisions were frequently litigated and, by the 1980s, were the subject of an increasingly large body of case law.

At this time, the legislation and its application by the courts was underpinned by three key democratic principles: representative democracy in union leadership; the fullest possible participation by union members in the affairs of the union; and prevention of the arbitrary exercise of discretionary power. With respect to the third principle in particular, one can see the influence of techniques that we might usually associate with the field of administrative law at play. The case law reveals that decisions made by trade union decision makers were subjected to *ultra vires* type testing and administrative law standards of procedural propriety through the application of the principles of natural justice.

At the same time, however, a secondary regulatory goal was emerging: the accountability of trade unions and their officials, particularly with respect to financial matters. To this end, the legislature and the courts began to draw on regulatory techniques and principles typically associated with corporations and fiduciary law. The legislation contained detailed provisions requiring the keeping of accounting records and financial auditing. The courts likened union officials to company directors and found that they were the donees of fiduciary power.

In recent decades, the regulatory orientation has shifted. Since the late 1980s, numerous cycles of legislative change have fundamentally altered the position and role of trade unions in the industrial relations system and society more generally. As the structural supports offered by the conciliation and arbitration system have been dismantled, and governments and employers have sought progressively to decollectivise employment relations, trade unions have found themselves under serious threat, with declining density. At the same time, there have been several rounds of legislative change directly impacting upon the internal affairs of trade unions. Ostensibly, the primary goal of many of these changes has been to make trade unions more accountable by extending to trade unions the duties and liabilities applied to corporations and their officers. Indeed, the application of standards from corporations law to trade unions has been elevated in political discourse to such a degree as to have become a regulatory goal in and of itself. Several principles or themes underpin the corporate model – ensuring financial propriety; prevention of corruption; and reshaping the respective roles of trade unions and the state. With respect to the third, less obvious, theme, the 'corporate model'[1] of regulation focuses not upon the content and performance of unions rules but, rather, imposes positive statutory duties and empowers external state regulatory bodies to investigate and enforce compliance. It is also centred upon a narrow view of the purpose of unions as the handling of members' money and the maximising of returns. Meanwhile, the goal of ensuring democratic control by members has become an ancillary one. While the provisions concerned with democratic control enacted before the 1970s remain largely intact in the current *Fair Work (Registered Organisations) Act 2009* (Cth) (*Fair Work (RO) Act*), they are no longer the frequent subjects of published judgments or public discussion.

The first three parts of this chapter seek to trace this shift in regulatory orientation, analysed against the backdrop of changes in the wider industrial relations landscape. The final part of this chapter then makes a number of observations. First, it argues that the rise of the corporate model – and the decline in focus on democratic control – has occurred in sync with the devaluation of collective institutions more generally. Second, it observes that the predominance of the corporate model of regulation can be seen as one of the ways in which labour law – especially since the mid-1990s – has become increasingly corporatised. Third, while regulatory mechanisms and principles from corporations law might validly play some contained role in regulating the financial management of trade unions, the blunt and extensive adoption of the model is problematic in a number of respects. It ignores the imbalance of power between employers and employees which lies at the heart of labour law; it overlooks the purpose and democratic mandate of trade unions; and it curbs union autonomy to an unacceptable degree by imposing a complex regime of positive statutory obligations rather than obligations contained in the union's own rules. Fourth, this chapter suggests that the decline in the use of provisions directed to democratic control of unions and, in particular, the content and performance of union rules is also troubling. While this is by no means an accurate barometer for the state of union democracy – and there may be a number of reasons as to why union members and officials are not utilising these provisions as frequently as they once did – it might indicate a degree of passivity in holding union decision making to account. It has also meant that administrative law principles – which at one time played a significant role in regulating decision making in unions – are now rarely deployed in the trade union context. Fifth, it is suggested that more attention should be dedicated to understanding the context from which principles are drawn and applied to the context of the internal affairs of trade unions. With this in mind, this chapter finally argues that the possible role of administrative law principles deserves renewed attention. Administrative law principles provide one mechanism by which the rank-and-file membership can hold the exercise of power in trade unions to account whilst preserving a margin of appreciation for union decision makers and an appropriate level of union autonomy more generally.

Early Federation: Conciliation, Arbitration and Registration

The internal affairs of Australian trade unions have traditionally been subject to statutory regulation in a way that has 'set Australia apart from other comparable countries in which the degree of external control of the affairs of trade unions has been relatively low'.[2] As Forsyth has highlighted, unions in Australia have tended to accept a relatively extensive level of regulation 'as the price to be paid for the substantial benefits that they have obtained from participation in the formal industrial relations framework.'[3] From the beginning of Australia's federal arbitration system, there was recognition of the fact that 'a trade union is not […] an institution that is tolerated by the state, but an institution whose existence is encouraged by the state and which is given the opportunity of co-operating with the state in the making of legislation to apply in industry'.[4] Indeed, one of the objects of the original *Conciliation and Arbitration Act 1904* (Cth) (*C&A Act*) was to 'facilitate and encourage the organisation of representative bodies of employers and employees'. As Henry Bourne Higgins observed, 'the system of arbitration adopted by the Act' was 'based on unionism [...] without unions it is hard to conceive how arbitration could be worked'.[5] The process of registration under the Commonwealth system thus enabled trade unions to acquire various rights, including to be party to industrial agreements or awards and to 'sue for subscriptions, fines and levies due to it by its members'.[6] The *C&A Act* also provided that upon registration a trade union becomes a corporate body and takes on 'an independent existence as a legal person'.[7]

As Boulton argues, it was thought that because the conciliation and arbitration system cultivated the growth of Australian unions, the Parliament must assume responsibility for ensuring that workers were not 'being encouraged or forced to join objectionable organisations' and that unions were 'democratic and properly managed organisations so that they could speak for, and enter into obligations on behalf of, their members within the system'.[8] In other words, by choosing to register under the federal system and to accept the privileges that process confers, unions must also subject their internal affairs to state regulation. Thus, the *C&A Act* of 1904 imposed restrictions (albeit limited) on trade unions to ensure democratic process and proper management. It provided for the cancellation of trade union registration in limited circumstances including, for example, where the rules of a trade union had not been bona fide observed;[9] where the rules of a trade union did not provide reasonable facilities for the admission of new members or imposed unreasonable conditions upon the continuance of their membership or were in any way tyrannical or oppressive;[10] or where the accounts of a registered organisation had not been audited in accordance with the rules or did not disclose the true financial position of the organisation.[11]

Twentieth-Century Regulation of the Internal Affairs of Trade Unions

The rise of 'democratic control' and the influence of administrative law principles

The conciliation and arbitration system formed at the turn of the century laid the groundwork for the growth of unionism in Australia over the course of the twentieth century. While it was not a 'simple history'[12] of continuous growth, and there were 'several periods of rise and decline',[13] the power and density of trade unions increased significantly in the years between 1904 and the early 1980s. In particular, as Bramble has argued, the years 1968–74 represent the 'flood tide' of union strength – unions 'began an offensive for higher wages, improved working conditions and political reform' and 'began to use the strike weapon in earnest'.[14] Union density was high and rising, and there was a considerable degree of political consensus about the role of trade unions in society.

Over this period of time, and in response to the growing power of the union movement, a number of new legislative changes were introduced to strengthen 'internal trade union controls in order to make the leadership truly accountable to the rank and file membership',[15] some of which are examined in more detail below. In 1928, the conservative Bruce Page Government (in the context of a broader reform package, some of which was repealed soon after in 1930) introduced provisions empowering the court to declare union rules invalid and to order union officials to obey their union's rules. In 1949, the Chifley Labor Government introduced, among other things, legislation enabling the court to conduct inquiries into electoral irregularities and in 1950 the Menzies Government introduced further amendments including the requirement that all union elections be held by secret ballot.

By the 1970s, there was an extensive regulatory regime in place. The Minister for Labour in the Whitlam Labor Government explained that legislative initiatives were based on the philosophy that 'as unions become larger, and their governing bodies become more remote from the membership, it will be important to safeguard against the development of bureaucratic relations between the leadership and the rank-and-file'.[16] He called upon the government to 'ensure a system of democratic control of all unions, allowing the fullest participation by members in their affairs'.[17] Encouraging 'the democratic control of organisations [...] and the full participation of members of such an organisation in the affairs of the organisation' was introduced as an object of the *C&A Act* in 1973. Many key aspects of the regime regulating union internal affairs by this time were 'generally propounded in terms of democracy'.[18] Bipartisan support for the idea that trade unions should be 'controlled "democratically" by their members'[19] continued into the mid-1980s. By this time there was a very large body of case law[20] considering and applying the key provisions of the legislative regime, due in part to the increasing willingness of the courts throughout the 1970s to scrutinise union elections, rules and governance. Democracy in trade unions was also the subject of a significant body of academic work. For example, the literature concerning the reality of union democracy, for example, 'as measured by such indices as membership participation levels, the presence within unions of factions or parties and the degree to which opposition is tolerated by union officials' was said by Tracey in 1985 to be 'so extensive that no attempt [could] be made to set it out in full'.[21]

Taking this point as a high watermark of concern with the democratic control of trade unions, it is useful to examine in further detail some key aspects of the legislative regime in place. The starting point of the regime was that 'decision-making processes of Australian unions are governed by rules adopted by their members from time to time' and that those rules 'form the basis of the relationship between individual members and between members and their union'.[22] Its key provisions introduced a 'measure of statutory control' to be exercised 'over the contents of union rule books and over the exercise of powers conferred by rule'.[23] As Tracey highlighted, three sets of statutory controls were particularly significant.[24]

The first set of controls related to the conduct of elections. The *C&A Act* stipulated that the rules of registered organisations must provide for certain matters with respect to elections. This included the election of the holder of each office within the union either by a direct voting system or through a one-tier collegiate electoral system.[25] Union rules were also required to address issues such as returning officers, defective nominations and limits on the holding of office for more than four years without re-election. Every election by direct voting system was required to be conducted by secret ballot.[26] The Federal Court had jurisdiction to inquire into 'alleged irregularities in or in connection with a ballot'.[27] Irregularity was defined widely to include any breach of union rules in relation to an election or ballot and any act, omission or other means whereby the full and free recording of all votes or a correct ascertainment or declaration of the results of the voting is, or is attempted to be, prevented or hindered. In the event that an irregularity was found, the court was empowered to order that any step in or in connection with the ballot be taken again, or that a fresh ballot be conducted and to make such further orders as necessary. The statutory remedies available admitted 'a flexible and appropriate response to irregularities that would otherwise be unavailable'.[28]

The second set of controls related to union rules. Section 140 of the *C&A Act* provided, among other things, that the rules of an organisation 'shall not be contrary to, or fail to make a provision required by, a provision of this Act, the regulations or an award or otherwise be contrary to law' and that they 'shall not impose upon applicants for membership, or members, of the organization, conditions, obligations or restrictions which, having regard to the objects of this Act and the purposes of the registration of organizations under this Act, are oppressive, unreasonable or unjust'. Earlier decisions of the Federal Court, prior to the 1970s, reveal a 'laissez faire' approach to the interpretation of section 140 as it was thought that 'organizations knew what rules were best for them'.[29] Decisions after that time, however, reflect increased readiness on the part of the court to find rules invalid.[30] This provision generated 'an enormous volume of case law' and provided 'wide scope for the expression of judicial views on the practice of democracy in trade unions'.[31]

The third significant statutory control was section 141 of the *C&A Act* which provided that a member of an organisation may apply to the court for an order giving 'directions for the performance or observance of any of the rules of an organisation by any person who is under an obligation to perform or observe those rules'. In some early cases, the court expressed the view that it would not interfere in 'domestic disputes unless there are allegations of fraud or of some violent breach of the rules which may disturb the peace of industry, or prevent the organizations properly functioning under the Act'.[32] The court later adopted the view expressed by Kelly CJ in *Wilson v. Heydon* that the section operates as a 'safeguard specially designed by the Legislature' to protect against 'action taken without authority, express or implied in the rules' which 'if unchecked, may destroy [...] members' confidence in the administration of the organization and so impair its effectiveness [...] as a body representative of their interests'.[33] Accordingly, the provision operated to ensure performance of the express terms of a union's rules. This included the protection of members against prejudicial action by a body that lacked the power to so act under the rules.[34]

However, when applying section 141 the court began to look not only to the express terms of the relevant rules but to 'what is seen to be implicit in them having regard to the relevant circumstances' in order to 'ascertain the meaning of rules upon their true construction'.[35] Particularly important was the implication of the principles of natural justice in 'decisions affecting a wide range of rights' including 'the right to continued membership of an organization, the right of continued employment, and the right not to be penalized unjustly'.[36] Whilst the early approach of the courts was cautious,[37] from the 1970s the courts began to draw upon cases concerning administrative tribunals in order to determine whether the principles of natural justice applied in the trade union context and, if so, what they required. With respect to the former question, the courts looked to the terms of the relevant rules in their own 'context and circumstances' – just as the courts look to the terms of the relevant statute in the administrative law context – as well as to seminal administrative law cases such as *Ridge v. Baldwin*.[38] With respect to the latter question of what natural justice requires in a particular case, the courts looked again to the position in administrative law reflected in the following statement of Tucker LJ in *Russell v. Duke of Norfolk* that:

> there are [...] no words which are of universal application to every kind of enquiry and every kind of domestic tribunal. The requirements of natural justice must depend on the circumstances of the case, the nature of the enquiry,

the rules under which the tribunal is acting, the subject matter being dealt with and so forth.[39]

Indeed, Tracey argued in 1982 that the Federal Court and its predecessor had taken 'advantage of the wide scope offered by Lord Justice Tucker to tailor natural justice requirements to the needs of Australian trade unions and their members'.[40] The decisions of the court between 1975 and 1982, he argued, could be seen 'collectively as providing a fairly clear code', particularly for the conduct of disciplinary proceedings.[41] There were a number 'essential elements' of this code, including the provision of notice of the details of the relevant charges and the hearing which was to take place. The notice provided was also required to be sufficiently detailed in order for the member to understand the case against them,[42] though the 'adequacy of notice will vary with the complexity of the charges and the ease with which the evidence for the defence can be marshalled'.[43] The hearing was to allow the member an opportunity to present a defence and was only to deal with charges of which the member had been notified.[44] The conduct of the hearing was to be fair and the member not to be inhibited from properly presenting their case: a hearing which is conducted in an 'emotionally charged atmosphere' or during which 'statements exhibiting hatred and contempt' for the relevant member with 'no proper control from the chairman' would constitute a denial of natural justice.[45] The hearing of evidence was also to be kept separate from any deliberations. Importantly, the tribunal could not be openly or 'invincibly' biased against the relevant member. Invincible bias is 'bias that is incapable of being remedied by reason or argument during the period up to the making of the tribunal's decision'.[46]

Under the regime's overarching goal of democratic control, three interrelated democratic sub-principles can be detected. First, the regime sought to ensure representative, as opposed to direct or 'primitive',[47] democracy in trade union leadership. Second, it sought to ensure the fullest possible participation of members in the affairs of their unions. The third principle, which has received altogether less attention, is protection of members from the arbitrary exercise of power. In this sense, this model of regulating union decision making affecting the interests of members bears similarity in some respects to the process of judicial review. In particular, parallels can be drawn with the *ultra vires* model of decision making imposed on administrative decision makers. In administrative law, the *ultra vires* principle requires that a body to which power has been granted pursuant to legislation must not exceed the powers so granted. This means, in a narrow sense, that the relevant body 'must have legal capacity to act on that subject matter' and, in a broader sense, that the relevant body is constrained in the way in which the power is exercised.[48]

That is, an administrative decision maker must comply with the rules of procedural fairness, act for proper and not improper purposes, take into account all relevant and not irrelevant considerations and must act reasonably (at least in the *Wednesbury* sense).[49]

Just as administrative decision makers derive decision-making power from legislation, decision makers in the trade union context derive power from union rules. A trade union committee or tribunal taking prejudicial action against a member must be empowered under the rules to do so or its decision may be found void. In *Magner v. Fowler*,[50] for example, the court found that the decision by the Administrative and Clerical Officers Association to establish a Committee of Inquiry to determine whether improprieties had taken place was not within the power conferred by any rule of the association and was contrary to the general intention of the rules. As Davies and Freedland once highlighted in the UK context, it is possible to see this as the importation of 'public principles into the construction of the contract of membership of the trade union [...] as expressed in the rule book [...] of the trade union'.[51] A decision-making body empowered by a union's rules is also constrained in the way in which it exercises the power conferred insofar as it must, as outlined above, accord natural justice to persons affected unless the union's rules provide to the contrary.[52] The courts will consider whether the decision was one that 'reasonable [people] acting honestly could have come to'.[53] The courts have also found that express powers conferred must be exercised for proper purposes and that irrelevant considerations must not be taken into account, although, as will be discussed below, they have drawn upon fiduciary and not administrative law in order so to find.

The extent to which this regime was successful in ensuring democratic control of trade unions by members was not settled among commentators. As Tracey highlighted, the 'effectiveness of legal intervention' in the field was doubted by some because 'no amount of legislation can force individuals to embrace democratic ideals'.[54] Whilst the law can ensure that members have access to mechanisms by which to exercise control over union officials, 'a union may well slip into a state of passive democracy' whereby members are 'unwilling and/or unable to exercise their rights'.[55]

Some such as Howard went further, suggesting that the imposition of democratic practices was a masked attempt to inhibit 'the tactical effectiveness of unions confronting employers': 'democratic processes can be detrimental to unions' because they 'retard [unions'] progress' in reducing 'managerial discretion'.[56] The periods during which the legislative amendments described above were introduced – in particular 1928–30 and 1949–50 – were marked by 'political, economic and industrial struggles'[57] and were periods during which governments were introducing 'increasingly harsh measures against trade unions' and, some argue, were moving more generally 'away from the labourist view of labour law to a disciplinarian version'.[58] Others have also argued that such reforms emphasised individual rights at the expense of collective rights.[59] Perhaps, following the 'growth of trade unions through favourable laws' in the period between 1904 and 1928, it was 'only natural for future governments, in the two later periods, to adopt a solution of more all-embracing and complex laws to curb the excesses of real or perceived union power'.[60]

It is important, though, that the regime at this time existed within the context of an industrial relations system which, as a whole, facilitated unionism. To the extent the regime conferred rights on individuals in this context it is arguable that it did so primarily to advance collectivist aims. In enacting provisions governing the status and powers of trade unions – and providing a floor for internal democracy – the legislature arguably gave unions 'a logical foundation in law' in recognition of 'the great changes that, in the course of their development, have come over the trade unions, transforming them into forces of great and growing importance in the social structure and in the life of the community'.[61] Further, as McCallum has argued, 'no one would deny' that the enactment of controls on the content of union rules, the performance of union rules and the power to conduct election inquiries were both necessary and worthwhile.[62] Such controls help not only to protect the rights of individual members, but to safeguard the 'functional usefulness of the union itself, in relation both to the objects for which it was formed and the purposes of the law' against the 'impairment and decay that would almost inevitably follow an excess of concentration of authority'.[63] Indeed, scholars such as Bramble have argued that during the relevant period (particularly in the early 1970s) rank-and-file members were 'driving the agenda' in many Australian trade unions, with the lively participation by members in union affairs creating pressure from below to democratise further.[64]

An additional problem was that many of the hundreds of actions brought under the provisions outlined above where 'various eligibility, election and expulsion rules have been pronounced upon' were 'not brought by single distraught individuals but [...] by union officials and factional groups anxious to see fair play and to enhance their intra-union causes'.[65] However, such actions 'established ground rules and norms of union behaviour and [...] forced such bodies to give careful thought to every union rule and to all of their internal procedures'.[66] Indeed, it is uncontentious that the legislative controls outlined above were 'influential in making more union structures conform, on paper at least' to a model of representative democracy and that the Australian experience 'indicates that [...] the law can operate constructively to prevent some undemocratic practices occurring and to remedy the effects of such practices when they do occur'.[67]

The emergence of 'accountability' and the influence of corporations and fiduciary law

While democratic control was the primary focus of the regulation of the internal affairs of trade unions during the mid-to-late twentieth century, it is clear that a regulatory focus on the accountability of trade unions and their officers was also emerging. By 1986, trade unions were subject to increasingly extensive requirements related to financial accountability and auditing. In addition to this, as Forsyth has noted, the imposition of 'standards of accountability and financial propriety on individual union office holders' was 'achieved through a combination of the common law, union rules and further legislative provisions'.[68] As noted above, in the context of applying section 141 of the *C&A Act*, the courts found an implied duty to exercise power conferred by union rules bona fide and for proper purposes, with the failure to do so resulting in a failure to comply with the rules as a whole.[69]

Furthermore, by the 1980s, it was possible to say that the application of fiduciary principles to trade union officials was emerging in general law. As Tracey highlighted in 1985, the courts, 'after some initial hesitance' had 'been prepared to imply a fiduciary duty which rests on those officials who have charge of a union's funds'.[70] Christie stated in 1986 that it could be said 'with some certainty that union officials owe fiduciary obligations identical to those owed by directors to companies'.[71] In the leading case of *Allen v. Townsend*, the Federal Court found that 'members of the committee of management of an organization [...] owe a fiduciary duty to members of the organization'.[72] The court said that trade union officials 'are to be compared with directors of incorporated bodies [...] under legislation such as the Companies Acts' and that, subject to 'necessary adaptations', principles of law 'regulating the manner in which directors of companies are required to exercise power conferred on them' should apply to those officials.[73] The court went on to highlight the similarities 'between organizations and legal persons incorporated under the *Companies Acts*'.[74] Among other things, each is 'a creature of statute' and has 'a legal personality separate [...] from its members'; each 'has perpetual succession' and 'the property of each does not belong to its members'; each must 'act at the direction of individuals who manage its activities' and the 'powers of these individuals depend upon the rules which regulate the affairs of the incorporated body'.[75] Although, theoretically, the 'ultimate control is conferred upon and retained by the members of the incorporated body', in practice, the group 'managing the affairs of the incorporated body has a very substantial control over the affairs of that body, the affairs of its members, and the privileges and obligations affecting different groups of members within that body'.[76]

These statements are a stark illustration of the growing influence of standards from corporations and fiduciary law in the regulation of trade union affairs. The extension of fiduciary duties mirroring those applying to company directors, however, was not codified until later.

The Regulation of Internal Trade Union Affairs in Recent Decades

Treatment of unions as corporations

Since the late 1980s, there have been numerous rounds of legislative change that have fundamentally altered the position and role of trade unions in the wider industrial relations landscape. Peetz has argued that since 'around the mid-1980s' unionism in Australia has been experiencing a 'paradigm shift' or 'institutional break' caused, in large part, by 'a change in strategies by employers and governments towards unions'.[77] As successive governments have sought to decollectivise employment relations, structural and institutional supports for trade unionism have been removed and density has declined. After 'nearly a century in which collective employment relationships were accepted, often grudgingly, as the norm',[78] trade unions have found themselves struggling to operate in an environment increasingly hostile to collective institutions.

Some have argued that the declining role of trade unions and collective institutions began with the introduction of the 1983 Prices and Incomes Accord between the Australian Council of Trade Unions (ACTU) and the Hawke Labor Government. Bramble, for example, has argued that the Accord marked 'the onset of the ebb tide in union affairs' and began a 'period of retreat', particularly at the level of grassroots organising.[79] Others such as Peetz, however, have argued that there are limits to the analysis that the Accord was 'a betrayal of unions' interests', ignoring among other things 'the benefits that accrued to union members through the Accord' and 'broader economic forces that led to policy changes'.[80] Putting this to one side, it is widely accepted that the shift in 1993 under the Keating Labor Government of 'the entire basis of the system away from dispute settlement and award regulation' to enterprise level bargaining as 'the primary means of setting wages and working conditions' was profound.[81] The election of the Howard Coalition Government in 1996 'heralded a new attack on collectivism'.[82] The *Workplace Relations Act 1996* (Cth) (*WR Act*) introduced a raft of changes including increased focus on contracts between employers and individual employees; prohibition of compulsory unionism and abolition of union preference clauses; stringent restrictions on union workplace entry rights; enactment of so-called freedom of association provisions (which in reality strengthened the right *not* to join a union); and increased sanctions for unprotected industrial action. As Fenwick and Howe have observed, changes from the mid-1990s onwards were characterised by two themes – emphasis on individualisation of the law, 'representing a marked shift from the previous emphasis on collective methods of regulation and dispute settlement', and the reconfiguration of 'the role of the state in the enforcement or policing of labour law norms'.[83]

Within that broader context, there are several rounds of legislative change that have impacted directly upon the internal affairs of trade unions. A consistent theme that runs through each of these is the emphasis upon increasing trade union accountability by extending to trade unions the duties and liabilities applied to corporations and their officers. Indeed, the desirability of doing so has been an 'abiding political message'[84] since the 1990s.

The *WR Act* did not deal directly with 'matters of internal union regulation', nor did it 'significantly alter the level of accountability of unions under federal law'.[85] Reform of that kind, however, followed in 2002 when the provisions of the *WR Act* concerning the internal affairs of organisations were incorporated into a schedule to the *WR Act*[86] and were amended under the pretence of providing 'greater choice and flexibility to registered organisations and their members'[87] and ensuring that 'industrial organisations become more competitive, open and accountable in their internal activities'.[88] This involved, among other things, the alignment of 'financial accounting and reporting requirements of organisations with those applicable under the Corporations Act'.[89] It also involved the introduction of 'a range of statutory fiduciary duties for officials of organisations in relation to financial management functions' which were 'broadly in line with those that apply to company directors and employees under the Corporations Act'.[90] The Coalition Government argued that such duties were 'appropriate, given that officials of registered organisations are entrusted with substantial funds on behalf of their members'.[91] Beyond this, however, little explanation of or justification for the statutory fiduciary duties was provided. The legislation provided that officers must exercise their powers and discharge their duties with care and diligence, in good faith in what they believe to be in the best interests of the organisation, and for a proper purpose; and not improperly use their position or information obtained in that position, to gain an advantage for themselves or someone else or to cause detriment to the organisation or someone else. Those duties are now contained in the *Fair Work (RO) Act*.

Several years after the introduction of these provisions, the Howard Government introduced *Work Choices*, commonly treated 'almost universally by commentators as the most significant [reform] since the establishment of the federal arbitration system in 1904'[92] and a 'major assault on unions'.[93] Among other things it 'finally laid to rest'[94] the system of compulsory arbitration;

strengthened the predominance of individual contracts; abolished the no-disadvantage test; introduced new, burdensome procedures for the taking of protected industrial action; and further limited the capacity of unions to enter workplaces. It did not, however, alter in any substantial way the provisions regulating internal union affairs.

Rather, the next significant wave of change did not come until several years after the *Fair Work Act 2009* (Cth) (*Fair Work Act*) came into force under the leadership of Rudd Labor Government. The *Fair Work Act* itself provided far wider scope for collective bargaining and the role of trade unions than *Work Choices*. It sought to 'place collective bargaining at the enterprise level at the heart of the workplace relations system'.[95] But in other respects – industrial action, for example – there were 'few substantive changes'.[96] Similarly, while the provisions regulating internal union affairs were transferred into a separate legislative instrument (the *FW(RO) Act*), it retained almost entirely the provisions previously in place.

Then, in 2011, details of corruption scandals within the Health Services Union (HSU) emerged involving a 'series of revelations of misuse of credit cards, misappropriation of unions funds and other forms of corruption' by senior HSU officials Craig Thomson, Michael Williamson and Kathy Jackson.[97] A 'range of legal consequences arose'[98] from these events, including an investigation by the Office of the General Manager of Fair Work Australia and criminal and/or civil proceedings against all three officials. Jackson, for example, was found by the Federal Court to have breached her obligation not to use her position to gain an advantage for herself under section 287 of the *FW(RO) Act*. Justice Tracey found that it was 'strongly arguable' that she had also contravened her obligations to act with care and diligence and in good faith under sections 285 and 286 of the *Fair Work (RO) Act*.[99] In 2012, in the wake of the scandal, the Gillard Labor Government introduced new provisions requiring that the rules of registered organisations deal with disclosure of remuneration, pecuniary and financial interests, strengthening the investigative powers of the Fair Work Commission and requiring compulsory education and training for all officials involved in financial administration.

The Abbott Coalition Government was elected in 2013 and in 2014 established the Royal Commission into Trade Union Governance and Corruption, appointing former High Court judge Dyson Heydon AC QC as Royal Commissioner. In its final report in December 2015, the Royal Commission found that corruption in unions was 'not the work of a few rogue officials' but was, rather, 'deep-seated'[100] and made numerous recommendations for reform of the law regulating the internal affairs of unions. The Royal Commission recommended, among other things, the establishment of an agency with powers similar to those conferred on the Australian Securities and

Investments Commission (ASIC) to regulate registered organisations; more onerous requirements for financial disclosure and record keeping; expansion of the range of offences leading to disqualification of union officials; new criminal offences relating to 'corrupting benefits'; and several initiatives to regulate separate entities or 'slush funds'.

It also recommended that the duties imposed on the officers of trade unions be brought further into line with those imposed upon the directors of companies given the 'strong analogy' between the two.[101] This included, for example, expansion of the definition of 'office'; expanding the statutory duties of union officers beyond financial management to 'the entire field of possible activity by officers of the organisation';[102] substantial increases in civil penalties for breach of statute and the imposition of criminal liability on officers who dishonestly or recklessly breach their statutory duties; and the introduction of an objective, rather than subjective, standard in relation to the duty of good faith contained in section 286 of the *Fair Work (RO) Act*.

The Parliament took up a number of the Royal Commission's recommendations. First, in 2016, the *Fair Work (Registered Organisations) Amendment Act 2016* (Cth)[103] established the Registered Organisations Commission (ROC) and endowed it with investigative powers in line with those of ASIC; implemented many of the recommendations relating to increased financial reporting, transparency and training; increased the maximum civil penalties; and introduced new criminal offences for breaches of union officers' duties. Second, in 2017, the *Fair Work Amendment (Corrupting Benefits) Act 2017* (Cth) was introduced to enact the recommendations of the Royal Commission with respect to 'corrupting benefits'.

There are several themes that can be detected in the corporate regulatory model implemented through the reforms outlined above. First is the concern to ensure financial propriety. Second is the related concern to address corrupt conduct. The third, less obvious, theme is the remodelling of the respective roles of trade unions and the state. The corporate model casts trade unions in a narrow role. It is not concerned with bolstering the legitimacy of trade unions as collective institutions serving the broad public function of representing workers' voices, not only in the workplace but in politics and civil society. It is not concerned with increasing the participation of members in union affairs. Rather, the focus (as with corporations and shareholders) is upon the union's role in handling members' money and maximising returns for members. However, the corporate model expands the role of the state as commander, investigator and enforcer. It is focused upon the use of statutory, rather than rule-based, regulation that is directory rather than enabling in nature, and enforcement by external agencies such as the ROC, rather than by members.

The attempted reforms of 2019 can be seen as an extreme extension of this third theme. In 2019, the Fair Work (Registered Organisations) Amendment (Ensuring Integrity) Bill 2019 (Ensuring Integrity Bill) was introduced under the guise of responding further to the recommendations of the Royal Commission. In fact, however, the Ensuring Integrity Bill sought to go much further than those recommendations by introducing a number of radical changes to intensify the influence of the corporate model of regulation. These included, among other things, introducing a 'discretionary regime' allowing the Federal Court to disqualify union officials from office for contravention not only of the *FW(RO) Act* itself but the *Fair Work Act* more broadly, failing to take steps to prevent the organisation from breaking the law or where the official is not a 'fit and proper' person. It also sought to enable the Federal Court to deregister an organisation on numerous grounds including 'unlawful or improper conduct of the affairs of the organisation', 'repeated breaches of a range of industrial laws by its members' and the 'taking of obstructive unprotected industrial action by a substantial number of members'.[104] Further, the Ensuring Integrity Bill contained expanded grounds 'on which the Federal Court may order remedial action to deal with governance issues'.

As Forsyth has highlighted, it was claimed that the Ensuring Integrity Bill simply sought to apply to trade unions 'the same regulatory standards that apply to corporations'.[105] In reality, though, it would have enabled the disqualification of trade union officials and the deregistration of entire trade unions on 'much wider grounds' than are available for the disqualification of company directors and the winding up of companies.[106] The Ensuring Integrity Bill was defeated in the Senate in late 2019 and the Morrison Coalition Government pledged to reintroduce it in 2020. However, in the initial phases of the COVID-19 crisis in Australia, the government sought to distance itself from its anti-union rhetoric ahead of new efforts to reform Australia's industrial relations system and, accordingly, announced that it would shelve the Ensuring Integrity Bill as a 'sign of good faith'.[107]

Democratic control: diminished focus

The regime directed to the democratic control of trade unions which was in force in the mid-to-late twentieth century remains largely intact in the current *FW(RO) Act.* There are a number of new provisions. For example, since 1988 all union elections are required to be conducted by the Australian Electoral Commission (AEC) unless an exemption is granted.[108] The *FW(RO) Act* now provides that union rules must not discriminate between applicants for membership or members on the basis of certain protected attributes including race, sex, religion, age or marital status.[109] The court may now refuse to consider an application seeking the performance of union rules unless it is satisfied that all reasonable steps have been taken to have the matter resolved internally.[110] In essence, however, the three sets of democratic controls outlined earlier are still in force.

In contrast to the position in the 1970s and 1980s, though, when election inquiries, challenges to union rules and applications for the performance or observance of unions rules were commonplace, the modern equivalents of those provisions have only occasionally been the subject of published judgments in recent decades. The volume of cases dealing with enforcement and observance of union rules has decreased most markedly, with only a handful of judgments since 2000. While the possible reasons for this are discussed in further detail below, it is sufficient to note for present purposes that this has meant that the application of administrative law principles to the trade union context has also been a much less prominent feature in the regulatory landscape. Few recent examples of substance can be found. In *Rayner v. Ellery*,[111] for example, the court considered whether directions of the National Council of the Communications, Electrical, Electronic, Energy, Information, Postal, Plumbing and Allied Services Union of Australia (CEPU) were 'beyond the power of the National Council' under the union's rules.[112] The court found that one of the directions in question was a conditional authorisation and therefore 'necessarily within the four corners of the, more absolute power expressed' in the relevant rule, 'analogously with the reasoning deployed' in cases considering the validity of council by-laws.[113] In considering the proper construction of the union rules, then, the court subjected the decision of the National Council to an *ultra vires* assessment of the administrative law kind, drawing directly on administrative case law. In *Butler v. Setches*,[114] the court stated that when considering the validity of the decisions of the National Council of the CEPU it will ask 'whether reasonable [people] acting honestly could have come to the decision that the domestic tribunal did'.[115] It also found that the decision of the National Council in that case was tainted by 'invincible bias'.[116] These types of cases, however, are now less common than they once were.

Emerging Issues

On the basis of the foregoing analysis, the final part of this chapter seeks to draw out some of the emerging issues and problems that warrant further consideration.

First, it is clear that the rise of the corporate model of regulation and the declining focus upon democratic control has occurred in tandem with broader shifts in the Australian industrial relations system. As outlined above, when the concern to ensure that unions were controlled democratically by their members was at its peak, the role of trade unions was at the same time legitimised and underpinned by the federal industrial relations system, influenced as it still was by the conciliation and arbitration framework. As employment relations have been increasingly decollectivised, and the role of collective institutions has been delegitimised, the concern to ensure democratic control has diminished in prominence. There is no longer bipartisan political concern, for example, with empowering rank-and-file union members or ensuring that they are active participants in union life. Perhaps this is because highly democratic unions, within which the rank and file is active in influencing union strategy, policy and decision making are 'not necessarily pleasant neighbours'.[117] Meanwhile, the concern to ensure accountability of trade unions and their officers has become central and the corporate model of regulation has been deployed to that end. As outlined above, a key feature of the model is that it reshapes the roles of trade unions and the state in relation to one another. Where the role of trade unions under the corporate model is narrower and less autonomous; the state and its regulatory bodies have taken on the expanded role of commander, controller, investigator and enforcer.

Second, these developments are reflective of an increasingly corporatised labour law. Just prior to the introduction of *Work Choices*, McCallum predicted that the enactment of federal labour law under the corporations, as opposed to labour, power of the Commonwealth Parliament would shape the 'DNA' of labour law in the twenty-first century.[118] Just as the labour law of the twentieth century had been moulded by the wording of the labour power in section 51(xxxv) of the Constitution – focused as it is on 'industrial disputes and by its requirement that their settlement must occur either through conciliation and arbitration' – the labour law of this century would be moulded by the corporations power.[119] This would lead, McCallum said, to Australian labour law becoming 'little more than a sub-set of corporations law and this will inevitably lead to the corporatisation of Australian labour law'.[120] In saying this, McCallum argued that this would cause labour laws to be centred upon the economic needs of corporate employers, to the detriment of employees who would be 'viewed as but one aspect of the productive process in our globalized economy'.[121] Arguably, though, it has also resulted in the treatment of unions as corporations to be regulated in the same way as corporate employers.

This leads directly to the third point, which is that the blunt and extensive adoption of the corporate model of regulation ignores the imbalance in bargaining power between employers and employees and, accordingly, the unique role that unions play in representing the latter. As Forsyth argued in 2000, while the 'extension of the corporate model to trade unions' is usually based on the assumption 'that unions and corporations are similar types of organisations, and therefore they should be regulated in the same way', trade unions and corporations are actually 'very different types of organisations in terms of the reasons for which they are formed, the purposes that they serve and the interests that their members and shareholders respectively hold'.[122] Where companies are 'primarily vehicles for the carrying on of commercial activity', trade unions are formed 'predominantly for the purpose of improving the working conditions of their members and the social standing of workers generally'.[123] Where shareholders have a proprietary interest in a corporation, the interest of a member in a union is a '"democratic" interest in ensuring that the union is properly and fairly administered'.[124] As David Peetz argues in Chapter 2 in this volume, where corporations are 'collective formations of the capital owned by shareholders', unions are 'collective formations of labour, established largely to counter the power of these collective formations of capital to exploit those reliant on the sale of their labour power'.

There is a strong argument that certain regulatory mechanisms from corporations law are justified in order to regulate financial management of unions to prevent the kind of 'misappropriation and deceit'[125] which was uncovered at the HSU. Indeed, it is clear that some of the measures introduced in recent years to ensure financial transparency have been warranted. However, the corporate model has gone beyond this in Australia and, until recently, attempts to extend its reach further were on the table in the form of the Ensuring Integrity Bill, which, as Forsyth argued, was an 'opportunistic attempt, under the guise of protecting union members, to provide employers and the Government itself with new avenues to reduce union power'.[126] The final report of the Royal Commission, outlined above, contained recommendations to extend the corporate model which as yet have not been implemented. Particularly concerning, among those, is the suggestion that the statutory fiduciary duties of officers be extended to 'apply across the entire field of possible activity'.[127] This risks a significant chilling effect on the capacity of union officers to vigorously represent the interests of their members, particularly if such duties were to extend beyond management to advocacy or to the enterprise bargaining process.[128] It is clear that the avowed concern to ensure the accountability of trade unions and their officers has become the hook upon which to hang an increasingly broad regulatory regime which is divorced from the democratic mandate of trade unions and is intended fundamentally to curb union autonomy. This is achieved through the imposition of positive statutory obligations, rather than obligations contained in unions' own rules, enforced by external regulators such as the ROC rather than the members of a union. It is also achieved through the selective use of some of the most onerous aspects of corporations law – such as penalties which actually exceed those that apply under the equivalent provisions of the *Corporations Act* – without also applying to trade unions some of the protections it offers to companies, such as limited liability.[129] At the very least, attempts to advance the corporate model further must be treated with great caution.

Fourth, the declining use of provisions directed to democratic control of unions and, in particular, the content and performance of union rules, is important. While a more detailed review of recent case law – including the numbers of cases dealing with each provision, their grounds, considerations and outcomes – is beyond the scope of this chapter, the reduction in published judgments indicates that members (and/or officials) are not utilising these provisions as commonly as they once did. The reasons for this are no doubt complex and worthy of stand-alone research. There are, however, a number of possibilities worth noting. First, it is possible that other processes are being used to resolve conflict. As outlined above, the court may refuse to deal with an application under section 164, for example, unless it is satisfied that steps have been taken to resolve the matter internally. In addition, some cases which may previously have been brought under section 164 or its predecessors are now being brought under Chapter 9 of the *Fair Work (RO) Act* by the ROC as breaches of duty in relation to the financial management.[130] It seems likely that the involvement of the AEC and the ROC in union elections has played a role in reducing the number of applications for inquiries into electoral irregularities in the Federal Court. *Creighton and Stewart's Labour Law* also suggests that unions 'have utilised other, non-litigious forms of engaging in intra […] union conflict, such as the establishment of "slush funds" to support particular candidates'.[131] Second, it is also possible that declining membership and reduced resources have meant that the cost of litigation 'cannot be justified'.[132] *Creighton and Stewart's Labour Law* states that avoiding the commencement of proceedings relating to the content and enforcement of union rules is sensible and that 'such legal battles may […] be considered a distraction from the tasks of maintaining members and resisting efforts to diminish union influence in the establishment of employment conditions and the resolution of workplace disputes'.[133] This, however, presents a limited view of the function that those provisions play in providing a mechanism by which the rank-and-file membership of a union is able to challenge the arbitrary exercise of power within that union and the implications for the democratic state of a union in which that mechanism is not utilised. This, in turn, raises another possibility: that the decline in cases overturning or enforcing union rules reflects increasing apathy among union members. An apathetic union membership, as Jackson has highlighted, may mean that an exercise of power which is arbitrary or contrary to union rules 'may go unnoticed by a large majority of rank and file members'.[134] Indeed, this is the kind of 'passive democracy' to which Tracey referred where 'the right to control the officials remain[s] in theory but it [is] not meaningful because members [are] unwilling and/or unable to exercise their rights'.[135] The paucity of research in recent years means that we do not currently understand the reality of union democracy in Australia. But clearly the possibility of a state of passive democracy in unions is of concern – a union cannot perform its external democratic functions in representing the voices of workers in politics and in the workplace if its members are not able to bring their interests to bear internally in the running of the union and its priorities. For more on the different ways in which democracy in constitutive of trade unions, see Chapter 1 in this volume.

Fifth, the above reveals that inadequate attention has been devoted to understanding, explaining and justifying the use of principles, doctrines and regulatory techniques from other fields of law in the regulation of trade union affairs. As this chapter has argued, principles have been drawn from both administrative and corporations law in regulating union internal affairs but little consideration has been given to the context from which those principles have been drawn and the impact of that context upon the way in which such principles are, or should be, utilised in the trade union context. Saunders, writing recently in the context of public law transplants across jurisdictional boundaries, has suggested that there are three critical stages in any decision about a transplant demand attention: the 'identification of a possible transplant', an 'evaluation of whether the transplant should proceed' and 'any adaption to the transplant in its original form that is deemed appropriate for the purpose'.[136] These observations apply with equal force to the issue of transplants from one field of law to another. Varuhas has similarly advocated, in the context of field-interaction within public law, the need to 'take heed of the distinctive nature' of the different fields in play.[137] This enables the answering of legal questions in a way that ' "fits" with the pre-existing rules and principles within the particular doctrinal context in which the question arises' and which, furthermore, is 'consonant with and does not work at cross purposes with the basic normative concerns of each field'.[138]

For example, as argued above, in deciding cases under what is now section 164 of the *Fair Work (RO) Act*, the courts have drawn upon administrative law, using an *ultra vires* mode of analysis and implying requirements of natural justice. However, they have incorporated into this analysis principles of fiduciary law in order to imply a duty to act for proper purposes. It is not clear why fiduciary and not administrative law is the source of the relevant obligation in this context, which has often involved a decision taken by a trade union body, purportedly under the rules of the union, to take disciplinary action against a member. Arguably it would make more sense in this context – particularly where the rights of individual members are concerned – to say that a decision maker must exercise powers under the rules for proper purposes, rather than to say that in not doing so they have breached a fiduciary duty owed to the union as a whole. The very fact that the rules of natural justice have been found to apply to decision making in trade unions further suggests the exercise of discretion in this context is more readily susceptible to the application of administrative law principles rather than fiduciary law. As Gageler J has observed extrajudicially, it is telling that the administrative law doctrine of procedural fairness which is concerned 'at its core' with 'ensuring that those potentially affected by an exercise of power have the opportunity to speak for themselves to influence its exercise' has 'no equitable parallel' – the 'trust paradigm is too managerial to be consistent with contemporary expectations about the appropriate role of judicial oversight of the actions of administrators'.[139]

Finally, it is suggested that the role of principles drawn from administrative law deserve renewed consideration in this context. As this chapter has argued, such principles already play an (increasingly limited) role in applications for the performance of union rules. That has not, to date, been the subject of detailed scholarly interrogation. It is plausible that administrative law doctrines have found expression in the law regulating trade union affairs because the two fields share a normative concern with the concentration, distribution and regulation of discretionary power and its abuse. To some extent, it can also be said that fiduciary duties 'guard against abuse of power'[140] but unlike beneficiaries in the fiduciary context, both the citizens of a state and the members of a trade union have a *democratic* interest in its governance and in holding the exercise of its power to account. According to Kahn-Freund, just like the contract of employment, the contract of membership conceals (though perhaps to a lesser degree) an '[act] of submission' by the worker who stands 'between the powers of management and of the unions'.[141] It is the role of the law in this context to protect the worker 'against abuse of power by either'[142] and to subject the arbitrary exercise of power by either trade unions or employers to the rule of law. Administrative law principles provide one mechanism by which to achieve this by ensuring that trade union officials exercise their discretionary powers under union rules lawfully and not arbitrarily, capriciously, for improper purposes, on the basis of irrelevant considerations or with procedural impropriety. In the trade union context, this recognises the importance of union membership to the worker, without which they may have no way of 'being an active participant in the shaping of [their] own occupational existence'.[143]

Such an approach, however, is also capable of balancing the democratic rights of members with the need for trade union autonomy. This is because it takes the rules of the union – rather than positive statutory obligations – as providing the source and limits of decision-making power. This protects the need for trade unions to remain autonomous in two ways. First, at a broad level it protects the union's ability, within certain parameters, to draw its own constitution and formulate its own rules. Second, it provides in individual cases an increased scope to accord union decision makers an appropriate margin of appreciation, particularly where polycentric decision making is involved, necessitating the weighing of conflicting interests within the membership. There is a further important question – for another time – about whether administrative law principles can play a valuable role in labour law more generally, including with respect to the exercise of discretion by employers.

Notes

The author would like to thank Professors Anthony Forsyth and Joo-Cheong Tham for their valuable feedback on an earlier draft of this chapter and the anonymous reviewers for their helpful comments. This chapter is dedicated to the memory of the Honourable Justice Richard Ross Sinclair Tracey AM, RFD, QC who was a mentor and held a long-standing interest in the regulation of the internal affairs of trade unions.

1 Anthony Forsyth, 'Trade Union Regulation and the Accountability of Union Office-Holders: Examining the Corporate Model', *Australian Journal of Labour Law* 13, no. 1 (2000): 28–49.

2 R. R. S. Tracey, 'The Legal Approach to Democratic Control of Trade Unions', *Melbourne University Law Review* 15, no. 2 (1985): 177–210 (177).

3 Forsyth, 'Trade Union Regulation and the Accountability of Union Office-Holders', 29–30.

4 J. H. Portus, *The Development of Australian Trade Union Law* (Melbourne: Melbourne University Press, 1958), 168.

5 Justice Henry Bourne Higgins, *A New Province for Law and Order* (London: Constable, 1922), 15.

6 Portus, *The Development of Australian Trade Union Law*, 168.

7 *Williams v. Hursey* (1959) 107 CLR 30 per Fullager J.

8 Alan Boulton, 'Government Regulation of the Internal Affairs of Unions', in *Power, Conflict and Control*, ed. Kathryn Cole (Melbourne: Penguin Books, 1982), 216–36 (217).

9 *Conciliation and Arbitration Act 1904* (Cth), assented to 15 December 1904, s 60(c).

10 Ibid., s 60(d).

11 Ibid., s 60(f).

12 David Peetz, *Unions in a Contrary World* (Cambridge: Cambridge University Press, 1998), 25.

13 Ibid.

14 Tom Bramble, *Trade Unionism in Australia: A History from Flood to Ebb Tide* (Cambridge: Cambridge University Press, 2008), 3.

15 Ron McCallum, 'Secret Ballots and the Industrial Relations Bureau: Old Wine in New Bottles', in *Australian Labour Relations: Readings Third Edition*, ed. Gordon Ford, June Hearn and Russell Lansbury (Melbourne: Macmillan, 1980), 368–94 (389).

16 The Honourable C. Cameron, Minister for Labour (Debates, House of Representatives, 12 April 1973), 1431, as cited in Dianne Yerbury, 'Legal Regulation of Unions in Australia: The Impact of Compulsory Arbitration and Adversary Politics' (University

of New South Wales Australian Graduate School of Management Working Paper No. 82–018, University of New South Wales, Sydney, October 1982), 28.

17 Ibid.

18 Ibid., 26.

19 Tracey, 'The Legal Approach to Democratic Control of Trade Unions', 177.

20 See generally, Andrew Stewart, Anthony Forsyth, Mark Irving, Richard Johnstone and Shae McCrystal (eds), *Creighton and Stewart's Labour Law* (Sydney: Federation Press, 2016), 847; Tracey, 'The Legal Approach to the Democratic Control of Trade Unions'.

21 Tracey, 'The Legal Approach to the Democratic Control of Trade Unions', 178.

22 Ibid., 182.

23 Ibid., 183.

24 Ibid.

25 *Conciliation and Arbitration Act 1904* (Cth), as at 16 December1985, s 133.

26 Ibid, s 133AA.

27 Ibid, s 158P.

28 Tracey, 'The Legal Approach to the Democratic Control of Trade Unions', 185.

29 R. C. McCallum and R. R. S. Tracey, *Cases and Materials on Industrial Law in Australia* (Melbourne: Butterworths, 1980), 382. See, for example, *Cameron v. AWU* (1959) 2 FLR 45.

30 McCallum and Tracey, *Cases and Materials on Industrial Law in Australia*, 382. See, for example, *Leveridge v. SDAEA* (1977) 17 ALR 145, which concerned a rule that to be eligible for election to office, a candidate had to have been a financial member for two years which, in the context of high turn-over within the union membership, had the effect of preventing over two-thirds of the membership from holding office. This was found to impose unreasonable restrictions on members in contravention of s 140.

31 Tracey, 'The Legal Approach to the Democratic Control of Trade Unions', 186.

32 *Griffin's Case* (1928) 27 CAR 1064 per Beeby J; *Chapman v. Sear* (1931) 30 CAR 165. See Portus, *The Development of Australian Trade Union Law*, 193.

33 *Wilson v. Heydon* (1944) 53 CAR 482, 488.

34 Tracey, 'The Legal Approach to the Democratic Control of Trade Unions' 206. See *Magner v. Fowler* (1979) 26 ALR 671.

35 *Porter v. Dugmore* (1984) 7 IR 120, 129.

36 R. R. S. Tracey, 'Section 141 of the Conciliation and Arbitration Act and Natural Justice', *Journal of Industrial Relations* 18, no. 1 (1976): 58 (59).

37 See, for example, *AWU v. Bowen (No 2)* (1948) 77 CLR 601.

38 *Ridge v. Baldwin* (1964) AC 40. In *Barnes v. Oliver* (1970) 16 FLR 366, for example, the Commonwealth Industrial Court found, drawing on Lord Reid's speech in *Ridge v. Baldwin*, that the branch executive of the Australian Worker's Union was 'bound to observe the principles of natural justice in seeking to exercise its power to remove the branch secretary'.

39 *Russell v. Duke of Norfolk* (1949) 1 All ER 109, 118.

40 R. R. S. Tracey, 'The Conduct of Union Disciplinary Hearings', *Journal of Industrial Relations* 24, no. 2 (1982): 204, 206.

41 Ibid.

42 See, for example, *Campbell v. Gorman* (1977) 18 ALR 108; *O'Donoghue v. ASCJA* (1979) 41 FLR 197.

43 Tracey, 'The Conduct of Union Disciplinary Hearings', 208.

44 *Annamunthodo v. Oilfield Workers' Trade Union* (1961) AC 945; *Clark v. PKIU* (1976) 9 ALR 621. See Tracey, 'The Conduct of Union Disciplinary Hearings', 211.
45 *Clark v. PKIU* (1976) 9 ALR 621.
46 *Cains v. Jenkins* (1979) 42 FLR 188.
47 Tracey, 'The Legal Approach to the Democratic Control of Trade Unions', 178.
48 Paul Craig, *Administrative Law*, 7th ed. (London: Sweet & Maxwell, 2012), 5.
49 This refers to the formulation of unreasonableness set out by Lord Greene MR in *Associated Provincial Picture Houses Ltd v. Wednesbury Corp* (1948) 1 KB 223, 299, where it was said that judicial review might be available on the grounds that a decision was 'so unreasonable that no reasonable authority could ever have come to it'.
50 *Magner v. Fowler.*
51 Paul Davies and Mark Freedland, 'The Impact of Public Law on Labour Law 1972–1997', *Industrial Law Journal* 26, no. 4 (1997): 311 (320).
52 *Australian Workers Union v. Bowen (No 2)* (1948) 77 CLR 601, 631.
53 Ibid., 615; *Cleworth v. Barrow* (1978) 20 ALR 359, 369.
54 Tracey, 'The Legal Approach to the Democratic Control of Trade Unions', 209.
55 Ibid., 210.
56 W. A. Howard, 'Democracy in Trade Unions', in Ford et al., *Australian Labour Relations: Readings*, 3rd ed, 162–78 (166–67).
57 McCallum, 'Secret Ballots and the Industrial Relations Bureau', 390.
58 Laura Bennett, *Making Labour Law in Australia: Industrial Relations, Politics and Law* (Sydney: The Law Book Company Limited, 1994), 23.
59 See, for example, Boulton, 'Government Regulation of the Internal Affairs of Unions', 217.
60 McCallum, 'Secret Ballots and the Industrial Relations Bureau', 373.
61 Orwell de R. Foenander, *Trade Unionism in Australia: Some Aspects* (Melbourne: The Law Book Co of Australasia, 1962), 168.
62 McCallum, 'Secret Ballots and the Industrial Relations Bureau', 389–90.
63 Ibid.
64 Bramble, *Trade Unionism in Australia*, 47.
65 McCallum, 'Secret Ballots and the Industrial Relations Bureau', 374.
66 Ibid.
67 Tracey, 'The Legal Approach to the Democratic Control of Trade Unions', 209.
68 Forsyth, 'Trade Union Regulation and the Accountability of Union Office-Holders', 5.
69 *Scott v. Jess* (1984) 56 ALR 379.
70 Tracey, 'The Legal Approach to the Democratic Control of Trade Unions', 206.
71 Michael Christie, 'Legal Duties and Liabilities of Federal Union Officials', *Melbourne University Law Review* 15, no. 4 (1986): 591–617 (598).
72 (1977) 31 FLR 431.
73 Ibid., 483–84.
74 Ibid., 484.
75 Ibid.
76 Ibid.
77 Peetz, *Unions in a Contrary World*, 112.
78 Ibid.
79 Bramble, *Trade Unionism in Australia*, 125.
80 Peetz, *Unions in a Contrary World*, 162.

81 Anthony Forsyth and Andrew Stewart, 'The Journey from Work Choices to Fair Work', in *Fair Work: The New Workplace Laws and the Work Choices Legacy*, ed. Anthony Forsyth and Andrew Stewart (Sydney: Federation Press, 2009), 1–18 (3).
82 Colin Fenwick and John Howe, 'Union Security after Work Choices', in Forsyth and Stewart, *Fair Work*, 164–85 (165).
83 Ibid., 166.
84 Peter Punch, 'Trade Unions – A Highly Regulated and Supervised Future …", *Workplace Review* 8, no. 2 (2017): 88–93 (92).
85 Forsyth, 'Trade Union Regulation and Accountability of Union Office Holders', 7.
86 *Workplace Relations Amendment (Registration and Accountability of Organisations) Act 2002* (Cth).
87 Revised Explanatory Memorandum, Workplace Relations Amendment (Registration and Accountability of Organisations) Bill 2002 (The Parliament of the Commonwealth of Australia, 2002).
88 Second Reading Speech, Workplace Relations (Registration and Accountability of Organisations) Bill 2002 (House of Representatives, 21 March 2002), 1837.
89 Revised Explanatory Memorandum, Workplace Relations Amendment (Registration and Accountability of Organisations) Bill 2002.
90 Ibid.
91 Second Reading Speech, Workplace Relations (Registration and Accountability of Organisations) Bill 2002, 1836.
92 Forsyth and Stewart, 'The Journey from Work Choices to Fair Work', 3.
93 Fenwick and Howe, 'Union Security after Work Choices', 166.
94 Ibid., 4.
95 Explanatory Memorandum, Fair Work Bill 2008 (The Parliament of the Commonwealth of Australia, 2008), [178].
96 Shae McCrystal, 'A New Consensus: The Coalition, the ALP and the Regulation of Industrial Action', in Forsyth and Stewart, *Fair Work*, 141–63 (142).
97 Anthony Forsyth, 'Law, Politics and Ideology: The Regulatory Response to Trade Union Corruption in Australia', *UNSW Law Journal* 40, no. 4 (2017): 1336–65 (1338).
98 Ibid.
99 *Health Services Union v. Jackson (No 4)* [2015] FCA 865, [19].
100 *Royal Commission into Trade Union Governance and Corruption Final Report: Volume One* (Commonwealth of Australia, December 2015), 12 [9].
101 *Royal Commission into Trade Union Governance and Corruption Final Report: Volume Five* (Canberra: Commonwealth of Australia, December 2015), 166 [27].
102 Ibid., 178 [54].
103 For a helpful summary of these changes, see Forsyth, 'Law, Politics and Ideology', 1349–50.
104 Explanatory Memorandum, Fair Work (Registered Organisations) Amendment (Ensuring Integrity No. 2) Bill 2019 (The Parliament of the Commonwealth of Australia, House of Representatives, 2019).
105 Anthony Forsyth, 'The Ensuring Integrity Bill and the Chimera of "Regulating Unions Just Like Companies"', *Labour Law Down Under*, 14 October 2019, https://labourlawdownunder.com.au/?p=755.
106 Ibid.

107 'Scott Morrison Takes Aim at Australia's Industrial Relations System, Reaches Out to Business and Unions', *ABC News*, 26 May 2020, https://www.abc.net.au/news/2020-05-26/scott-morrison-industrial-relations-business-unions-coronavirus/12287072.
108 *Fair Work (RO) Act*, s 182–83.
109 Ibid., s 142(1)(d).
110 Ibid., s 164(3).
111 *Rayner v. Ellery* (2016) FCA 771.
112 Fenwick and Howe, 'Union Security after Work Choices', 165.
113 *Rayner v. Ellery*, 5. See *Country Roads Board v. Neale ADS Pty Ltd* (1930) 43 CLR 126; *Foley v. Padley* (1984) 154 CLR 349.
114 *Butler v. Setches* [2017] FCA 1538.
115 Ibid. See also *Cleworth v. Barrow* (1978) 20 ALR 359.
116 *Butler v. Setches*, [54]–[56] For the most recent example at the time of writing, see *Difelice v Dettmer* [2021] FCA 631 where the court found there was a 'strong prima facie case' that certain resolutions of the National Council of the Automotive, Food, Metals, Engineering, Printing and Kindred Industries Union were invalid because they purported to 'confer upon the National Council powers that it does not have' under the union's rules.
117 Howard, 'Democracy in Trade Unions', 177.
118 Ron McCallum, 'The Australian Constitution and the Shaping of Our Federal and State Labour Laws' 10, no. 2, *Deakin Law Review* (2005): 460–69 (461).
119 Ibid.
120 Ibid., 467.
121 Ibid., 469.
122 Forsyth, 'Trade Union Regulation and the Accountability of Office-Holders', 11.
123 Ibid., 12.
124 Ibid., 11–12.
125 *Royal Commission into Trade Union Governance and Corruption Final Report: Volume One*, 89 [237].
126 Anthony Forsyth, 'Submission to the Senate Education and Employment Legislation Committee', Fair Work (Registered Organisations) Amendment (Ensuring Integrity) Bill, 5.
127 *Royal Commission into Trade Union Governance and Corruption Final Report: Volume Five,* 178 [54].
128 See Jill Murray, 'In Whose Interests? Fiduciary Obligations of Union Officials in Bargaining', *Sydney Law Review* 40 (2018): 123.
129 See further, Forsyth, 'Submission to the Senate Education and Employment Legislation Committee', 3–5.
130 In *Registered Organisations Commissioner v. Australian Workers' Union* [2019] FCA 1852, for example, the relevant conduct constituted a breach of the rules of the union. The relevant contraventions, however, which were agreed between the parties, were breaches of the duties of care and diligence and of good faith.
131 Forsyth et al., *Creighton and Stewart's Labour Law*, 847.
132 Ibid.
133 Ibid.
134 Michael P. Jackson, *Trade Unions* (New York: Longman, 1988), 57.
135 Tracey, 'The Legal Approach to the Democratic Control of Trade Unions', 179.

136 Cheryl Saunders, 'Transplants in Public Law', in *The Unity of Public Law? – Doctrinal, Theoretical and Comparative Perspectives*, ed. Mark Elliott, Jason Varuhas and Shona Wilson Stark (Oxford: Hart Publishing, 2018), 257–77 (258).

137 Jason Varuhas, 'Taxonomy and Public Law', in Elliott, Varuhas and Stark, *The Unity of Public Law?*, 39–78 (48).

138 Ibid.

139 Stephen Gageler, 'The Equitable Duty of Loyalty in Public Office', in *Finn's Law: An Australian Justice*, ed. Tim Bonyhady (Sydney: Federation Press, 2016), 126–46 (136).

140 Jason Varuhas, *Damages and Human Rights* (Oxford: Hart Publishing, 2016), 175. See also Matthew Conaglen, 'Public-Private Intersection: Comparing Fiduciary Conflict Doctrine and Bias' 58 *Public Law* (2008).

141 Otto Kahn-Freund, *Labour and the Law: The Hamlyn Lectures Twenty-Fourth Series* (London: Stevens, 1972), 5, 195.

142 Ibid.

143 Ibid., 184.

Chapter 5

TRADE UNIONS AND THE REGULATION OF ELECTION FUNDING: BETWEEN LIBERTARIANISM AND EGALITARIANISM

Joo-Cheong Tham

Two overarching goals are central to the role of trade unions in society: social justice and democracy (see Chapter 1 of this volume). Both imply a range of functions and strategies that invariably stamp trade unions as political organisations (should politics be understood as activity aimed at influencing the exercise of power). Trade unions seek to influence the exercise of power at the workplace by providing a countervailing force to employer power.[1] This typically occurs through the institution of collective bargaining and the regulatory function it performs in laying down labour standards[2] – standards critical for workers to receiving a 'just share of the fruits of progress'.[3] Through the same processes, and more generally, the representative function of trade unions, organisations of working people seek to give workers a voice in the workplace and society at large.[4]

It is not only industrial-political activities that characterise trade unions as political organisations but also their political-political activities (those aimed at influencing the exercise of governmental power). While the nature and extent of trade union involvement in such activities depends on a range of factors,[5] there is no doubt that all trade unions will be involved in *some kind* of political-political activity. As Hyman has noted:

> Regulating the labour market involves political issues [...] The state is not only the ultimate guarantor of contracts, including employment contracts; whether by active intervention or by default, it underwrites a particular (im)balance between different participants in market relations. At a very minimum, unions have to influence the ways in which the state shapes the rules of the game in the

> labour market, including their own right to exist, to bargain collectively and to mobilize collective action.[6]

That is to say that political-political activity will be significant, whatever the model of trade unionism. It is clearly so with social movement unionism (aimed at socialising the capitalist economy) or radical unionism (directed at an anti-capitalist agenda) but also the case with business unionism (focused on collective bargaining).[7] The importance of political-political activity is similarly recognised by the International Labour Organization (ILO) jurisprudence on the right to strike which does not sharply distinguish such activity from industrial-political activity. For instance, in its criticisms of the rules governing industrial action under the *Fair Work Act 2009* (Cth), the ILO Committee on Freedom of Association observed that 'the occupational and economic interests which workers defend through the exercise of the right to strike do not only concern better working conditions or collective claims of an occupational nature, but also *the seeking of solutions to economic and social policy questions and problems* facing the undertaking which are of direct concern to the workers'.[8]

A key political-political strategy, one at the heart of this chapter, is influencing the agenda and outcomes of elections. This is typically effected through support for particular candidates and political parties as well as through independent campaigning. In Australia, trade union engagement in such activities is patent and long-standing. Trade unions were key to the establishment of the Australian Labor Party (ALP)[9] and most trade unions remain affiliated to the ALP as organisational members. Australian trade unions, through the peak union body, the Australian Council of Trade Unions (ACTU), have run major campaigns in recent federal elections; notably, 'Your Rights at Work' in the 2007 federal election[10] and 'Change the Rules' in the 2019 federal election.[11]

These activities have not only involved millions of dollars but have also resulted in trade unions counting among the biggest spenders in Australian elections. In the 20-year period of 1998–99 to 2018–19, trade union contributions (affiliation fees and political donations) constituted nearly a third of total contributions to the ALP (31.8%) and totalled $173.6 million (in 2018–19 dollars). Also significant is direct spending on union campaigns. Total third party campaign expenditure (electoral expenditure by groups other than political parties and candidates) for the past five elections (2007, 2010, 2013, 2016, 2019) is estimated to be $183.4 million (in 2018–19 dollars) of which trade union spending constituted 45 per cent.[12]

Such large amounts of spending (in absolute and relative terms) give rise to acute difficulties arising from the laissez-faire regulation of money in federal elections.[13] The same (lax) rules that enable Australian trade unions to spend freely in federal elections also allow commercial interests to use their money to influence candidates, political parties and elections. The absence of contribution and expenditure caps enable Australian trade unions to expend millions on contributions to the ALP and campaigns such as 'Rights at Work' and 'Change the Rules'; they also breed unfairness and corruption in the Australian political process.[14]

Such corrosion of Australian democracy, in turn, has prompted calls for more robust regulation including caps on political contributions and spending in federal elections. How should Australian trade unions respond to these calls? Specifically, how should they do so in a way that is faithful to the social justice and democratic rationales of the union movement?

This chapter takes up these questions through two normative perspectives on the regulation of election funding. It begins with a libertarian approach. Such an approach has found expression in the successful constitutional challenges made by Unions NSW to political funding laws and, indeed, has powerful appeal. I, however, argue in favour of the second perspective, an egalitarian approach, and show how such an approach can effectively address the legitimate concerns that Australian trade unions have with caps on contributions and expenditure.

The Lure of Libertarianism

A libertarian approach is evident in the constitutional challenges brought by Unions NSW in 2013 and 2018 to provisions of New South Wales election funding laws, particularly the challenge in *Unions NSW (No 1)*.[15] In both cases, Unions NSW argued that the challenged provisions breached the freedom of political communication implied under the Commonwealth Constitution. In *Unions NSW (No 1)*, the challenge was to two provisions: one restricting the ability to donate to those on the electoral rolls (thereby, prohibiting donations from legal entities such as trade unions) and the other, a provision that aggregated the spending of organisations affiliated to a political party to the cap applying to the party. The latter measure would have meant that spending in New South Wales elections by trade unions affiliated to the New South Wales branch of the ALP would count towards the cap applying to the New South Wales ALP. In *Unions NSW (No 2)*,[16] the challenge was to the reduction of spending caps that applied to third party campaigners (organisations and individuals engaged in election campaign spending but who were not political parties or candidates) from $1.05 million to $0.5 million and a provision that aggregated spending when organisations were said to 'act in concert'.

Table 5.1 summarises the provisions challenged and the outcome of the decisions.

Table 5.1 *Unions NSW (No 1)* and *Unions NSW (No 2)*

Case	Challenged provisions	Outcome
Unions NSW v. New South Wales (2013) 252 CLR 530 (*Unions NSW (No 1)*)	• Section 96D of the *Election Funding, Expenditure and Disclosures Act 1981* (NSW) which restricted the ability to donate to those on the electoral rolls. • Section 96G(6) of the *Election Funding, Expenditure and Disclosures Act 1981* (NSW) which aggregated spending of organisations affiliated to a political party to that of political party.	• Invalid • Invalid
Unions NSW v. New South Wales (2019) 93 ALJR 166 (*Unions NSW (No 2)*)	• Section 29(10) of *Election Funding Act 2018* (NSW) which reduced third party campaigners' spending limits from $1.05 million to $0.5 million. • Section 35 of *Election Funding Act 2018* (NSW) which aggregated spending of third party campaigners when 'acting in concert'.	• Invalid • Unnecessary to decide

These provisions, particularly those challenged in 2013, were definitely problematic. Before the High Court handed down its decision in *Unions NSW (No 1)*, I wrote an opinion piece that said the following:

> [The challenged laws] constitute one of the most serious attacks on Australia's democratic process in recent times. In all likelihood, they will render the historic structure of ALP unviable by prohibiting affiliation fees, and by strongly discouraging affiliation through the aggregation of spending. Amounting to a de facto ban of the ALP's party structure, they are an egregious breach of freedom of association. They are also grossly unfair as they have a selective – and dramatic – impact on the ALP.[17]

At the same time, I said:

> [There are] risks of victory, even if less apparent. Should the laws be struck down through endorsement of US supreme court jurisprudence – especially *Buckley v Valeo*, which rejected equality and fairness as legitimate grounds for restricting 'free' speech – attempts to regulate the electoral process to ensure its democratic integrity may be imperilled through constitutional obstacles.[18]

This was said in a context where the submissions of Unions NSW dripped with references to the US First Amendment jurisprudence, particularly, *Buckley v. Valeo*[19] and *Citizens United*.[20] Such reliance on US First Amendment jurisprudence brings us into the treacherous terrain of a liberal-democratic approach to regulating money in politics – or what the Canadian Supreme Court has characterised as a libertarian model.[21]

In such a model, the pre-eminent democratic value is liberty or freedom. Freedom is, however, understood in a particular way – as 'freedom from' state regulation. The reason for such an understanding of freedom is not difficult to find: as the US Supreme Court in *Citizens United* emphasised in relation to the First Amendment, it was 'premised on mistrust of governmental power'.[22] Hence, a libertarian model is founded upon hostility to state regulation.

At the same time, it is sanguine about the exercise of private power – private regulation – for three reasons. First, it almost exclusively focuses on the dangers of state regulation. Second, it rejects equality as a rationale for regulation. The most striking statement here is from *Buckley v. Valeo* where it was said that 'the concept that government may restrict the speech of some elements of our society in order to enhance the relative voice of others is wholly foreign to the First Amendment'.[23] Third, it sanctifies the use of money in politics as democratic by characterising money as speech – the use of money for political expression is, according to this approach, fundamentally an exercise of democratic freedom.[24]

It is not hard to see and feel the appeal of a libertarian approach. There is its adoption by the US Supreme Court. Its rhetoric of freedom resonates in an age where neoliberalism has particular sway.[25] More than this, the principle of freedom is central to the rationale and effectiveness of trade unions. As affirmed by the *International Covenant on Civil and Political Rights*, the ability to form and act through trade unions is an incident of freedom of association.[26] This same freedom together with effective recognition of the right to collective bargaining are fundamental rights at work (as recognised by the ILO).[27] These are rights integral to the democratic effectiveness of trade unions and to their ability to give voice to the concerns, grievances and aspirations of working people. Not only that, freedom of association is essential for pursuit of the social justice goal of trade unions. T. H. Marshall, for instance, placed this freedom at the centre of 'industrial citizenship' where freedom of association, a civil right in Marshall's view, is extended through the right to collective bargaining which, in turn, aims to secure social rights, particularly, the right to a living wage.[28] Indeed, the *ILO Declaration of Philadelphia* states more generally that 'freedom of expression and of association are essential to sustained progress'.[29]

We can also appreciate here the appeal of hostility to state regulation embodied in a libertarian approach. Freedom of association requires suspicion of state regulation or, put more precisely, it requires autonomy for trade unions from laws that interfere with this freedom. As the ILO *Freedom of Association and Protection of the Right to Organise Convention* puts it, 'the law of the land shall not be such as to impair, nor shall it be so applied as to impair, the guarantees provided for in this Convention'.[30] We can all the more appreciate the hostility to state regulation among Australian trade unions given the continuous attempts to increase regulation of their internal affairs, undermining their democratic purpose and organisational security: see, further, Chapter 4 by Caroline Kelly in this volume.

Most significantly perhaps, a libertarian approach would seem to provide a way of addressing legitimate concerns that some unions have in relation to the regulation of money in politics – concerns that particularly apply to caps on political contributions and spending. As it is, there is considerable momentum to adopting these measures in relation to federal elections. The 2018 ALP National Platform commits to 'seek[ing] to limit the level of federal campaign expenditure, through the introduction of spending caps'.[31] Federal ALP leader, Anthony Albanese, has furthermore given in-principle support to caps on political donations because 'democracy shouldn't be for sale'.[32] Nearly all states and territories have one or both of these measures. Caps on political contributions have been adopted in New South Wales and Victoria.[33] Caps on spending already apply in New South Wales, Queensland, South Australia, Tasmania, the Australian Capital Territory and Northern Territory,[34] and, at the time of writing, the Western Australian Parliament is considering the Electoral Amendment Bill 2020 (WA) which seeks, among others, to put in place caps on spending.

Standing against this tide are two formidable concerns:

- First, that contribution caps will prohibit trade union affiliation fees going to the ALP – this was the underlying concern of the challenge in *Unions NSW (No 1)*;
- Second, that spending caps will prevent trade unions from mounting effective election campaigns – this was the key concern in *Unions NSW (No 2)*.

These are clearly salient concerns given the significance of trade union political spending, both in the form of contributions to the ALP and also in the form of independent third party campaign spending.[35] Through its trenchant opposition to regulation, a libertarian approach would allow all these contribution and spending practices to proceed apace. In the same breath, it addresses the concerns regarding trade union affiliation fees and election campaigns. A full-blooded libertarian approach, such as that adopted by US Supreme Court Justice Clarence Thomas, and cited in the submissions of Unions NSW in *Unions NSW (No 1)*,[36] would consider caps on both contributions and spending as constitutionally illegitimate. And if there were no such caps, the concerns regarding trade union affiliation fees and election campaigns would naturally disappear.

Electing for Egalitarianism

There is, however, an alternative perspective more consonant with the social justice and democratic goals of trade unions and more supportive of the regulation of electoral funding. This perspective finds expression in ACTU Secretary Sally McManus's book, *On Fairness*, where she notes:

> A powerful incentive to corruption, hard and soft, exists in the dynamics of [...] economic and political relationships. Big corporations have a direct interest in politics and the political system; their political donations reward those who promise them favourable conditions, and neither the community benefit nor the national interest comes into it.[37]

After the last federal election, Sally McManus also called for serious consideration of controls on election spending.[38]

These statements point to a social democratic approach – what the Canadian Supreme Court has dubbed an egalitarian model.[39] In this model, the pre-eminent democratic value is political equality[40] – the notion that each member of the community has equal political status. Correspondingly, wealth and resources should not determine the extent of political influence. As Robert Dahl, a key theorist of democracy, has said:

> If income, wealth, and economic position are [...] political resources, and if they are distributed unequally, then how can citizens be political equals? And if citizens cannot be political equals, how is democracy to exist?[41]

Under an egalitarian model, freedom is central but is understood as both 'freedom from' (state regulation) and 'freedom to' (meaningfully exercise freedom). As John Rawls puts it, it is not just the formal conferral of political freedoms that matters but also their fair value.[42] Understanding freedom in this more subtle way connects to what is universally accepted as the benchmark for democratic elections: that they be free *and* fair.

Under an egalitarian model, there is suspicion of state regulation, particularly abuse of power by governing parties, but also an embrace of state regulation in order to give effect to the principles of political equality and fairness in the context of inequalities of wealth and resources. As the High Court opined in *McCloy*, 'the risk to equal participation posed by the uncontrolled use of wealth may warrant legislative action to ensure, or even enhance, the practical enjoyment of popular sovereignty'.[43]

The suspicion and embrace of state regulation under an egalitarian approach parallels similar sentiments under a nuanced understanding of freedom of association. True, freedom of association requires suspicion of state regulation. At the same time, it also needs state regulation. The ILO *Right to Organise and Collective Bargaining Convention*, for instance, requires state signatories to provide machinery 'for the purpose of ensuring respect for the right to organise',[44] as well as 'to encourage and promote the full development and utilisation of machinery for voluntary negotiation between employers or employers' organisations and workers' organisations, with a view to the regulation of terms and conditions of employment by means of collective agreements'.[45]

Moreover, as will be seen below, an egalitarian approach can effectively address the two key concerns that Australian trade unions have with the regulation of electoral funding (that contribution caps will prohibit trade union affiliation fees going to the ALP and that spending caps will prevent trade unions from mounting effective election campaigns).

An Egalitarian Approach to Caps on Contributions[46]

Under an egalitarian model, caps on contributions – which were upheld by the High Court in *McCloy* – seek to address corruption broadly understood: not just quid pro quo corruption as accepted by the US Supreme Court, but also clientelism which, according to the High Court, 'arises from an office-holder's dependence on the financial support of a wealthy patron to a degree that is apt to compromise the expectation, fundamental to representative democracy, that public power be exercised in the public interest';[47] and 'war-chest' corruption, which arises when 'the power of money [...] pose[s] a threat to the electoral process itself'.[48]

Under such a model, we can make a principled distinction between political donations and membership fees on the basis that membership fees have much less risk of corruption due to an open declaration of support for the aims of a political party and are, moreover, integral to a vital form of political participation, namely, participation within political parties.

This distinction supports an exemption for genuine membership fees from caps on contributions. This exemption, in turn, should extend to organisational members such as trade unions affiliating to the ALP. There is no reason to view membership solely in individualistic terms. Further, a failure to extend exemptions to organisational membership will mean banning particular party structures; specifically, indirect parties comprising organisational members only and parties with mixed structures consisting of individual and organisational members. These party structures are not unique to parties of the 'left'. For instance, the predecessor of the National Party, the Country Party, had farmers' organisations as members; similarly, the New South Wales Shooters and Fishers Party has had shooting and fishing clubs as members.[49]

It might, however, be said that in the world of realpolitik, there is no way the Liberal Party and the National Party will agree to caps with an exemption for organisation membership fees. On the contrary, this is precisely what occurred when I put similar arguments to the New South Wales Legislative Council Select Committee on Electoral and Political Party Funding. The six member committee, which had only two ALP members and had as its chair the Christian Democratic Party's Reverend Fred Nile, and as its deputy chair, the Liberal Party's Don Harwin (the current Minister for the Public Service and Employee Relations for New South Wales) said this:

> The Committee considers that membership fees should not be encompassed by the Committee's proposed ban on all but small individual donations [...] Similarly, the Committee believes that trade union affiliation fees should be permissible, despite the proposed ban on union donations. To ban union affiliation fees would be to place unreasonable restrictions on party structures.[50]

It is these views that explain the exemption in section 26 of the *Election Funding Act 2018* (NSW) for organisational membership fees, including trade union affiliation fees.

An Egalitarian Approach to Caps on Spending

There are two reasons for caps on election spending under the egalitarian approach: it levels the playing field by preventing excessive spending to dominate electoral contests, and it reduces the risk of corruption by staunching the demand for campaign funds.

Once spending limits are placed on contestants in elections (parties and candidates), it is imperative that controls are also placed on what are called third party campaigners (individuals and organisations which participate in election campaigns but are not parties and candidates). The need for this was well explained by the Canadian Supreme Court in *Harper v. Canada*. Drawing upon the 1991 Canadian Lortie Royal Commission Report, the Court explained that third party campaign spending limits were needed on the following grounds: it prevents the dominance of political discourse by the wealthy; it prevents parties and candidates from circumventing the limits that apply to them by creating a front organisation; and it reduces the risk of third party spending having an unfair effect on the outcome of an election.[51]

What then about the concern that spending limits will prevent effective election campaigns by trade unions? The short answer is that this does not *necessarily* result from third party campaign spending limits. The experience of New South Wales unions in the first two state elections where spending limits applied (in 2011 and 2015) supports this point.[52]

Whether spending limits will prevent effective election campaigns by trade unions very much depends on the level at which the limits are set. Indeed, it is well accepted that third party campaign spending limits should, as the High Court made clear in *Unions NSW (No 2)*, be high enough to allow third party campaigners to reasonably present their case. Equally, the limits should not be too high so that they allow the wealthy to dominate political discourse and elections through third party campaign spending.

We are inevitably in Goldilocks territory where third party campaign spending limits should not be too low nor too high. And that is why the process of setting the level of the limits should be robust. For my part, I have suggested the initial levels be set through a Royal Commission process and changed subsequently by the Australian Electoral Commission.[53]

There are two other noteworthy principles in setting the level of third party campaign spending limits; one may be palatable to those involved in union election campaigns, and the other perhaps less so. First, from a democratic perspective, mass mobilisation should be encouraged in the design of spending limits. This can be done by exempting volunteer labour from spending. It may also be desirable to provide for an increase in third party campaign spending limits according to the number of members of a third party campaigner when there is an authorisation from its members for such spending.

Second, third party campaign spending limits should be set at a level lower than that which applies to political parties, as is the case with Canadian and UK spending limits. As the Canadian Supreme Court in *Libman* has said, 'owing to their numbers, the impact of [third party] spending on one of the candidates or political parties to the detriment of the others would be disproportionate'.[54] Moreover, as Gageler J rightly recognised in *Unions NSW (No 2)*, there is a 'functional distinction' between political parties and third party campaigners: 'During a period leading up to an election, a political party which aims to form government must be in a position to communicate on the whole range of issues of potential concern to voters whereas a third-party campaigner can concentrate its resources on a single issue of concern to it'.[55] His Honour then went on to say:

> To ensure that the political party is able to communicate on the range of issues of potential concern to voters without being overwhelmed by the targeted campaigns of any number of third-party campaigners acting alone or in concert, the cap on the third-party campaigner must be substantially lower than the cap on the political party.[56]

Conclusion

It is highly likely that the questions taken up by this chapter will grow in significance in the immediate and medium-term with the political-political strategies of trade unions, including election campaigns, becoming increasingly important. This is not just because of the existential need for trade unions to protect their organisational security and to institute durable institutions for collective bargaining. It is also because political-political strategies are necessary in order for trade unions to secure protection for workers where union density is low, for instance, migrant workers and those working in the gig economy; industrial-political strategies do not suffice in these contexts. For further commentary on migrant workers and on the gig economy, see Chapters 8 and 7 by Joanna Howe and Anthony Forsyth respectively in this volume . The same applies to regulating international trade for decent work, for instance, through trade agreements: see further, Chapter 10 by Patricia Ranald in this volume.

The COVID-19 pandemic will further deepen the importance of trade union political-political strategies. It has brought about a crisis in the world of work with staggering levels of unemployment and underemployment, together with widespread industry and workforce restructuring.[57] Political-political strategies will be vital for trade unions in addressing this crisis. They would, for instance, be critical to effectively implementing the four-pillar policy framework promulgated by the ILO: Pillar 1: Stimulating the economy and employment; Pillar 2: Supporting enterprises, jobs and incomes; Pillar 3: Protecting workers in the workplace; and Pillar 4: Relying upon social dialogue for solutions.[58] They would be all the more so should efforts be directed to bringing about coordinated international action needed to avoid a global recession: see further discussion in Chapter 11 by K. D. Ewing in this volume.

All this deeply connects with the main crisis in the world of work, the climate crisis. And again, political-political strategies will be pivotal for trade unions, whether it be to bring about a just transition for workers (see Chapter 10 by Jeremy Moss in this volume) or to institute some degree of economic democracy (see Chapters 2 and 3 by David Peetz and Julian A. Sempill respectively in this volume).

These overlapping crises reinforce the need for a principled approach to the regulation of election funding, which this chapter has argued should be grounded in an egalitarian approach. Happily, this approach is also aligned in the longer-term interests of Australian trade unions. True, a libertarian approach might yield short-term gains. The challenges in *Unions NSW (No 1)* and *Unions NSW (No 2)*, after all, were successful.

The longer-term prognosis for the union movement can, however, only be bleak in a world where the use of money in politics is unrestricted. However much money unions amass, there is no conceivable way they can match the funds available to commercial corporations. Take, for instance, the 2019 federal election where Clive Palmer through his party, Clive Palmer's United Australia Party, spent $89.5 million (in 2018–19 dollars), nearly matching the *combined* spending of the ALP and the Coalition parties ($94.2 million) and was 37 times trade union third party campaign spending ($2.4 million).[59]

Clive Palmer, however, is only a single mining magnate – only the twentieth richest person in the country – and yet with an estimated wealth of $1.8 billion,[60] his 2019 federal election spending shows how big money in elections is small change for the mega-rich.[61] It should also be remembered that when the mining billionaires combined to oppose the Resources Super Profits Tax, they contributed to the ousting of a Prime Minister.[62]

You cannot beat owners of capital when it comes to money – that is why they are the capitalists.

Notes

1 Karl Klare, 'Countervailing Workers' Power as a Regulatory Strategy', in *Legal Regulation of the Employment Relation*, ed. Hugh Collins, Paul Davies and Roger Rideout (London: Kluwer Law International, 2000), 63–82.

2 K. D. Ewing, 'The Functions of Trade Unions', *Industrial Law Journal* 34, no. 1 (2005): 1–22.

3 *Constitution of the International Labour Organisation*, annex 'Declaration Concerning the Aims and Purposes of the International Labour Organisation (Declaration of Philadelphia)' (1944), art. III(d).

4 K. D. Ewing, 'Democratic Socialism and Labour Law', *Industrial Law Journal* 24, no. 2 (1995): 103–32 (116–18); Alan Bogg, *The Democratic Aspects of Trade Union Recognition* (Oxford: Hart Publishing, 2009).

5 Hyman and Gumbrell-McCormick single out four (ideology, opportunity structures, organisational capacity and contextual challenges): Richard Hyman and Rebecca Gumbrell-McCormick, 'Trade Unions, Politics and Parties: Is a New Configuration Possible?', *Transfer: European Review of Labour and Research* 16, no. 3 (2010): 315–31.

6 Richard Hyman, *Understanding European Trade Unionism: Between Market, Class and Society* (London: Sage, 2001), 13–15.

7 For these three ideal types, see Hyman, *Understanding European Trade Unionism.*

8 International Labour Office, Case No. 2698 (Australia): *Complaint against the Government of Australia Presented by the Communications, Electrical, Electronic, Energy, Information, Postal,*

Plumbing and Allied Services Union of Australia (CEPU), June 2010, para. 224 (emphasis added).

9 Phil Larkin and Charles Lees, 'The Australian Labor Party and the Trade Unions', in *Left-of-Centre Parties and the Trade Unions in the Twenty-First Century*, ed. Elin Haugsgjerd Allern and Tim Bale (Oxford: Oxford University Press, 2017), 54.

10 Kathie Muir, *Worth Fighting For: Inside the 'Your Rights at Work' Campaign* (Sydney: UNSW Press, 2008); Tom Bramble, *Trade Unionism in Australia: A History from Flood to Ebb Tide* (Cambridge: Cambridge University Press, 2008), chapter 8.

11 Anthony Forsyth, 'Where to Now for Unions and Change the Rules?', *The Conversation*, 23 May 2019, https://theconversation.com/where-to-now-for-unions-and-change-the-rules-117583.

12 Analysis from 'Dollars and Democracy' database by Malcolm Anderson (copy on file with author). Election spending estimates have been derived from total spending in relevant financial years.

13 Graeme Orr, 'Political Finance Law in Australia', in *Party Funding and Campaign Financing in International Perspective*, ed. K. D. Ewing and Samuel Issacharoff (Oxford: Hart Publishing, 2006), 99, 100.

14 Joo-Cheong Tham, *Money and Politics: The Democracy We Can't Afford* (Sydney: UNSW Press, 2010).

15 *Unions NSW v. New South Wales* (2013) 252 CLR 530.

16 *Unions NSW v. New South Wales* (2019) 93 ALJR 166.

17 Joo-Cheong Tham, 'NSW Election Funding Laws Are a Serious Attack on Freedom of Association', *Guardian,* 7 November 2013, https://www.theguardian.com/commentisfree/2013/nov/07/nsw-election-funding-laws-are-a-serious-attack-on-freedom-of-association.

18 Tham, 'NSW Election Funding Laws'.

19 Unions NSW, 'Plaintiff's Written Submissions', *Unions NSW v. State of New South Wales*, S70 of 2013, 18 September 2013, [15], [21], [33], [42] ('Unions NSW Submissions').

20 Unions NSW Submissions, [31], [33], [40], [57]–[59].

21 *Harper v. Canada (Attorney General)*, [2004] 1 S.C.R 827, 868.

22 *Citizens United v. Federal Election Commission* 558 U.S. 310, 340 (2009).

23 *Buckley v. Valeo* 424 U.S. 1, 48–49 (1976).

24 *Buckley v. Valeo*, 19, as cited in Unions NSW Submissions, [42].

25 David Harvey, *A Brief History of Neoliberalism* (New York: Oxford University Press, 2005).

26 *International Covenant on Civil and Political Rights*, 23 March 1976, 999 U.N.T.S. 171, art. 22(1).

27 *ILO Declaration on Fundamental Principles and Rights at Work and Its Follow Up*, 18 June 1998, art. 2(a).

28 T. H. Marshall, *Class, Citizenship, and Social Development* (Westport, CT: Greenwood Press, [1950] 1973), 94–103. For discussion, see Guy Mundlak, 'Industrial Citizenship, Social Citizenship, Corporate Citizenship: I Just Want My Wages', *Theoretical Inquiries in Law* 8, no. 2 (2007): 719–48.

29 *ILO Declaration of Philadelphia*, art. I(b).

30 *Freedom of Association and Protection of the Right to Organise Convention*, No. 87, 1948, art. 8(2).

31 Australian Labor Party, *A Fair Go for Australia: National Platform* (2018), [73], https://www.alp.org.au/media/1539/2018_alp_national_platform_constitution.pdf.

32 Paul Karp, '"Obscene Amount of Money": Anthony Albanese Backs Potential Cap on Political Donations', *Guardian*, 23 February 2020, https://www.theguardian.com/australia-news/2020/feb/23/obscene-amount-of-money-anthony-albanese-backs-potential-cap-on-political-donations.
33 *Election Funding Act 2018* (NSW); *Electoral Act 2002* (Vic), part 12.
34 *Election Funding Act 2018* (NSW); *Electoral Act 1992* (Qld), part 11; *Electoral Act 1985* (SA), part 13A; *Electoral Act 2004* (Tas), part 6; *Electoral Act 1992* (ACT), part 14; *Electoral Act 2004* (NT), part 10, div. 4. See also, Joo-Cheong Tham, 'Democracy before Dollars: The Problems with Money in Politics and How to Fix Them', *Australian Quarterly* 90, no. 2 (April 2019): 20–32.
35 Refer to figures in Introduction.
36 Unions NSW Submissions, [16], [22].
37 Sally McManus, *On Fairness* (Carlton: Melbourne University Press, 2019), 69–70.
38 David Crowe, '"We'll Be the Resistance": Unions Defend Their Campaign, Vow to Take on Morrison', *Sydney Morning Herald*, 22 May 2019, https://www.smh.com.au/federal-election-2019/we-ll-be-the-resistance-unions-defend-their-campaign-vow-to-take-on-morrison-20190522-p51q7i.html.
39 *Harper v. Canada*, 868.
40 Canada Royal Commission on Electoral Reform and Party Financing, *Reforming Electoral Democracy: Final Report*, vol. 1 (1991), 321.
41 Robert Dahl, *Democracy and Its Critics* (New Haven, CT: Yale University Press, 1989), 326.
42 For this distinction, see John Rawls, *A Theory of Justice*, rev. ed. (Oxford: Oxford University Press, 1999), 225; John Rawls, *Justice as Fairness: A Restatement* (Cambridge, MA: Harvard University Press, 2001), 149.
43 *McCloy v. New South Wales* (2015) 257 CLR 178, 207 [45].
44 *Right to Organise and Collective Bargaining Convention*, no. 98, 1949, art. 3.
45 Ibid., art. 4.
46 The following analysis relating to trade union affiliation fees draws upon Joo-Cheong Tham, *Establishing a Sustainable Framework for Election Funding and Spending Laws in New South Wales: A Report for the New South Wales Electoral Commission* (Sydney: New South Wales Electoral Commission, 2012), 142–52.
47 *McCloy v. New South Wales*, 204–5 [36].
48 Ibid., 205 [38].
49 Tham, *Establishing a Sustainable Framework*, 148–51.
50 Legislative Council Select Committee on Electoral and Political Party Funding, Parliament of New South Wales, *Electoral and Political Party Funding in New South Wales* (2008), 113.
51 *Harper v. Canada*, 875.
52 The following analysis relating to trade union affiliation fees draws upon Tham, *Establishing a Sustainable Framework*, 171–77.
53 Joo-Cheong Tham, 'The Crisis of Political Money; Or, What the Rest of Australia Can Learn from New South Wales', *Meanjin* 74, no. 3 (2015): 69–76.
54 *Libman v. Quebec (A.G.)* [1997] 3 S.C.R. 569, 601.
55 *Unions NSW (No 1)*, 630 [89].
56 Ibid., 630–31 [90].
57 See International Labour Organization, *ILO Monitor: COVID-19 and the World of Work* 6th ed (Geneva: ILO, 23 September 2020).

58 International Labour Organization, 'A Policy Framework for Tackling the Economic and Social Impact of the COVID-19 Crisis' (Briefing Note, 20 May 2020).

59 Analysis from 'Dollars and Democracy' database by Malcolm Anderson (copy on file with author).

60 Lucinda Schmidt, 'Australia's Richest 2019: In a Down Year, Two Miners Break Back into the Top 50', *Forbes*, 16 January 2019, https://www.forbes.com/sites/forbesasia/2019/01/16/australias-richest-2019-in-a-down-year-two-miners-break-back-into-the-top-50/#63c1bdab7090.

61 Marian Sawer, 'After Clive Palmer's $60 Million Campaign, Limits on Political Advertising Are More Important than Ever', *The Conversation*, 21 May 2019, https://theconversation.com/after-clive-palmers-60-million-campaign-limits-on-political-advertising-are-more-important-than-ever-117099; Paul Karp, 'Clive Palmer $60m Election Spend Shows Need for Cap, Advocates Say', *Guardian*, 23 September 2019, https://www.theguardian.com/australia-news/2019/sep/23/clive-palmer-60m-election-spend-shows-need-for-cap-advocates-say.

62 Mark Davis, 'A Snip at $22m to Get Rid of PM', *Sydney Morning Herald*, 2 February 2011, https://www.smh.com.au/business/a-snip-at-22m-to-get-rid-of-pm-20110201-1acgj.html.

Chapter 6

TRADE UNIONS AND PRECARIOUS WORK: IN SEARCH OF EFFECTIVE STRATEGIES

Iain Campbell

Trade unions in Australia, as in many other industrialised societies, are facing a major challenge as a result of the expansion of precarious work. How unions respond will be crucial both for precarious workers and for the future of unions.

Precarious work, also called 'insecure work' or 'bad jobs', is best understood as work that exhibits precariousness or insecurity across all or most characteristics of a job. One useful definition refers to (1) lack of regulatory protection; (2) low wages; (3) high employment insecurity; and (4) low levels of employee control over wages, hours and working conditions.[1] Scholars rightly caution that precarious work should not be identified just with non-standard employment, since precariousness can also emerge within standard full-time permanent employment. Nevertheless, it is true that precariousness tends to be concentrated in certain non-standard forms of employment. In Australia, this would include forms of self-employment such as freelancing, but it mainly concerns forms of wage labour such as casual work, fixed-term employment, temporary agency work ('labour-hire'), bogus self-employment (including much 'platform work') and even part-time permanent employment.[2] The list includes several highly commodified forms of work, new and old, and their recent proliferation highlights the continuing relevance of the principle announced in the opening passage of the *ILO Declaration of Philadelphia*: 'labour is not a commodity'.[3]

One pitfall in discussing this topic should be flagged at the start. From a union point of view, it is vital to keep in mind a distinction between precarious work and precarious workers. The distinction is not always hard and fast, but it is an essential heuristic device. It is the key to avoiding dangerous errors of conflation, whereby (1) hostility to the work is taken to imply hostility to the worker currently in that form of work; or (2) a positive approach to the worker is taken to imply a positive approach to the work. Instead, effective union strategy may require different approaches for the work and for the worker. For example, zero-hours work arrangements may need to be proscribed, but action to achieve a prohibition can be compatible with, and may indeed demand, organisation of zero-hours workers and representation of their interests.

The distinction between precarious work and precarious workers overlaps with a second distinction between representation and regulation. Representation of *workers* is a crucial starting point for trade union action. However, determined representation of workers' material interests inevitably leads towards a sphere of regulation, in the first instance regulation of the terms and conditions of *work* through formal instruments such as collective agreements and legislation.[4] From the point of view of labour market theory, the aim here is regulation oriented to worker interests in place of other, competing types of regulation, whether formal or informal.[5] The regulatory ambitions of trade unions are under pressure in many societies, often displaced by encouragement of servicing to members and narrow visions of representation ('organising'), but regulation is aptly described by Keith Ewing as the most important function of trade unions and 'the most visible manifestation of the trade union role in promoting fairness and social justice not only at work but within the economy as a whole'.[6]

Description of precarious work and its recent expansion has made good progress in Australia, accurately coming to grips with long-standing peculiarities such as the prominent place of casual work.[7] Description is by no means complete, partly due to conceptual and data problems,[8] and some aspects are only lightly covered. Nevertheless, there is widespread agreement that precarious work has indeed increased, mainly, though not exclusively, in low-paid sectors of the economy. With the exception of some employer associations, who insist that precariousness is a synonym for 'flexibility' and should be viewed as a benefit for both employers and employees, there is also widespread agreement that the growth of precarious work is a substantial problem with significant negative impacts.[9]

This chapter is primarily concerned with strategies for *regulation* of precarious work. This dimension of union action is poorly developed in Australia but it is central to beneficial outcomes for precarious workers. The chapter does not propose specific new regulatory initiatives but instead aims to raise questions and outline possible paths forward. It draws extensively in the early sections on international literature, but the aim is to set the scene for a focus on Australian unions.[10] The first section explores motives for union engagement with the issue of precarious work, while the second section considers two influential but mistaken theories that dismiss the potential of union action.

The third section dips into the rich European debate, seeking to identify the strategic options available to unions. Select union initiatives in Germany, successfully bridging representation and regulation, are summarised in the fourth section. Union responses in Australia are reviewed in the fifth section, which notes that, in spite of widespread concern and the development of a few promising initiatives, the crucial dimension of regulation is lagging badly. The sixth section examines barriers to action. I suggest that it is possible to identify a two-fold blockage at the level of union agency, which involves (1) neglect of regulation as an objective; and (2) a narrow choice of levers for action. The conclusion suggests that effective strategies for precarious work in Australia need to place more emphasis on a goal of regulation and to move beyond traditional levers, such as negotiating collective agreements and making claims before industrial tribunals, in order to build political campaigns aimed at extending and strengthening *statutory protective standards*.[11]

The Challenge of Precarious Work

For trade unions, the three main motives for responding to precarious work are:

1. concern that precarious work is a threat to existing wages and conditions, especially for full-time regular employees, who form the core of union membership;
2. a desire to pursue new sources of union membership; and
3. a commitment to representing all workers and advancing social justice.[12]

The first motive, the threat posed by precarious work, is the most important. The immediate danger is linked to employer strategies, primarily at the level of the enterprise, which aim to use the varied 'flexibilities' of precarious work to reduce unit labour costs and secure a competitive advantage, either by direct conversion of existing jobs to more precarious forms or by indirect replacement through mechanisms such as outsourcing, subcontracting, use of subsidiaries and use of temporary agencies. In directly affected enterprises, existing jobs stand at risk, and unionised workforces are often forced into concession bargaining. This is a threat not only to existing wages and conditions but also to union organisation and any realistic prospect of action to improve wages and conditions. Though employer cost-minimisation strategies are felt most immediately by workers at individual enterprises, the impact readily spills over to other workplaces, especially when wage differentials between competing enterprises spark a dynamic of wage competition. This wider impact undermines good employers and fragments the workforce in new ways, posing a threat to a broad range of workers, whether unionised or non-unionised, including even most precarious workers themselves. In addition, insofar as expansion of precarious work damages the quality of the product or service, it harms the interests of workers as customers, clients and citizens. More broadly, the presence of precarious work acts as a menace that chills employment relations throughout an entire society. As this discussion indicates, union responses may start with self-interest, but they also draw on broader imperatives of societal concern and solidarity.[13]

The second and third motives are less to do with precarious work and more to do with precarious workers. The desire to pursue new sources of recruitment certainly plays a part in the thinking of many unions, drained of traditional membership, but it is largely a pragmatic, tactical calculation based on organisational self-interest. The third reason, however, is more fundamental, drawing attention to central elements of union purpose. Precarious workers are difficult to organise, often falling outside both union membership and the sphere of union influence. This is perhaps particularly true for workers in the gig economy, as noted in Chapter 7 by Anthony Forsyth in this volume. Moreover, as well as common interests, precarious workers often have distinct interests, in tension with the interests of other workers, whether because of characteristics of the work or because of characteristics of the worker, such as youth, gender and migrant status. Yet, irrespective of any other motives, union engagement with precarious workers is justified because of their location within the most exploited layers of the workforce. Scholars and activists note that unions cannot shrink into mere 'business unionism', serving just their membership, without losing much of their influence, their legitimacy and their purpose. True unions are champions of social justice, both in the workplace and in the broader society, and they are inevitably entangled in relations of solidarity with the wider workforce, especially the weakest sections.[14]

Trade unions are on the defensive in most industrialised societies, faced with a formidable range of challenges. As well as presenting a major challenge in itself, precarious work is implicated, either directly or indirectly, in the many other challenges documented by researchers, such as (1) long-term structural changes, based on product market shifts and advances in production and product technologies, which favour the decline of industry and the rise of services; (2) the diversification of patterns of participation and individual needs within the workforce, which generates interest in new ways of working; (3) increasingly aggressive employer strategies, especially in the private sector; (4) neoliberal governments, which have eroded the institutional framework of labour regulation, opening up more and wider loopholes that employers can use to avoid labour standards and unions; (5) the environmental crisis and the wasteful over-exploitation of cheap (or free) natural resources; and (6) the intensification of social and economic inequalities in most domains of life.[15]

The challenge of precarious work in Australia has been underlined by the COVID-19 pandemic. Precarious work in settings such as security firms, abattoirs and aged care residences has proven to be an important vector for transmission of the virus. At the same time, the pandemic and the government response have boosted the numbers of precarious workers, intensified precariousness for already precarious workers and introduced new types and levels of insecurity for many workers in the remainder of the workforce. The long-term implications will become clearer as the health threat recedes and economic activity recovers. However, the current outlook is dark. On the one hand, the government response has offered a useful reminder of the importance of politics. On the other hand, the federal government is promising a pro-business agenda for recovery, and employer groups have responded by dusting off old proposals for policy changes to further increase 'workplace flexibility', restrain union action, and enhance management discretion. Much will depend on the capacity of unions, in collaboration with other groups, to present a clear, alternative reform agenda. For a perspective on paths forward in the United Kingdom, see Chapter 11 by K. D. Ewing in this volume.

Two Mistaken Theories

Trade unions, both in the past and in the present, are crucial vehicles in the struggle against precarious work. Two recent theories, however, summarily dismiss the value of union action. The first, somewhat elastic but often coloured by politics of the neoliberal Right, refers to 'insiders' and 'outsiders'; the second, anchored in politics of the left, is structured around the notion of a 'precariat'.[16] In both cases, the basic argument starts with the notion of a *dualistic divide* within labour markets, which has become deeper and more fundamental as a result of the growth of precarious work alongside a standard model of secure and regular work (*dualisation*). The argument suggests that trade unions, embedded in the old model and pressed back into their heartlands, represent the interests of relatively privileged 'core' workers on one side of the dualistic divide, while precarious workers are left outside union protection, either because these workers are neglected or, more strongly, because union action to defend the interests of core workers inevitably undermines the interests of less privileged workforce groups. In short, the argument asserts that unions are locked into exclusionary attitudes and actions. Both theories advocate policy initiatives that would bypass unions but still supposedly serve the interests of precarious workers, such as further labour market deregulation or state provision of a basic income.

There is no room to develop a critique of these two theories. General weaknesses are well canvased in recent literature. Though the theories usefully highlight economic inequalities and precarious work, critics point out that contemporary labour market changes and workforce segmentation processes are poorly captured by the notions of dualism and dualisation. It is difficult, for example, to distinguish two relatively homogenous but separate groups, which can be labelled either 'insiders' and 'outsiders' or the 'working class' and the 'precariat'. A better descriptive term for the outcome of current labour restructuring is not dualism but *fragmentation*, which involves multiple workforce groups, stretched out on a continuum of socioeconomic inequality. Similarly, dualisation is a poor synonym for what is better defined at the policy level as a process of *liberalisation*, anchored in neoliberal philosophies.[17]

What about the dualist argument dismissing unions? It is easy to concede that a significant deficit in representation separates most precarious workers from the mainstream of the union movement. Moreover, it is true that some trade unions, especially in the past, have displayed exclusionary attitudes, marked by indifference or even hostility to precarious workers. However, exclusion is not a necessary component of union attitudes and actions; it is better seen as a contingent response, indeed a response that is often the unfortunate result of analytical misjudgements, such as the belief that precarious work should be tolerated or even encouraged because it might function as a stable buffer for the wages and conditions of current union members. Scholars note that exclusionary attitudes and actions are in fact waning in many industrialised societies, displaced by alternative approaches that more accurately analyse labour market trends and aim to engage with precarious workers.[18] Alternative approaches can be aptly described as solidaristic and *inclusive*, in the first instance inclusive of precarious workers, but often embedded in broader analytical judgements that recognise the importance of inclusive institutions of labour regulation and indeed inclusive labour markets.[19]

European Discussion

The most useful analysis of unions and precarious work comes from Europe, where the concept of precarious work is familiar and research has benefited from solid funding and support, both through unions themselves and through other bodies such as national governments and the European Union (EU). The research is rich and varied, with many accounts situated at the national level,[20] some at a broader cross-national level[21] and an increasing number examining industry sectors across nations.[22] Some studies seek to cover all forms of precarious work, while others focus on particular types such as temporary agency work or zero-hours contracts.[23] Several studies focus on trade

Table 6.1 Union strategies in response to precarious work

Strategies for representing precarious workers:

- Exclusion from union;
- Inclusion in mainstream of union;
- Inclusion with special forms of representation;
- Inclusion with specialist labour market services.

Strategies for regulating precarious work:

- Elimination (total or partial);
- Limits in conditions of use and quantitative limits;
- Limits to worker duration in precarious work, for example, transition rules;
- Improved wages and conditions, aimed at narrowing a deficit with standard workers, lessening precariousness or compensating for specific disabilities.

Strategic choice of levers of action:

- Developing individualised services, for example, insurance, access to training and labour market services;
- Bargaining with employers to insert clauses in binding collective agreements;
- Promoting voluntary codes of conduct among employers;
- Pressuring indirect employers (including government);
- Advocating legislation for minimum protective standards;
- Advocating regulatory changes through independent tribunals or other authorities;
- Litigation;
- Collaborating with government agencies, for example, labour inspectorate;
- Organising and mobilising precarious workers;
- Working with community groups, NGOs, social movements (including 'alt-labour' organisations);
- Developing media-based campaigns, for example, 'name and shame' campaigns.

unions and precarious workers, considering vulnerable groups such as migrant workers who are disproportionately concentrated in precarious work.[24]

Most important, discussion and research in Europe is accompanied by union action. The initiatives are varied, reflecting the many strategies that trade unions have adopted in response to precarious work. It is useful to disaggregate the strategies in terms of three dimensions, which correspond to precarious workers, precarious work and levers of action (Table 6.1).[25]

The typology in Table 6.1 points to the multiplicity of approaches that can be taken by unions. The first dimension allows us to situate the familiar contrast between exclusive and inclusive approaches to precarious workers. The second dimension outlines broad options for the regulation of precarious work, generally based on restricting either the form of employment or its negative consequences for workers. Improving wages and conditions is a commonly chosen option, appropriate for many, though not all, forms of precarious work. This approach has achieved success in many countries in the pivotal case of part-time work, where legal regulation requiring equality of treatment, backed up by union action in collective bargaining, has helped to reduce the marginality of part-time work and to integrate most part-time workers into the mainstream of the workforce.[26]

Perhaps the most thought-provoking aspect of the typology is the third dimension. I refer here to 'levers', but they can be equated with the 'repertoires of collective action' mentioned in the union renewal literature, or indeed with the union 'methods' identified by Sidney and Beatrice Webb over one hundred years ago.[27] Some levers concern servicing or representation but most are closer to objectives of regulation.

In discussing levers, scholars and activists often note the limitations of traditional methods of collective bargaining and the related structures of workplace unionism.[28] Collective bargaining is never universal. Access to collective bargaining is impeded for many precarious workers, given that they are concentrated in small workplaces, engaged in irregular schedules (perhaps with minimal hours), and are fearful of dismissal or loss of shifts, because of their limited rights. Difficulties are compounded in the case of the 'fissured workplace', where outsourcing, subcontracting, franchise arrangements and temporary work agencies have led to an externalisation of employment.[29] Externalised jobs, especially those at the end of long, cost-driven subcontracting chains, are often hidden from view, highly precarious and mainly occupied by vulnerable workforce groups.[30]

In the light of such difficulties, European scholars argue that representation of precarious workers needs to move beyond the workplace and to use alternative levers alongside or instead of collective bargaining.[31] The main supplement or alternative to collective bargaining is 'legal regulation' or 'legal enactment', which was the union method recommended for low-wage workers by the Webbs. It is important to clarify that what is meant here is legislation for *minimum protective standards*, rather than legislation for *participative standards*, which is linked to state support for collective bargaining.[32] From a union point of view, both types of legal regulation are important and necessary, but it is the former, involving legislation that sets standards such as minimum wages, maximum working hours and restrictions on dismissal, which is most relevant for precarious workers. Indeed, such regulation is particularly relevant for precarious workers because of the way in which precarious work is often located within gaps in the system of minimum protective standards. New legislation for protective standards can seek to (1) plug the gaps; (2) raise the level of existing protective standards; or (3) introduce entirely new protective standards. Political action aimed at achieving such legislation cannot be confined to lobbying; in a context of social contestation, where employers are resistant to minimum standards and governments of all complexions are tempted by neoliberal prescriptions, political action generally requires public campaigning with a 'social justice' frame, often in alliance with other civil society groups.[33]

Statutory minimum protective standards are prominent in most European societies, including even those with a strong tradition of reliance on collective bargaining. Moreover, they are becoming more important, as societies seek to respond to new forms of work and to employer interest in loopholes and 'exit options' that would allow them to avoid the cost and burden of existing standards. National and regional regulation is usefully augmented by regulation at EU level, where unions have succeeded, first, in negotiating with employer associations two important European directives that aim at narrowing the deficit in protection for workers in part-time employment and fixed-term employment, and, second, in paving the way for a third directive on temporary agency work.[34] A recent Directive on Transparent and Predictable Working Conditions[35] marks a further advance by introducing new rights for a broader group of workers, including zero-hour, voucher-based and platform workers.[36]

What influences union strategic choice across the three dimensions in Table 6.1? One factor is union identity and ideology.[37] Opposing strategies adopted by powerful actors such as employers and the state are another important factor. Power resources, which can be usefully disaggregated into four types (structural, associational, institutional and societal), are crucial.[38] At the same time, it is important not to overlook *union agency* – starting with the ability of unions to define their objectives (long term and short term), analyse labour markets and class relations, and accurately assess their power resources in relation to opposing forces. This set of tasks is demanding at the best of times, but incorporating precarious workers sharpens the challenge. Representation, for example, is never an automatic process. Unions must decide which interests to represent; they must articulate different interests and construct solidarities and then push new ideas and interests within the available institutions of regulation.[39] There is plenty of room here for diverse strategies and tactics. There is also plenty of room for miscalculation and poor choices, leading to failure rather than success.

German Examples

Union initiatives in response to precarious work, some successful, are common in Europe. It is worth citing a couple of German examples, since Germany is often presented as a classic national case of entrenched dualism, marked on the one hand by strong industrial unions, firmly embedded in the workplace and involved in sectoral collective bargaining on behalf of 'core' workers, and on the other hand by a large and growing periphery of unorganised workers with markedly inferior wages and conditions.[40] Yet German unions in recent years have undertaken several inclusive initiatives that incorporate legislation for minimum protective standards and effectively respond to the threat of precarious work.

A good starting point is the powerful manufacturing union, IG Metall, which, in the course of changing employer strategies and the liberalisation of labour regulation, has confronted two main threats: (1) the erosion of collective bargaining, as more employers take opportunities to opt out of collective agreements and to unilaterally set wages and conditions at reduced levels; and (2) increases in the proportion of lower-wage workers supplied through either temporary work agencies or subcontracting. Both trends widen wage differentials and thereby threaten the security of workers throughout the sectors covered by the union. IG Metall, and indeed other blue-collar unions, responded to the erosion of collective bargaining and the associated growth of wage competition by drawing on solidaristic traditions, existing power resources and robust research in order to support the public campaign, led by service sector unions, for a statutory minimum wage.[41] At the same time – after a few false starts – the union tackled temporary agency work by organising temporary agency workers, developing new clauses in collective agreements with host employers to entrench principles of equal pay, 'naming and shaming' host employers that exploited wage differentials, and campaigning for stricter legal regulation (e.g. to impose a maximum limit on the duration of assignments and to promote equal pay). Similar techniques were used to tackle the growth of subcontracting.[42] The result is described as a virtuous circle in which better outcomes for workers were secured through a combination of coordinated bargaining and strict national legislation.[43] Both union support for the minimum wage and union action on temporary agency and subcontracted work fit a model of inclusive trade unionism. Both initiatives have been successful in shaping the forms and effects of precarious work, in reconfiguring solidarity at workplace and sectoral levels and in helping to renew the strength and influence of IG Metall.[44]

Also worth mentioning are the efforts by the service sector union, NGG (Nahrung–Genuss–Gaststätten), to meet the challenge posed by the deterioration in wages and conditions in meat processing. Deterioration was linked to a surge after 2004 of 'posted' workers, mainly from Poland, Hungary, Romania and Bulgaria, who were organised and supplied under markedly inferior wages and conditions to German meat processing plants by labour subcontractors based in the source countries. In contrast to other EU countries, the institutional framework governing posted workers in German meat processing was porous, but reversal of the spiral of wage competition seemed blocked because the union was relatively weak, migrant workers were generally unwilling to organise and employers, split among multiple employer associations, were hostile to negotiations. Nevertheless, the union has been able to make advances in recent years, primarily by campaigning at local and national levels and by using tighter legislation, especially in connection with the minimum wage, to force encompassing agreements with employers. The result is a more favourable regulatory regime, which helps to equalise wages and conditions. This new regime rests on a mix of hard regulation, public awareness and media attention, and voluntary agreements with a selection of larger companies, which act to limit posting and indeed to discourage most subcontracting arrangements.[45]

Union Initiatives in Australia

To what extent have Australian unions produced effective strategies to deal with precarious work? The record over the past 20 years is mixed. There seems to be a broad commitment to inclusiveness. The peak union body, the Australian Council of Trade Unions (ACTU), has drawn attention to general features and experiences of precarious work, most ambitiously by sponsoring a public inquiry into insecure work, which reported in 2012.[46] It has persistently called for a 'reduction in insecure work', but it has struggled to take the further step to a plausible programme of action. Some individual unions have launched initiatives, focused on specific forms of precarious work, but efforts have been rather desultory and success has proved elusive.

There is no space for a complete review, but it is useful to refer to one or two instances of action and inaction. The main examples of success have occurred in the context of lengthy and complex supply chains, where unions have been able to add new layers of protective regulation to improve wages and conditions and mitigate the risk of unfair wage competition.[47] One positive initiative, with a lengthy history that stretches back to the 1980s, concerns the actions of the clothing workers' union to improve wages and conditions for 'outworkers', that is, homeworkers, in clothing manufacture. Outworkers, generally migrant women, were organised by subcontractors to supply apparel manufacturers or retailers. They worked from home under precarious conditions, ostensibly as independent contractors paid according to meagre piece rates. The union, in collaboration with a non-government organisation, Asian Women at Work, founded and supported a broad-based community organisation (FairWear), which used varied campaigning techniques to mobilise outworkers, spread information, build public support as well as lobby employers and policy makers. The campaign was able to achieve a 'suite of regulatory mechanisms', much of it targeting lead firms in the supply chain, extending from special provisions in the *Fair Work Act 2009* (Cth), special provisions in the Textile, Clothing, Footwear and Associated Industries Award, state legislation and a voluntary Code of Practice for firms at the head of the supply chain. Key regulatory features included deeming provisions (which treated homeworkers as employees for the purposes of protection), requirements of record keeping as well as clarification of several and joint liability along the links in the supply chain.[48]

Union initiatives to deal with subcontracting arrangements and precarious work have also taken place in other sectors, though with more qualified results.[49] Some legislation to address bogus self-employment has been achieved, for example, in relation to 'sham contracting', though a clear statutory definition of the distinction between employee and self-employed worker is still missing.[50] Beyond this realm, however, the cupboard is rather bare, marked by a distinctive absence of worker-oriented regulation. One striking feature of the Australian context, in comparison with most European examples, is the failure of unions to shape in any substantial way the central categories of non-standard waged work: namely, part-time work, fixed-term work, temporary agency work and casual work. Though far larger than bogus self-employment as a proportion of the workforce, and more significant as sites for the expansion of precarious work, these forms of waged work have evolved freely in recent years independent of regulatory initiatives from trade unions.[51]

The record regarding regulation of *part-time work* has been particularly disappointing. Most part-time waged work in Australia is categorised as casual and suffers the multiple disadvantages of that status (see below). But even the segment that is categorised as permanent or 'regular' part-time work, and which has traditionally been the channel for *good quality* part-time work, subject since the 1990s to standard award provisions that elevate a principle of equal treatment, has experienced a significant process of degradation (or 'casualisation') in recent years. In some sectors, this occurs as a direct result of employer practices such as intensification and 'flexing up' of working hours. In sectors such as aged care, disability support and hospitality, such cost-minimisation practices have been supported by regulatory changes that preserve pro rata entitlements but weaken crucial working-time protections concerning roster regularity and employer obligations to obtain worker agreement before changes.[52] Not only have unions failed to disseminate good quality part-time work, but even the limited advances of an earlier period are now under retreat. This constitutes a major setback for the many employees, often women with care responsibilities, who desire reduced weekly hours of work but with regular and predictable schedules.[53] Their chances of obtaining good quality part-time work are increasingly dependent on the selective favours of enterprise management.

The most glaring union failure concerns casual work, the central category of precarious work in Australia, which was set aside when the Commonwealth Arbitration Court began to consolidate decent wages and conditions for 'weekly hire' employees in the 1920s.[54] Casual work, whether full-time or part-time, spread rapidly in the 1980s and 1990s, and it currently accounts for around one in five workers (or one in four employees).[55] The category is found throughout the workforce structure, primarily in low-wage sectors, though in a multiplicity of forms. One familiar division is between 'regular casual' (or 'permanent casual') workers, who are on regular working-time schedules and who tend to be used for extended periods and in a similar way to permanent employees, and what can be called 'on-demand' casuals, who have an irregular schedule and may be called in, often at short notice, as and when they are needed. Casual workers are deprived of most of the standard protections and benefits enjoyed by permanent employees, and they are paid by the hour (notionally with a 'casual loading') for each hour of labour performed. Because casual work is highly commodified work, characterised by a sharp imbalance of power between employee and employer, it is often a platform for systematic employer non-compliance, as indicated by recent evidence of underpayment ('wage theft') in low-wage sectors such as food services and seasonal work in horticulture.[56] Apart from a significant wage penalty, most casual employees suffer numerous other disadvantages, including hours variability, ease of dismissal and lack of career progression. Casual work constitutes the largest and most significant hole in the Australian system of protective standards.[57]

The persistence of casual work in Australia, apart from that small proportion that might be required to meet objective needs for short-term and irregular tasks, is hard to justify. Certainly the existence of 'regular casual' work is a startling anomaly in a modern society. Yet, in spite of the prominence of casual work and a widespread awareness of its negative consequences, unions have been unable to mount an effective response. This failure can be observed at each of the three crucial regulatory levels in Australia: (1) enterprise agreements; (3) awards; and (3) statute.[58] Several unions, most notably the National Tertiary Education Union (NTEU), have tried to insert clauses regarding casual work in *enterprise agreements*, but the results have been modest and have failed to slow casualisation in the sector.[59] At the level of modern *awards*, unions, in the present, as in the past, have pursued claims before the industrial tribunal for amendments to the standard award clause that permits casual employment (with a casual loading).[60] But outcomes over the past 20 years have been slight. Some minor improvements for long-term regular casuals have been secured, for example, in relation to unpaid parental leave and severance pay.[61] In addition, a tribunal case in 2000 achieved an amendment in several awards that entitled some regular casual workers, after a qualifying period, to *ask* their employer if they could convert their contract of employment to standard full-time or part-time employment. A subsequent case that began in 2014 led to a generalisation of a similar right to request conversion into the 85 modern awards that lacked provision for such a right. The introduction of this right is of strictly limited significance as a regulatory tool, confined to certain 'regular casuals' and preserving strong rights for management to refuse employee requests on business grounds. Most importantly, it shifts the challenge of casual work away from the realm of protective regulation towards a separate realm of purported individual choice. In a context of stark power imbalance between the employer and the casual employee, and without any procedural supports, an individual right to request conversion is feeble, and it is not surprising that it has been rarely used, even within unionised settings.[62]

Finally, it is difficult to identify *any* significant union initiatives at the level of *statute*. This absence is surprising, given the increasing importance of statute in the Australian system and the role of legislation, including the National Employment Standards (NES), in reinforcing exclusions of casual employees from most basic employment standards.[63] It is particularly surprising in the current period, given the outcome of litigation led by the CFMEU Mining and Energy Division on behalf of a casual employee, employed on a regular, predictable and continuous roster with a labour-hire firm at a coal-mining site.[64] The litigation found that the employee had been misclassified; he was not a casual in the common-law understanding of the term, and as a result he was entitled to paid annual leave as prescribed by the NES. Together with other, similar cases from mining,[65] this case has been winding its way through the courts since late 2016 and a High Court challenge remains on the agenda.[66] Federal legislation to establish a definition of 'casual' is clearly required. The federal government responded in late 2020 with the Fair Work Amendment (Supporting Australia's Jobs and Economic Recovery) Bill 2020, which picked up employer association proposals to preserve and extend employer discretion in designating their regular employees as casual. Many unions prepared submissions opposing the proposals. But the opportunity to take a more positive political stance, by advocating for an alternative legislative definition that would consolidate the common-law understanding of 'casual' and would align with the long-standing union goal of restricting 'regular casual' work, was spurned.[67]

Barriers to Effective Action

Several barriers hamper union responses to precarious work. Structural barriers exercise a powerful influence. Australian unions, like unions in many other industrialised societies, have been clearly on the defensive since the early 1990s, forced to wrestle with labour market changes, more hostile employer strategies and the consequences of neoliberal policies. Frequent alterations to the institutional framework for industrial relations, involving a slow and stuttering transformation of the previous award system to a new hybrid system, made up of legislated protective standards, modernised awards and a new sphere of 'enterprise bargaining' (with or without unions), have had a major negative impact.[68] In the course of this transformation, union activities have been directed away from 'inclusive' awards to 'exclusive' enterprise agreements, and unions themselves have been officially redefined from representatives of workers in a particular occupation or sector to agents just of their members.[69] At the same time, tight restraints have been imposed on union action, including in relation to industrial action, multi-employer bargaining, access to arbitration, secondary action ('secondary boycotts'), union entry, union preference, enforcement of protective standards, and the permitted content of awards and agreements.[70] Partly as a result of such unfavourable contextual changes, union density and collective bargaining coverage have declined sharply.[71] Moreover, as union strength and influence have dwindled, divisions among unions have intensified, and at least some unions have turned inwards, confining their ambition to institutional survival.

There is no space to analyse these structural barriers, though they undoubtedly play a major role in inhibiting union action on precarious work. But it may be useful to offer a few comments on barriers at the level of union agency, since these also have an important effect and yet may be more easily overcome by discussion and analysis. The example of casual work points to two major blockages at this level. The first is linked to hesitancy in determining objectives and strategies for regulation. A simplistic opposition of 'servicing' and 'organising', inherited from debates of the 1990s, remains influential and obscures the importance of identifying and pursuing regulatory goals.[72] As a result, unions appear uncertain about the scale and content and indeed legitimacy of their regulatory ambitions. In relation to casual work, for example, it is unclear whether unions are seeking elimination or just reduction of 'regular casual' work, and it is unclear what they aspire to do with 'on-demand casual' work, which comes with its own problems for workers and labour markets.[73] Nor is it clear how they are representing the material interests of casual workers. In this fog of uncertainty, unions have been corralled into the dead-end of an individual right to request conversion, which has little to do with effective regulation and indeed cannot even be described as appropriate representation. This general uncertainty about goals is not confined to casual work, and it can be seen as a long-standing problem in Australian unions, linked to a shortfall, in contrast to European movements, of both research capacity and confidence in mediating policy disagreements within the union movement.[74]

The second blockage is related to the first, but it is less to do with policy formulation and more to with policy implementation. It concerns the narrow choice of levers to deal with precarious work (see Table 6.1 above). As indicated by the case of casual work, union initiatives around precarious work tend to rely on just two levers: (1) efforts via enterprise bargaining to insert clauses in binding collective agreements with single employers; and (2) claims to industrial tribunals to modify awards.

This is not to say that other levers are entirely absent. Some unions, as in apparel manufacture and cleaning services, have experimented with various forms of 'soft regulation', primarily negotiated with individual employers. More broadly, some unions have sought to bypass the legal restrictions on the content of enterprise agreements by using arrangements such as memoranda of understanding and deeds of settlement to conclude bargaining with individual employers. Public campaigning by unions has been developed, most dramatically in the 'Your Rights at Work' campaign, coordinated by the ACTU before the 2007 federal election, which targeted the Coalition government's Work Choices legislation and sought to mobilise electoral support for the opposition Labor Party.[75] Public campaigns have also been used at sectoral level, as in the example above of regulating outwork. In one promising development, campaigning techniques and political lobbying, together with coalitions with client and customer groups, have been used to pressure public sector employers, either as direct employers or as lead employers in privatised or outsourced services, such as child care, aged care and community services.[76] Other levers, however, are much harder to find. For example, in spite of the evidence of a 'vast enforcement gap', which particularly disadvantages precarious workers, unions appear divided on the value of monitoring and enforcement and on the merits of collaboration with the official enforcement body, the Fair Work Ombudsman (FWO).[77] Nor is there much evidence of working with community groups, NGOs and social movements on issues of precarious work.[78]

The most startling omission, noted in relation to casual work, concerns *legal regulation for protective standards*. This is the very lever, often crudely summed up as 'political action', which is prioritised by union movements in Europe as the most appropriate approach for responding to the challenge of precarious work. It is true that unions in Australia habitually engage in politics, but this remains politics of a particular, narrow type, which starts and often finishes with lobbying, primarily through the dusty corridors of the Australian Labor Party. Moreover, such political action is generally focused either on specific policy areas outside of employment relations or on the participative standards that support collective bargaining.[79] It rarely has anything to do with political action in the European sense of campaigning for improvements in statutory protective standards.

The absence of attention to legal regulation for protective standards constitutes a major blind spot in current union perspectives. One explanation for the blind spot, linked to enterprise bargaining and union enthusiasm for organising, may be a fear that legislated minimum standards obscure the need for unionism and undermine the incentive for workers to join.[80] But perhaps the more plausible explanation is simply to do with the power of institutional legacy. Throughout much of the twentieth century, employment regulation in Australia was characterised by a relative lack of legislated standards, based on 'abdication' of responsibility from governments and political parties to industrial tribunals.[81] Most protective standards were developed through awards, set out by independent industrial tribunals, often by means of test cases, and then clarified through litigation.[82] As awards have declined as a site for the development of protective standards and as statute has assumed more importance, unions seem to have missed the institutional shift and overlooked the need to adapt their strategies. They remain committed to two levers of union action, which have been inherited from the prior labourist tradition – workplace bargaining and claims before industrial tribunals. These functioned well in the past, but they are failing in the present, in relation to both standard workers and precarious workers. It could be argued that, in relying so heavily on these two traditional levers to confront the problem of precarious work, Australian trade unions are stuck in a rut, or, in more academic language, 'stuck in a path dependency'.[83]

Conclusion

The challenge of precarious work to Australian unions is pressing, but the response so far has been weak. Though part of the blame can be sheeted home to the survival of exclusionary attitudes, many unions have adopted an inclusive approach, and indeed some have invested substantial resources in engaging with precarious workers, for example, the NTEU efforts to mobilise casual teaching staff in higher education[84] and the campaign by the United Workers Union to recruit among seasonal workers in horticulture, discussed in further detail in Chapter 8 by Joanna Howe in this volume.[85] The main explanation for the disappointing record would seem to lie with external and internal blockages.

This chapter focuses on internal blockages at the level of union agency. It suggests that union action to confront the challenge of precarious work could benefit from greater attention to an objective of regulation, as a supplement to servicing and organising. In addition, as Barbara Pocock notes, there is a need for a 'a rebalancing of the traditional repertoire of union tools'.[86] Neither of the two levers currently favoured by unions have been effective in regulating precarious work; indeed, they seem to be increasingly ineffective. The enterprise bargaining system is currently in crisis, declining in coverage, riddled with restrictions, easily avoided by most employers, large and small, or else misused by a minority of large employers to bypass union pressure, either through friendly agreements with compliant unions or through non-union agreements.[87] Even as a vehicle for serving the day to day needs of current union members, it appears inadequate, and it is even more poorly suited to dealing with the challenge of precarious work.[88] Similarly, the federal industrial tribunal has been hampered by a loss of powers, including the crucial test case function, and by a surge of unbalanced appointments, biased to employer interests.

Collective bargaining and industrial tribunals are important features of the Australian system and should be strengthened. Nevertheless, even if strengthened, international experience and labour market analysis indicate that they would remain poorly suited to the challenges posed by precarious work. The most promising lever for tackling the threat of most forms of precarious work is legal regulation, especially when backed by clear objectives, robust research, open discussion and vigorous public campaigning. This is not a new lever, nor is it free from all weaknesses. But it is a lever that has been unjustifiably overlooked in Australia. There are numerous starting points for putting the lever into action, including the pressing need in the current context for paid pandemic leave. Other starting points could include: (1) a new approach to the annual minimum wage review;[89] (2) efforts to plug the gaping holes in the NES; (3) promotion of clear legislative definitions to help to resolve the problems of bogus self-employment and regular casual work; and (4) advocacy for new protective standards, starting with a requirement for employers to provide employees with a written statement of the terms and conditions of their employment.[90]

Notes

1 Gerry Rodgers, 'Precarious Work in Western Europe: The State of the Debate', in *Precarious Jobs in Labour Regulation: The Growth of Atypical Employment in Western Europe*, ed. Gerry Rodgers and Janine Rodgers (Geneva: International Institute for Labour Studies, 1989), 1–16.

2 International Labour Organization, *Non-Standard Employment Around the World: Understanding Challenges, Shaping Prospects* (Geneva: International Labour Office, 2016). For Australia, see Iain Campbell and John Burgess, 'Patchy Progress? Two Decades of Research on Precariousness and Precarious Work in Australia', *Labour and Industry* 28, no. 1 (2018): 48–67.

3 Valerio De Stefano, 'Labour Is not a Technology – Reasserting the Declaration of Philadelphia in Times of Platform-Work and Gig-Economy', *IUSLabor* 2 (2017): 1–16; Jill Rubery, Damian Grimshaw, Arjan Keizer and Mathew Johnson, 'Challenges and Contradictions in the "Normalising" of Precarious Work', *Work, Employment and Society* 32, no. 3 (2018): 509–27.

4 Peter Gahan, 'Trade Unions as Regulators: Theoretical and Empirical Perspectives', in *Labour Law and Labour Market Regulation: Essays on the Construction and Regulation of Labour Markets and Work Relationships*, ed. Chris Arup, Peter Gahan, John Howe, Richard Johnstone, Richard Mitchell and Anthony O'Donnell (Sydney: Federation Press, 2006), 261–81. In Australia, awards, set down by industrial tribunals, are also important regulatory instruments: Mark Bray and Andrew Stewart, 'What Is Distinctive about the Fair Work Regime?', *Australian Journal of Labour Law* 26, no. 1 (2013): 20–49.

5 Jamie Peck and Nik Theodore, 'Labour Markets from the Bottom Up', in *Handbook of Employment and Society: Working Space*, ed Susan McGrath-Champ, Andrew Herod and Al Rainnie (Cheltenham: Edward Elgar, 2012), 87–105.

6 Keith Ewing, 'The Function of Trade Unions', *Industrial Law Journal* 34, no. 1 (2005): 1–22 (13).

7 Campbell and Burgess, 'Patchy Progress'; Tanya Carney and Jim Stanford, *The Dimensions of Insecure Work: A Factbook* (Canberra: The Australia Institute, 2018); Inga Laβ and Mark Wooden, 'Trends in the Prevalence of Non-Standard Employment in Australia', *Journal of Industrial Relations* 62, no. 1 (2020): 3–32; Paula McDonald, Penny Williams, Andrew Stewart, Robyn Mayes and Damian Oliver, *Digital Platform Work in Australia: Prevalence, Nature and Impact* (Brisbane: Queensland University of Technology, 2019).

8 Wayne Lewchuk 'Precarious Jobs: Where Are They, and How Do They Affect Well-being?', *Economic and Labour Relations Review* 28, no. 3 (2017): 402–19.

9 Employer viewpoints are summarised in Raymond Markey and Joseph McIvor, 'Regulating Casual Employment in Australia', *Journal of Industrial Relations* 60, no. 5 (2018): 593–618. For recent scholarly opinion, see also Campbell and Burgess, 'Patchy Progress'; Iain Campbell, Fiona Macdonald and Sara Charlesworth, 'On-Demand Work in Australia', in *Zero Hours and On-call Work in Anglo-Saxon Countries*, ed. Michelle O'Sullivan, Jonathan Lavelle, Juliette McMahon, Lorraine Ryan, Caroline Murphy, Thomas Turner and Patrick Gunnigle (Berlin: Springer, 2019), 67–90.

10 Recent research warns against 'methodological nationalism' and advocates more attention to other levels of analysis, such as industry sector and the transnational sphere. See, for example, Virginia Doellgast, Nathan Lillie and Valeria Pulignano, 'From Dualization to Solidarity: Halting the Cycle of Precarity', in *Reconstructing Solidarity: Labour Unions, Precarious Work, and the Politics of Institutional Change in Europe*, ed. Virginia Doellgast, Nathan Lillie and Valeria Pulignano (Oxford: Oxford University Press, 2018), 1–41; Maarten Keune and Marcello Pedaci, 'Trade Union Strategies against Precarious Work: Common Trends and Sectoral Divergence in the EU', *European Journal of Industrial Relations* 26, no. 2 (2020): 139–55. A sectoral approach is undoubtedly useful, especially if we want to grasp employer strategies. Nevertheless, I focus here on the national level, because of the historical importance of the national institutional framework, which shapes the opportunities for and the precise forms of precarious employment, and because of the continued relevance of state action in improving job quality: Gerhard Bosch and Claudia Weinkopf, 'Reducing Wage Inequality: The Role of the State in Improving Job Quality', *Work and Occupations* 44,

no. 1 (2017): 68–88; Chris Howell, 'Rethinking the Role of the State in Employment Relations for a Neoliberal Era', *ILR Review* 74, no. 3 (2021): 739-72.

11 I refer to effective strategies in the loose sense of strategies that succeed in meeting union objectives to improve workers' working and living conditions. For a more intensive discussion of the concept of union effectiveness, see Gregor Gall and Jack Fiorito, 'Union Effectiveness: In Search of the Holy Grail', *Economic and Industrial Democracy* 37, no. 1 (2016): 189–211.

12 Maarten Keune, 'Trade Unions, Precarious Work and Dualisation in Europe', in *Non-Standard Employment in Post-Industrial Labour Markets: An Occupational Perspective*, ed. Werner Eichhorst and Paul Marx (Cheltenham: Edward Elgar, 2015), 378–400. See also Doellgast et al., 'From Dualization to Solidarity'; Lisa Dorigatti, 'Trade Unions in Segmented Labor Markets: Evidence from the German Metal and Chemical Sectors', *ILR Review* 70, no. 4 (2017): 919–41; Maarten Keune and Marcello Pedaci, 'Trade Union Strategies against Precarious Work', 3.

13 Doellgast et al., 'From Dualization to Solidarity'.

14 Keune 'Trade Unions, Precarious Work and Dualisation in Europe'; Richard Hyman, *Understanding European Trade Unionism: Between Market, Class and Society* (London: Sage, 2001).

15 Jelle Visser, 'Can Unions Revitalize Themselves?', *International Journal of Labour Research* 9, nos 1–2 (2019): 18–48. For Australia, see Bradley Bowden, 'The Rise and Decline of Australian Unionism: A History of Industrial Labour from the 1820s to 2010', *Labour History* 100 (2011): 51–82; David Peetz, *The Realities and Futures of Work* (Canberra: ANU Press, 2019); David Peetz and Janis Bailey, 'Dancing Alone: The Australian Union Movement over Three Decades', *Journal of Industrial Relations* 54, no. 4 (2012): 525–41.

16 Assar Lindbeck and Dennis Snower, 'The Insider-Outsider Theory: A Survey', (Discussion Paper No. 534, IZA, Bonn, 2002); Guy Standing, *The Precariat: The New Dangerous Class* (London: Bloomsbury Academic, 2011).

17 Useful critiques are in Richard Hyman and Rebecca Gumbrell-McCormick, 'Resisting Labour Market Insecurity: Old and New Actors, Rivals or Allies?', *Journal of Industrial Relations* 59, no. 4 (2017): 538–61; Jill Rubery, 'Reregulating for Inclusive Labour Markets', in *Regulating for Equitable and Job-Rich Growth*, ed. Colin Fenwick and Valerie Van Goethem (Cheltenham: Elgar, 2017), 31–62; Rubery et al. 'Challenges and Contradictions'; Erik Olin Wright, 'Is the Precariat a Class?', *Global Labour Journal* 7, no. 2 (2016): 123–35.

18 Doellgast et al., 'From Dualization to Solidarity'; Damian Grimshaw, Mat Johnson, Jill Rubery and Arjan Keizer, *Reducing Precarious Work: Protective Gaps and the Role of Social Dialogue in Europe* (Brussels: European Commission, 2016); Edmund Heery, 'Trade Unions and Contingent Labour: Scale and Method', *Cambridge Journal of Regions, Economy and Society* 2 (2009): 429–42; Hyman and Gumbrell-McCormick, 'Resisting Labour Market Insecurity'; Keune and Pedaci, 'Trade Union Strategies against Precarious Work'.

19 Bosch and Weinkopf, 'Reducing Wage Inequality'; Doellgast et al., 'From Dualization to Solidarity'; Rubery, 'Reregulating for Inclusive Labour Markets'.

20 For example, Heery, 'Trade Unions and Contingent Labour'.

21 For example, Keune, 'Trade Unions, Precarious Work and Dualisation in Europe'.

22 Several studies are grouped together in *Reconstructing Solidarity: Labour Unions, Precarious Work, and the Politics of Institutional Change in Europe*, ed. Virginia Doellgast, Nathan Lillie

and Valeria Pulignano (Oxford: Oxford University Press, 2018); see also Keune and Pedaci, 'Trade Union Strategies against Precarious Work'.

23 Chiara Benassi and Tim Vlandas, 'Union Inclusiveness and Temporary Agency Workers: The Role of Power Resources and Union Ideology', *European Journal of Industrial Relations* 22, no. 1 (2016): 5–22; Caroline Murphy, Thomas Turner, Michelle O'Sullivan, Juliette MacMahon, Jonathan Lavelle, Lorraine Ryan, Patrick Gunnigle and Mike O'Brien, 'Trade Union Responses to Zero Hours Work in Ireland', *Industrial Relations Journal* 50, nos 5–6 (2019): 468–85.

24 Gabriella Alberti, Jane Holgate and Maite Tapia, 'Organising Migrants as Workers or as Migrant Workers? Intersectionality, Trade Unions and Precarious Work', *International Journal of Human Resource Management* 24, no. 22 (2013): 4132–48; Miguel Martinez Lucio, Stefania Marino and Heather Connolly, 'Organising as a Strategy to Reach Precarious and Marginalized Workers. A Review of Debates on the Role of the Political Dimension and the Dilemmas of Representation and Solidarity', *Transfer* 23, no. 1 (2017): 31–46.

25 Keune, 'Trade Unions, Precarious Work and Dualisation in Europe', 381–82; see also Heery, 'Trade Unions and Contingent Labour'.

26 Colette Fagan, Helen Norman, Mark Smith and Maria Gonzalez-Menendez, *In Search of Good Quality Part-Time Employment*, Conditions of Work and Employment Series no. 43 (Geneva: ILO, 2014); Edmund Heery and Hazel Conley, 'Frame Extension in a Mature Social Movement: British Trade Unions and Part-time Work, 1967–2002', *Journal of Industrial Relations* 49, no. 1 (2007): 5–29.

27 Gregor Murray, 'Union Renewal: What Can We Learn from Three Decades of Research?', *Transfer* 23, no. 1 (2017): 9–29. The Webbs list mutual insurance, collective bargaining and legal enactment as the three main union methods – Sidney Webb and Beatrice Webb, *Industrial Democracy* (London: Longman, Green and Co., 1920), 150.

28 Heery, 'Trade Unions and Contingent Labour', 433–38.

29 David Weil, *The Fissured Workplace: Why Work Became So Bad for So Many and What Can Be Done to Improve It* (Cambridge, MA: Harvard University Press, 2014); for Australia, see Richard Johnstone and Andrew Stewart, 'Swimming against the Tide? Australian Labour Regulation and the Fissured Workplace', *Comparative Labor Law and Policy Journal* 37, no. 1 (2015): 55–90.

30 Jane Wills, 'Subcontracted Employment and Its Challenge to Labor', *Labor Studies Journal* 34, no. 4 (2009): 441–60.

31 Heery, 'Trade Unions and Contingent Labour', 439. Collective bargaining may still be appropriate for some precarious workers: see Grimshaw et al., *Reducing Precarious Work*; Susan Hayter and Minawa Ebisui, 'Negotiating Parity for Precarious Workers', *International Journal of Labour Research* 5, no. 1 (2013): 79–96.

32 Gerhard Bosch, 'Shrinking Collective Bargaining Coverage, Increasing Income Inequality: A Comparison of Five EU Countries', *International Labour Review* 154, no. 1 (2015): 57–66.

33 Kerstin Hamann and John Kelly, 'Unions as Political Actors: A Recipe for Revitalization?', in *Varieties of Unionism: Strategies for Union Revitalization in a Globalizing Economy*, ed. Carola Frege and John Kelly (Oxford: Oxford University Press, 2004), 93–116.

34 Julia O'Connor, 'Precarious Employment and EU Employment Regulation', in *Social Policy Review 25: Analysis and debate in social policy*, ed. Gaby Ramia, Kevin Farnsworth and Zoe Irving (Bristol: Bristol University Press, 2013), 227–48.

35 Directive EU (2019/1152).

36 Agnieszka Piasna, 'The Space for Regulation Beyond Borders? The Role of the EU in Regulating Zero Hours Work', in O'Sullivan et al., *Zero Hours and On-call Work in Anglo-Saxon Countries*, 179–94.

37 Hyman, *Understanding European Trade Unionism.*

38 Each type can be mobilised at workplace, industry and societal levels: Stefan Schmalz, Carmen Ludwig and Edward Webster, 'The Power Resources Approach: Developments and Challenges', *Global Labour Journal* 9, no. 2 (2018): 113–34; see also Christian Lévesque and Gregor Murray, 'Understanding Union Power: Resources and Capabilities for Renewing Union Capacity', *Transfer* 16, no. 3 (2010): 333–50.

39 Glenn Morgan and Valeria Pulignano, 'Solidarity at Work: Concepts, Levels and Challenges', *Work, Employment and Society* 34, no. 1 (2020): 18–34; Melanie Simms, 'Unions and Job Quality in the UK: Extending Interest Representation Within Regulation Institutions', *Work and Occupations* 44, no. 1 (2017): 47–67.

40 Bruno Palier and Kathleen Thelen, 'Institutionalizing Dualism: Complementarities and Change in France and Germany', *Politics and Society* 38, no. 1 (2010): 119–48.

41 Gerhard Bosch, 'The Making of the German Minimum Wage: A Case Study of Institutional Change', *Industrial Relations Journal* 49, no. 1 (2018): 19–33; see also Heiner Dribbusch, Steffen Lehndorff and Thorsten Schulten, 'Two Worlds of Unionism? German Manufacturing and Service Unions Since the Great Recession', in *Rough Waters – European Trade Unions in a Time of Crises*, 2nd ed., ed. Steffen Lehndorff, Heiner Dribbusch and Thorsten Schulten (Brussels: ETUI, 2018), 209–33. The statutory minimum wage was introduced first at sectoral level before coming into full operation in 2015.

42 Dribbusch et al., 'Two Worlds of Unionism?' 224–26; see also Chiara Benassi and Lisa Dorigatti, 'Straight to the Core – Explaining Union Responses to the Casualization of Work: The IG Metall Campaign for Agency Workers', *British Journal of Industrial Relations* 53, no. 3 (2015): 533–55; Chiara Benassi, Lisa Dorigatti and Elisa Pannini, 'Explaining Divergent Bargaining Outcomes for Agency Workers: The Role of Labour Divides and Labour Market Reforms', *European Journal of Industrial Relations* 25, no. 2 (2019): 163–79; Dorigatti, 'Trade Unions in Segmented Labor Markets'.

43 Benassi et al., 'Explaining Divergent Bargaining Outcomes for Agency Workers', 175.

44 Stefan Schmalz and Marcel Thiel, 'IG Metall's Comeback: Trade Union Renewal in Times of Crisis', *Journal of Industrial Relations* 59, no. 4 (2017): 465–86.

45 Karen Jaehrling, Ines Wagner and Claudia Weinkopf, *Reducing Precarious Work in Europe through Social Dialogue: The Case of Germany* (Duisburg: University of Duisburg-Essen, 2016), 62–72; Ines Wagner, *Workers without Borders: Posted Work and Precarity in the EU* (Cornell: Cornell University Press, 2018); see also Ursula Mense-Petermann, 'Interest Representation in Transnational Labour Markets: Campaigning as an Alternative to Traditional Union Action?', *Journal of Industrial Relations* 62, no. 2 (2020): 185–209.

46 Brian Howe, Paul Munro, Jill Biddington and Sara Charlesworth, *Lives on Hold: Unlocking the Potential of Australia's Workforce. The Report of the Independent Inquiry into Insecure Work* (Melbourne: Studio Alto, 2012). See also ACTU, 'The Future of Work in Australia: Dealing with Insecurity and Risk' (ACTU Options Paper on Measures to Promote Job and Income Security, ACTU, Melbourne, 2011); ACTU, *Australia's Insecure Work Crisis: Fixing It for the Future* (Melbourne: ACTU, 2018).

47 Sarah Kaine and Cathy Brigden, 'Union Responses to Regulatory Change: Strategies of Protective Layering', *Economic and Labour Relations Review* 26, no. 4 (2015): 614–30.

48 Rosaria Burchielli, Annie Delaney and Kylie Coventry, 'Campaign Strategies to Develop Regulatory Mechanisms: Protecting Australian Garment Homeworkers', *Journal of Industrial Relations* 56, no. 1 (2014): 81–102. See also Johnstone and Stewart, 'Swimming against the Tide?', 83–84; Shelley Marshall, *Living Wage: Regulatory Solutions to Informal and Precarious Work in Global Supply Chains* (Oxford: Oxford University Press, 2018); Igor Nossar, Richard Johnstone, Anna Macklin and Michael Rawling, 'Protective Legal Regulation for Home-Based Workers in Australian Textile, Clothing and Footwear Supply Chains', *Journal of Industrial Relations* 57, no. 4 (2015): 585–603.

49 One example concerns the Transport Workers' Union (TWU) in New South Wales, which, through 'comprehensive campaigning', achieved new regulation at state level to establish 'safe rates' that would lift income and improve working conditions for self-employed owner-drivers: Kaine and Brigden, 'Union responses to regulatory change'; Sarah Kaine and Michael Rawling, 'Comprehensive Campaigning in the NSW Transport Industry', *Journal of Industrial Relations* 52, no. 2 (2010): 183–200. The TWU has also been active in responding to 'platform work': see Anthony Forsyth, 'Playing Catch-Up but Falling Short: Regulating Work in the Gig Economy in Australia', *King's Law Journal* 31, no. 2 (2020): 287-300.

50 Forsyth, 'Playing Catch-Up'; see also Anthony Forsyth, 'Is There an App for That? Worker Representation, Unions and the Gig Economy', in this volume.

51 Re-regulating the boundary between waged work and self-employment is undoubtedly important, highlighted in recent debates on 'platform work'. But from the point of view of unions and precarious workers, it is important to keep in mind that the number of 'bogus self-employed' is relatively small. Latest figures suggest that 'independent contractors' constitute around 8.2 per cent of the workforce, with less than half likely to be 'dependent contractors': Australian Bureau of Statistics, *Characteristics of Employment*, Cat. No. 6333.0, August 2019.

52 Campbell et al., 'On-Demand Work in Australia', 74–76; Sara Charlesworth and Alexandra Heron, 'New Australian Working Time Minimum Standards: Reproducing the Same Old Gendered Architecture', *Journal of Industrial Relations* 54, no. 2 (2012): 164–81.

53 Features of good quality part-time work are listed in Jenny Chalmers, Iain Campbell and Sara Charlesworth, 'Part-Time Work and Caring Responsibilities in Australia: Towards an Assessment of Job Quality', *Labour and Industry* 15, no. 3 (2005): 41–66; see also Judy Rose and Belinda Hewitt, 'Does Part-Time Employment Status Really Reduce Time Pressure?', *Journal of Sociology* 55, no. 2 (2019): 366–88. In August 2019, 15.8 per cent of all employees were classified as permanent part-time, while 17 per cent were casual part-time – ABS, *Characteristics of Employment*, August 2019.

54 Anthony O'Donnell, *Inventing Unemployment: Regulating Joblessness in Twentieth-Century Australia* (Oxford: Hart, 2019).

55 Carney and Stanford, *The Dimensions of Insecure Work*; Laβ and Wooden, 'Trends in the Prevalence of Non-Standard Employment in Australia'. In August 2019, 24.4 per cent of all employees were classified as casual (in their main job): ABS, *Characteristics of Employment*, August 2019.

56 Edward Cavanough and Lachlan Blain, *Ending Wage Theft: Eradicating Underpayment in the Australian Workplace* (Melbourne: The McKell Institute Victoria, 2019).

57 For an introduction to the category of casual, see Campbell et al. 'On-Demand Work in Australia', 71–74; Markey and McIvor, 'Regulating Casual Employment in Australia'.

58 Bray and Stewart, 'What Is Distinctive About the Fair Work Regime?'.

59 The NTEU has achieved minor improvements, for example, extra payments for marking. Most recently, the union has inserted clauses in enterprise agreements that introduce a new category of 'scholarly teaching fellow', designed partly to improve wages and conditions for casual ('sessional') teachers and partly to build a bridge that would allow a transition to more secure tenured employment. But numbers are small, and the programme seems to work poorly as a bridge: James Goodman, Kaye Broadbent, Tony Brown, Nour Dados, Anne Junor, Glenda Strachan and Keiko Yasukawa, *Scholarly Teaching Fellows as a New Category of Employment in Australian Universities*, Final Report, Department of Education, 2019, http://scholarlyteaching.net/.

60 For past strategies regarding award regulation, such as quantitative limits (including complete exclusions) and increases in the casual loading, see Iain Campbell, 'Casual Employment, Labour Regulation and Australian Trade Unions', *Journal of Industrial Relations* 38, no. 4 (1996): 571–99.

61 Rosemary Hunter, 'The Legal Production of Precarious Work', in *Precarious Work, Women and the New Economy*, ed. Judy Fudge and Rosemary Owens (Oxford: Hart Publishing, 2006), 283–304.

62 Rosemary Owens, 'The "Long-Term or Permanent Casual" – An Oxymoron or a "Well Enough Understood Australianism" in the Law?', *Australian Bulletin of Labour* 27, no. 2 (2001): 118–36. For evidence on why casual employees might not take up a right to request conversion, see Markey and McIvor, 'Regulating Casual Employment in Australia', 609–10; Barbara Pocock and Sara Charlesworth, 'Job Quality and Work-Life: Unsocial Working Hours, Casual Work and Work-Life Outcomes in Australia', in *Job Quality in Australia*, ed. Angela Knox and Chris Warhurst (Sydney: Federation Press, 2015), 103–26.

63 Iain Campbell and Sara Charlesworth, 'The National Employment Standards: An Assessment', *Australian Journal of Labour Law* 33 no. 1 (2020): 36–51; Charlesworth and Heron, 'New Australian Working Time Minimum Standards'.

64 *Workpac Pty Ltd v Skene* (2018) 264 FCR 536.

65 *Workpac Pty Ltd v Rossato* (2020) 278 FCR 179.

66 'Workpac Seeks to Take Rossato to High Court', *Workplace Express*, 17 June 2020.

67 A clear, limited definition of casual is recommended as a regulatory initiative in Howe et al., *Lives on Hold*, 30–32; see also ACTU, *The Future of Work in Australia*, 23–24; ACTU, *Australia's Insecure Work Crisis*, 27.

68 Bray and Stewart, 'What Is Distinctive about the Fair Work Regime?'. In the previous award system, awards supported union regulatory objectives by acting as a sort of 'extension mechanism' that functioned to generalise gains achieved by strong unions in collective bargaining to weaker groups. In the new hybrid system, awards survive but they have been 'converted' into a simple 'safety net' designed to underpin processes of enterprise bargaining and individual contracting: John Buchanan and Damian Oliver, ' "Fair Work" and the Modernisation of Australian Labour Standards: A Case of Institutional Plasticity Entrenching Deepening Wage Inequality', *British Journal of Industrial Relations* 54, no. 4 (2016): 790–814.

69 Buchanan and Oliver, ' "Fair Work" and the Modernization of Australian Labour Standards'.

70 Rae Cooper and Bradon Ellem, 'Cold Climate: Australian Unions, Policy, and the State', *Comparative Labor Law and Policy Journal* 38 no. 3 (2017): 415–35.

71 Union density has fallen to 15 per cent: ABS, *Characteristics of Employment*, August 2018. Estimates for collective bargaining coverage in 2016 vary according to the data source (and the underlying concepts) from 21.9 to 36.4 per cent – David Peetz and Serena Yu, *Explaining Recent Trends in Collective Bargaining* (Melbourne: Fair Work Commission, 2017); see also Alison Pennington, *On the Brink: The Erosion of Enterprise Agreement Coverage in Australia's Private Sector* (Sydney: The Centre for Future Work, 2018), 24.

72 Gerard Griffin and Rosetta Moors, 'Organising Works: Objectives, Evolution, Outcomes' (Working Paper No. 78, National Key Centre in Industrial Relations, Monash University, Melbourne, 2002).

73 Campbell et al., 'On-Demand Work in Australia'.

74 For a perceptive account of the changing role of the ACTU, see Chris Briggs, 'The End of a Cycle? The Australian Council of Trade Unions in Historical Perspective', in *Peak Unions in Australia: Origins, Purpose, Power, Agency*, ed. Bradon Ellem, Ray Markey and John Shields (Sydney: Federation Press, 2004), 236–60. Though the ACTU, as in the past, plays a valuable role in presenting credible submissions to inquiries and industrial cases, including the annual minimum wage adjustment process, this is not the same as formulation and implementation of effective strategies. Tim Lyons, previously an ACTU official, offers a rare insider critique of union weaknesses. He notes *inter alia* the anti-intellectual history of Australian unions and calls for more 'investment in ideas': Tim Lyons, 'The Labour Movement: My Part in Its Downfall', *Meanjin* 75, no. 3 (2016): 87–95.

75 Peetz and Bailey, 'Dancing Alone'.

76 For an example in community services, see Janis Bailey, Michelle Robertson and Lyndall Hulme, 'Challenging the "Care Penalty": The Queensland Pay Equity Campaign for Community Service Workers', *Journal of Industrial Relations* 56, no. 1 (2014): 43–61.

77 Ingrid Landau, Sean Cooney, Tess Hardy and John Howe, *Trade Unions and the Enforcement of Minimum Employment Standards in Australia* (Melbourne: Centre for Employment and Labour Relations Law, University of Melbourne, 2014); see also Tess Hardy and John Howe, 'Out of the Shadows and into the Spotlight: The Sweeping Evolution of Employment Standards Enforcement in Australia', in *Closing the Enforcement Gap: Improving Employment Standards Protections for People in Precarious Jobs*, ed. Leah Vosko and the Closing the Enforcement Gap Research Group (Toronto, University of Toronto Press, 2020), 221–41; Peetz, *The Realities and Futures of Work*, 292–98.

78 This largely reflects the fact that there has been little independent mobilisation by precarious workers and little involvement of community groups in employment matters: Rae Cooper and Bradon Ellem, 'Australian Unions: Crisis, Strategy, Survival', in *Trade Unions and Labour Movements in the Asia-Pacific Region*, ed. Byoung-Hoon Lee, Ng Sek-Hong and Russell Lansbury (London: Routledge, 2020), 35–54 (49).

79 A recent example of the focus on participative standards is the 'Change the Rules' campaign, initiated by the ACTU prior to the 2019 federal elections, which sought to pave the way for an incoming Labor government to loosen the harsh restrictions on collective bargaining: see Ken McAlpine and Sarah Roberts, 'The Future of Trade Unions in Australia' (unpublished paper, 2017); James Stanford, *Union Organising and Labour Market Rules: Two Sides of the Same Coin*, Briefing Note (Sydney: The Centre for Future Work, 2019). Unfortunately, the campaign came to nothing, because of the return of the Coalition government.

80 Cooper and Ellem, 'Australian Unions', 49; McAlpine and Roberts, 'The Future of Trade Unions'.

81 Ron McCallum, 'Legislated Standards: The Australian Approach', in *Work and Employment Relations: An Era of Change*, ed. Marian Baird, Keith Hancock and Joe Isaac (Sydney: Federation Press, 2011), 6–16; see also Campbell and Charlesworth, 'The National Employment Standards'.

82 Jill Murray, 'The AIRC's Test Case on Work and Family Provisions: The End of Dynamic Regulatory Change at the Federal Level?', *Australian Journal of Labour Law* 18, no. 3 (2005): 325–43.

83 Lévesque and Murray, 'Understanding Union Power', 345.

84 NTEU efforts to organise casual employees have used low membership fees, a dedicated website, surveys, special conferences and magazines, and encouragement of casual committees.

85 See further, Elsa Underhill, Dimitria Groutsis, Diane van den Broek and Malcolm Rimmer, 'Organising Across Borders: Mobilising Temporary Migrant Labour in Australian Food Production', *Journal of Industrial Relations* 62, no. 2 (2020): 278–303.

86 Barbara Pocock, 'Rethinking Unionism in a Changing World of Work, Family and Community Life', *Relations Industrielles/Industrial Relations* 66, no. 4 (2011): 562–84 (577). As well as statutory standards, Pocock advocates more union attention to procedural rights and social security and public services.

87 Pennington, *On the Brink*; Stanford, *Union Organising and Labour Market Rules*.

88 Proponents of collective bargaining as a method for 'negotiating parity' for precarious workers stress that collective bargaining should be encompassing: Hayter and Ebisui, 'Negotiating Parity for Precarious Workers', 91. The Australian system, oriented to single-employer bargaining under restrictive conditions, clearly does not qualify.

89 Union involvement in the minimum wage review is valuable, but it needs to be revamped to better meet the needs of precarious workers, who enjoy only a limited benefit from any annual increase in minimum hourly wage rates because of the prevalence of: (1) underemployment; (2) underpayment; and (3) bogus self-employment.

90 Campbell and Charlesworth, 'The National Employment Standards'.

Chapter 7

'IS THERE AN APP FOR THAT?' WORKER REPRESENTATION, UNIONS AND THE GIG ECONOMY

Anthony Forsyth

Of the many challenges for trade unions around the world noted in Chapter 1 of this collection by Joo-Cheong Tham and Caroline Kelly, one of the greatest is presented by the gig economy.[1] This form of delivering services and organising work through technology raises important questions about the nature of freedom of association – a foundational concept of the International Labour Organization – in the modern era. In Australia, the gig economy has shamelessly inverted traditional assumptions about employment regulation: that someone who performs labour is deserving of the law's protection, unless carrying on a genuine independent business of their own.[2] Instead, workers for platforms such as Uber, Lyft, Foodora, Deliveroo, Uber Eats, Freelancer and Airtasker are designated as independent contractors, unless they prove otherwise through legal challenges.[3]

This contracting model is usually buttressed by arcane contracts and service agreements which use Orwellian language to obscure the reality of gig work and who is performing it.[4] 'Flexibility' is held up by the platforms as a kind of holy grail,[5] to explain gig workers being prepared to sacrifice minimum wages, unfair dismissal rights and other protections that flow from employee status. For example, Deliveroo maintains 'that the basis of its engagement with self-employed riders is inconsistent with employment, whether full-time, part-time or casual. None of these employment relationships provide the flexibility inherent to the way in which self-employed riders work with Deliveroo.'[6] The contracting model has been adopted not only to absolve platforms from responsibility for minimum labour standards,[7] but also to keep unions at bay. Most gig operators flatly refuse to engage with unions. Instead they offer insipid forms of worker voice, which they control.

This chapter examines the ways in which platforms counter unionisation, despite the clear desire for collective representation manifested by many gig workers around the world. The next section provides an overview of these issues along with the difficulties faced by trade unions in seeking to organise workers in the platform economy. This is followed by an exploration of a couple of significant recent aspects of gig work regulation. The third section of the chapter considers the debate over Californian legislation which challenges the platform economy's contracting model, and which both galvanised and saw fractures emerge within the US labour movement; while the fourth section assesses the effects of the COVID-19 pandemic in highlighting the extreme vulnerability of gig workers and the necessity of collective representation to preserve their basic rights at work. The implications of these developments for Australian unions are analysed in the final section, emphasising the preconditions to ensuring genuine expression of collective worker power in the world of platform work. While the gig economy globally encompasses many different types of work and service delivery,[8] this chapter focuses mostly on platforms which function like brokers of services via an app[9] (best exemplified by rideshare and food delivery platforms).

The Hard Road: Organising Platform Workers

The rapid expansion of the gig economy across the world in the last 10 years has seen increasing attention focused on the deleterious outcomes for those performing platform work.[10] The assumed designation of gig workers as independent contractors[11] has enabled them to be subjected to below minimum wage levels of payment,[12] and the bypassing of other legal protections commonly afforded to employees (e.g. the right to challenge arbitrary or unfair dismissal;[13] the right to receive pension or superannuation payments;[14] and coverage under compensation schemes for workplace injuries or illnesses[15]). Generally, their putative contractor status also means that these workers are denied access to collective bargaining.[16]

This reflects a broader hostility on the part of many platforms to the notion that their 'partners' (or other euphemisms used to describe the workers who perform services through an app) might form or join a collective group to improve their position. The anti-unionism of gig companies takes several different forms: outright refusal to engage with unions including through litigation to prevent union recognition for collective bargaining;[17] dissuading workers from engaging in collective action and persuading them that they 'don't need a union';[18] and putting up alternative avenues for voice or participation.

Alternative voice mechanisms are promoted in the World Economic Forum's *Charter of Principles for Good Platform Work* (whose signatories include the

CEOs of Cabify, Deliveroo, Grab and Uber). It makes the banal suggestion that 'workers should be able to express their views on platform guidelines and practices to the platform, and platforms should provide processes, channels and/or forums as appropriate for those discussions to occur'.[19] In this vein, Uber Australia says it provides information and feedback channels for 'driver and delivery-partners' through newsletters, podcasts, roundtables and focus groups. In the United Kingdom, it has piloted 'Uber Engage': a network of local advisory groups with driver representatives that involves 'meeting with Uber staff monthly and working with internal Uber teams on new product features and changes to the App'.[20]

These kinds of limp worker participation structures fit within the long history in employment relations of 'company unions': bodies that cannot effectively represent workers because they are compliant and beholden to management.[21] Employer capture of something looking more like a real union is another tactic used to fend off authentic worker collectivism. This can be seen in the battle over representation of rideshare drivers that has been taking place in the United States. In 2016, the Independent Drivers Guild (IDG) was established by the International Association of Machinists and Aerospace Workers in New York city. The IDG has done some important work, including helping to obtain minimum wage increases for drivers from New York's Taxi and Limousine Commission[22] as well as publicly advocating on issues of concern to drivers such as safety, mental health and opposition to the city's traffic congestion tax.[23]

However, the IDG is partly funded by Uber. As Dubal has observed: 'Uber pays an undisclosed sum to the Machinists [Union] – which uses the money to fund the [...] IDG. The IDG has not been elected by workers [...] After [its] formation, the worker association agreed (for a period of five years) not to contest the status of drivers and not to go on strike.'[24] Clearly, this raises significant concerns about the autonomy and independence of the IDG. It has faced criticism, in particular, for giving up on contesting the categorisation of drivers as contractors, and for taking a more combative approach to Uber's competitors such as Lyft.[25] It has also been asserted that at least some of IDG's claimed gains for rideshare drivers would not have been achieved without the efforts of the rival New York Taxi Workers Alliance (NYTWA).[26] We will return to the debate over representation of US rideshare drivers below.

For now, the IDG example shows that there is a desire on the part of gig workers for some form of collective representation. This can also be seen in many other areas of the global platform economy, where workers have sought the assistance of mainstream unions and (in some instances) engaged in self-organised collective action to protest their low wages and poor working conditions.[27] Unions have been at the forefront of legal challenges to the misclassification of workers by platforms in many jurisdictions.[28] They have negotiated some (albeit modest) improvements in the terms of engagement of gig workers in a few instances, such as the agreements struck in 2017 between Unions New South Wales and Airtasker,[29] and in 2019 by the GMB Union with delivery company Hermes.[30] Unions have also used surveys and other measures of platform workers' experiences to inform public campaigns highlighting the need for law reform to close down the contracting model.[31]

More direct forms of collective action, such as protests and 'log off' strikes, have tended to emanate spontaneously from self-organised gig worker groups. For example, the online forum RideShare Drivers United has helped organise several global rideshare driver 'strikes'[32] (in Australia, with assistance from the Transport Workers Union (TWU)[33]), and various food delivery rider collectives (like Deliveroo Strike Raiders) have emerged in Italy.[34] The latter have evolved from workers simply gathering in central meeting places in northern Italian cities to discuss their gripes. Having attracted considerable publicity through lively protests and social media campaigning, they obtained a seat at the table in local and national policy debates about gig work regulation.[35] The activities of similar food delivery rider collectives in UK cities including London, Bristol and Brighton have been bolstered by support from the Independent Workers Union of Great Britain (IWGB),[36] formed in 2012 specifically to represent these kinds of precarious workers.[37]

In attempting to organise and advance the interests of gig workers, unions face several challenges.[38] De Stefano and Aloisi have highlighted the difficulty of building collective voice for platform workers, given factors such as 'the absence of a workplace'; a lack of 'class consciousness' among individuals who 'are geographically dispersed, isolated and sometimes highly mobile'; and workers' concerns about retaliation through dismissal or deactivation from the app if they are involved in union activism.[39] Further, as Vandaele et al. point out, gig workers in certain sectors (e.g. food delivery) tend to be younger and less inclined to understand the relevance of unions – although not hostile to the idea of joining if unions were more visible to them.[40] (Mis)classification as contractors may also impact on whether gig workers even seek collective representation.[41] These various factors require unions to innovate and adapt if they are to succeed in building membership among a new breed of workers. A united approach among union representatives is also critical. This has been tested in the face of the 'divide and rule' tactics of rideshare platforms in the United States, as we shall see in the next section.

Resisting Regulation through Union-Busting Tactics: The Platforms' Campaign against AB5 in California, and Its Aftermath

On 12 June 2019, the CEOs of Uber and Lyft wrote a joint opinion article in the *San Francisco Chronicle*, calling for the updating of 'century-old employment laws' so that 'we can make independent work better'. They indicated that their platforms would offer drivers more benefits if their independent contractor status was preserved, and further noted thus:

> We can also give workers more of a say in the decisions affecting their lives and livelihoods [...] We can start by forming a new driver association, in partnership with state lawmakers and labor groups, to represent drivers' interests and administer the sorts of benefits that meet their highly individual needs.[42]

Given what was stated earlier about the opposition of platforms to collective representation of workers, it may be asked: why were these two rideshare companies now talking about setting up driver collectives?

The answer is that the regulatory door was closing in on them. At the time of the joint op ed, there was a bill before the California legislature going by the short-hand title 'AB5',[43] which proposed to make it easier for platform workers to be categorised as employees. AB5 would enshrine in statute the April 2018 ruling in *Dynamex Operations West, Inc v. Superior Court of Los Angeles* ('*Dynamex*'),[44] where the Supreme Court of California found that on-demand couriers were employees covered by that state's minimum wage orders. In place of previous judicial approaches to distinguishing between employees and contractors under Californian Law, the Court articulated a new 'ABC test'[45] which deems a worker to be an employee unless:

(A) the worker is free from the control and direction of the hiring entity, both under the contract through which work is performed and in the practical operation of the working relationship; and
(B) the worker performs work outside the scope of the hiring entity's usual business operations; and
(C) the worker is normally engaged in an independent trade, occupation or business of the same kind as the work being performed.[46]

AB5 posed a significant threat to the operating model of Uber, Lyft and many other platforms operating in California.[47] As a result, they engaged in furious lobbying to prevent AB5 becoming law.[48]

The rideshare companies were especially vocal, using many of the tactics pioneered over a long period by union busting employers and the law firms and consultants who advise them.[49] For example, drivers were marshalled to protest against this legislative threat to the 'flexibility' they are said to treasure. Some drivers were offered up to US$100 to cover their costs of attending an anti-AB5 rally in Sacramento. The 'I'm Independent Coalition', funded by California Chamber of Commerce, covered these costs.[50] The rideshare companies also asked drivers to sign a petition against AB5. There is evidence to suggest that some drivers were confused when this appeared as an 'in-app message', thinking they had to accept it in order to keep using the app and therefore continue to perform driving work. Drivers with limited English language skills also claimed they feared retaliation from Uber and Lyft if they spoke in favour of AB5, and were worried the companies were keeping track of who had signed the petition.[51]

In the course of the debate over AB5, divisions arose within and between labour unions. The *New York Times* reported in late June 2019 that Californian officials of the Service Employees International Union (SEIU) had met with Uber and Lyft about establishing a drivers' organisation, again premised on retaining the classification of drivers as contractors (like the IDG, discussed above). National SEIU leaders rejected that approach because 'the union supported full employee status [for rideshare drivers], including the California bill that would enshrine it'.[52] Creating 'deep rancor within the labor ranks and set[ting] unions against one another' formed a key part of the rideshare companies' strategy to prevent AB5 entering the statute books.[53]

These efforts were unsuccessful: AB5 was passed by the Californian legislature and signed into law by the state governor in September 2019.[54] This was in no small part due to the very strong campaign mounted in support of AB5 by various labour groups and the workers they represent. Large numbers of rideshare drivers attended pro-AB5 rallies in cities including San Francisco and Sacramento.[55] Drivers also directly lobbied state law makers to convey their personal experiences of platform work.[56] This campaigning was coordinated by three major gig workers' groups in California: Rideshare Drivers United, Gig Workers Rising and Mobile Workers Alliance.[57] While the rideshare platforms were able to sow some division among workers' representatives, mostly they galvanised labour opposition to their plan to scuttle AB5.

Of course, this was not the end of the road for the platforms' opposition to the new law, which took effect on 1 January 2020. Uber and Postmates (along with two drivers) brought a legal challenge in the US District Court for the Central District of California, seeking a preliminary injunction to prevent the enforcement of AB5 pending a full trial.[58] On 10 February 2020, the

Court denied the motion for a preliminary injunction in *Olsen, et al. v. State of California, et al.*[59] The Court found that the plaintiffs' claim was unlikely to succeed on its merits (including arguments that AB5 breaches both the US and Californian constitutions). Judge Gee opined that 'AB 5 furthers the State's legitimate interest in addressing misclassification' of the workers whom it covers.[60] Her Honour also rejected the plaintiffs' contention that AB5 unfairly targeted companies in the gig economy for regulation.[61] Judge Gee concluded that 'the State's interest in applying AB 5 to Company Plaintiffs and potentially hundreds of thousands of California workers outweighs Plaintiffs' fear of being made to abide by the law'.[62] Since this judgement, California's attorney general and several city attorneys general have sued Uber and Lyft for misclassifying drivers in breach of AB5.[63]

However, the platforms enjoyed greater success with a different strategy to derail AB5: Uber, Lyft, DoorDash, Postmates, Instacart and others obtained more than one million signatures on a ballot initiative proposing an alternative regulatory scheme, which was submitted to Californian voters in late 2020. Under this proposal, known as 'Prop 22', gig workers would remain independent contractors but with an 'earnings guarantee', reimbursement for expenses and injury insurance (although these arrangements have been subjected to criticism by University of California Berkeley economists).[64] The push for this ballot initiative came through the US$90 million 'Protect App-Based Drivers and Services' campaign which is funded by the platforms.[65] Their tactics in support of Prop 22 in the lead-up to the 3 November 2020 ballot were just as robust as those adopted to stymie AB5, including more pounding of workers with in-app messages[66] and a public advertising spend in excess of US$200 million.[67] This time, the platforms' investment paid off, as Prop 22 was passed with a 58 per cent majority of those voting.[68] California's ground-breaking effort to shut down the gig economy's contracting model was ultimately overwhelmed by the sheer persistence, power and money marshalled by anti-regulation forces.

In the wake of Prop 22's passage, the enhanced protections it was meant to provide gig workers have not materialised and evidence has emerged of some companies outside the gig economy replacing permanent staff with contractors engaged via platforms (taking advantage of the flexibility offered by Prop 22).[69] More generally, the notion of providing any additional benefits to gig workers has usually been resisted as gig companies consider it would threaten their contracting model.[70] However, as will be shown in the next section, several platforms globally were compelled by the circumstances of the COVID-19 pandemic to take some steps to safeguard the workers without whose labour they could not function.

COVID-19: The Insecurity (and Danger) of Gig Work Laid Bare

In Australia, it was apparent very soon after the emergence of the coronavirus outbreak in March 2020[71] that workers in the gig economy would be highly vulnerable in many ways. First, workers like rideshare drivers and food delivery riders were directly exposed to contracting coronavirus given that contact with members of the community forms an essential part of their job, yet basic health and safety protections were not being provided. Second, if a worker felt so concerned about the risk of becoming ill that they decided not to log onto the app, or was required to self-isolate, they would not be paid. And third, if a worker contracted the virus and could not work, their assumed independent contractor status means they would have no entitlement to sick leave.[72] The TWU took up the cause of gig workers, pushing platforms like Uber to provide them with sick leave and suspend their ratings systems so drivers would not be penalised for taking steps to protect themselves (e.g. wearing face masks).[73]

Very soon after this, Uber and Deliveroo announced they would take some steps to protect their drivers and riders: Uber, by providing up to 14 days' compensation for drivers diagnosed with COVID-19 or required by a public health authority to quarantine; and Deliveroo, through a similar commitment and by providing face masks and hand sanitiser.[74] By early April, at the same time as demand for home food deliveries had catapulted, riders were still expressing concern that they had inadequate personal protective equipment. This, and the introduction by Deliveroo and Uber Eats of 'contactless delivery' to customers, left workers feeling that the platforms' safety measures were 'pure tokenism' and 'the 'bare minimum that they have to do'.[75] One platform, Uber's rideshare rival Ola, introduced more stringent safety measures (e.g. transparent hygiene screens in vehicles, 'driver hygiene packs' and regular driver temperature checks)[76] – but only for drivers opting into the 'Ola Pro Program', part of a new service marketed to customers wanting a 'super sanitised' ride service.[77]

In addition, the federal government's 'JobKeeper' wage subsidy scheme (introduced in response to COVID-19)[78] provided little support to gig workers, such as rideshare drivers whose work fell away because of government lockdown measures. The JobKeeper payment of A$1500 per fortnight only covered full-time, part-time and long-term casual employees – again, putative contractor status ruled out those in the platform economy.[79] Some gig workers could qualify for JobKeeper as sole traders, but only if they had maintained proper records to show the required reduction in turnover of at least 30 per cent.[80] For any able to establish they were employees, they were also ineligible for JobKeeper if working on an international student or working holiday visa.[81] A high proportion of those engaged in platform work in Australia are temporary migrant workers.[82] The position of migrant workers more generally is explored in Chapter 8 by Joanna Howe in this volume.

The Australian story outlined above has been replicated for gig workers all around the world.[83] A common thread also has been the advocacy of unions and other collectivist groups in highlighting the increased insecurity of these workers due to the pandemic, and demanding improved income, leave and safety protections. In the United Kingdom, IWGB threatened the government with legal action over the exclusion of self-employed workers from the 80 per cent wage subsidy under its Coronavirus Job Retention Scheme.[84] In California, Gig Workers Rising responded to Uber's and Lyft's granting of two weeks' compensation to drivers diagnosed with coronavirus or quarantined, with a demand for permanent healthcare and sick leave coverage (not just during the pandemic).[85] Rideshare Drivers United lobbied for a universal income payment and a moratorium on evictions for Californian drivers.[86]

In New York city, where many rideshare drivers died from COVID-19 infection, Uber's CEO fell back on the tired company line that the drivers' independent contractor classification constrained its ability to improve their position.[87] Never mind that the contractor model has been a deliberate choice, inherent in the business model of platforms like Uber since their inception, to avoid employment regulation. Both the IDG and NYTWA helped draw attention to the devastating plight of rideshare drivers in New York.[88] NYTWA had to apply pressure to ensure Uber took the simple step of providing drivers' details to the Labor Department so they could access the federal government's US$600 weekly unemployment benefit.[89]

Lessons from AB5/Prop 22 and COVID-19, and What Role for Australian Unions vis-à-vis Gig Workers?

The controversy over the enactment of increased protections for gig workers through AB5 in California (ultimately over-run by Prop 22), and the exposure of those engaged via platforms to heightened financial and health risks by the COVID-19 pandemic, both hold important lessons for Australian unions seeking to collectivise the gig economy. The Californian debate illustrates that employer anti-unionism has simply been developed and adapted to the world of gig work. The platforms will engage in massive public campaigns to thwart any attempt to regulate them, especially – as was the case with AB5 – if regulation imperils the contracting model. In the process, they will corral workers to join their cause, luring them in with false concerns that regulation will compromise their 'independence' and 'flexibility'. They will also seek to capture worker representative groups, and even mainstream unions, through peace pacts that involve major compromises on the goal of advancing workers' interests. Money may even change hands as occurred in the setting up of IDG in New York. When all that fails, the platforms will test the validity of any new legislation through litigation, then utilise avenues like California's public ballot mechanism to buy a regulatory reversal. Their resources for these counter-campaigns seem formidable.

As for the coronavirus crisis, it reinforces the vital role of an effective collective voice for gig workers. The implementation of the contracting model had already placed millions of workers around the world at the mercy of the platforms, which dictated the rules of engagement through interposed entities and contractual gimmicks. The pandemic has accentuated the brutal effects of this legal fantasy for workers who are denied employment status but do not operate genuine independent businesses either. They have been frozen out of wage subsidy schemes and sick leave entitlements, all the while working on the frontline of exposure to the virus with insufficient safety protections: see further, Chapter 11 by K. D. Ewing in this volume. Without unions and groups like the TWU and Gig Workers Rising, these workers would have no prospect at all of decent treatment in performing the kinds of work that is now being valued as essential.[90] The crisis has made the task of organising platform workers much harder: meetings must be held virtually (e.g. via Zoom or Facebook live sessions),[91] and social media has become a critical organising tool.[92] However, this kind of organising might just suit gig workers better (given some of the factors discussed earlier in this chapter). And in any case, some of Australia's more sophisticated unions have been utilising digital organising techniques effectively in recent years.[93] They have stepped this up significantly in the COVID-19 lockdown through 'virtual town halls' and adept marshalling of online resources for campaigning.[94]

More specifically, what role can Australian unions play in representing gig workers into the future? They can continue making stark the reality of platform work, through surveys and campaigns, as a basis for applying pressure for law reform (although legislative change to clarify the employment status of gig workers is unlikely in the foreseeable future). Unions can also keep supporting legal challenges to the platforms' contracting model. At the time of writing, the TWU is behind just such a case: a claim on behalf of a Deliveroo rider who alleges his engagement breached section 357 of the *Fair Work Act 2009* (Cth) prohibiting an employer from misrepresenting an employment relationship as one of principal and contractor.[95]

Even if the general trend of Australian case law continues to preclude gig workers from obtaining employment status, there remains some capacity for unions to organise and represent them – including through avenues that have been little explored to date. First, unions could run cases under Part 3 of the *Independent Contractors Act 2006* (Cth) that allow Federal Courts to review harsh or unfair contracts and order compensation or variation of contractual terms if unfairness is established. This mechanism, at least theoretically, offers 'valuable protection against harsh or exploitative arrangements'[96] and its potential as a source of redress for gig workers should be tested.

Second, in the state of Victoria, unions should consider their ability to assist food delivery riders and deliverers of freight (who operate up to three vehicles including their own) in accessing certain rights under recent amendments to the *Owner Drivers and Forestry Contractors Act 2005* (Vic). These rights include information about applicable rates and operating costs, minimum contractual requirements and dispute resolution processes through the Victorian Small Business Commission.[97] Unions in New South Wales can perform an even more expansive representative role under the 'contract determinations' and 'contract agreements' provisions in chapter 6, parts 2 and 3 of the *Industrial Relations Act 1996* (NSW).

Third, unions could seek to engage in collective bargaining with platform operators over pay rates, rest periods, safety standards and managerial control through algorithms, on behalf of gig workers. However, for this to occur, competition law constraints on collective negotiations by the self-employed or independent businesses would have to be lifted;[98] and of course, the companies would have to agree to negotiate or be compelled to do so through some legal mechanism. In respect of the latter, unions should bring forward a test case on platform workers' access to collective bargaining under the *Fair Work Act*[99] (which would require a determination of employment status). Any retaliatory actions by platforms against gig workers involved in collective bargaining efforts, whether as employees or independent contractors, could be contested using the general protections provisions in Part 3-1 of the *Fair Work Act*.[100]

Finally, unions can follow the TWU's lead in seeking to utilise the worker representation provisions in occupational health and safety (OHS) statutes.[101] The union requested that SafeWork NSW investigate Deliveroo, in early 2020, following the platform's alleged refusal to agree to geographical work zones for worker representation under state OHS law and alleged retribution against a union activist.[102] In rejecting the union's proposal, a Deliveroo spokesperson stated that the NSW safety legislation 'does not readily apply to the flexible nature of our relationship with independent contractors'.[103] On 17 May 2020, the TWU indicated (on Twitter) that SafeWork NSW had 'provided Deliveroo with a notice to comply' with the OHS legislation. Then in early 2021, it was reported that workers had elected health and safety representatives at Deliveroo,[104] illustrating the potential of federal, state and territory safety laws to build collective organisation among gig workers.

Whatever form it takes, the collective voice of platform workers must meet the essential preconditions for genuine freedom of association: it must be strong, independent from management, and grounded in legal rights and protections. Australian law is seriously deficient in the protection it offers for collective organisation and representation of employees,[105] let alone those designated as contractors in the gig economy. Redefining the statutory concept of 'employee', to ensure gig workers fall within the protective framework under the *Fair Work Act*, is an essential first step to building a suite of rights that will ensure they can be effectively represented by trade unions. Such representation is critical to ensure that platform workers have the same access to democratic representation and social justice at work as others in the workforce, and (in turn) the opportunity to improve the conditions of their labour.[106]

Notes

1 The latest manifestation of the broader phenomenon of insecure work. On insecure work, see Chapter 6 in this volume by Iain Campbell, 'Trade Unions and Precarious Work: In Search of Effective Strategies' .

2 See, for example, Richard Johnstone, Shae McCrystal, Igor Nossar, Michael Quinlan, Michael Rawling and Joellen Riley, *Beyond Employment: The Legal Regulation of Work Relationships* (Annandale, NSW: Federation Press, 2012), 54–56; Andrew Stewart, Anthony Forsyth, Mark Irving, Richard Johnstone and Shae McCrystal, *Creighton and Stewart's Labour Law*, 6th ed. (Annandale, NSW: Federation Press, 2016), 195.

3 See, for example, Anna Patty, '"It's Not Fair. It's Not Right": Rider Takes Deliveroo to Court', *Sydney Morning Herald,* 28 August 2019, https://www.smh.com.au/business/workplace/it-s-not-fair-it-s-not-right-rider-takes-deliveroo-to-court-20190815-p52hda.html; David Marin-Guzman, 'Sacked Driver Says Uber Eats Model Is "Based on a Fiction"', *Australian Financial Review*, 19 November 2019, https://www.afr.com/work-and-careers/workplace/later-ubereats-business-model-based-on-a-fiction-20191118-p53bmr.

4 'Ross-led FWC Bench Ruling on Gig Workers "Curious": Academics', *Workplace Express*, 22 April 2020; see also Anthony Forsyth, 'The Uber Eats Decision: Australia's FWC Full Bench Misses the Chance to See Through the Gig Economy's Sophistry', *Labour Law Down Under*, 28 April 2020, https://labourlawdownunder.com.au/?p=846.

5 See, for example, Uber, *Submission: Inquiry into the Victorian On-Demand Workforce* (2019): 5, 7–12.

6 Deliveroo, *Submission to the Victorian Government Inquiry into the On-Demand Workforce* (February 2019), 1. Compare the evidence of food delivery riders' experiences of work presented in Victorian Trades Hall Council (VTHC): Young Workers Centre (YWC)/Transport Workers Union (TWU), *Snapshot: On-Demand Food Delivery Riders* (November 2019); Alex Veen, Tom Barratt and Caleb Goods, 'Platform-Capital's "App-etite" for Control: A Labour Process Analysis of Food-Delivery Work in Australia', *Work, Employment and Society* (forthcoming).

7 Possibly the worst example in the Australian context is Foodora, which ceased operations in this country in August 2018 leaving around 5,000 riders with A$8 million in unpaid entitlements including wages and superannuation, as well as

over A$2 million owing to the Australian Taxation Office: see, for example, David Chau, 'Foodora Owes $8 million to Former Delivery Workers, Who Will Only Receive 29 Cents in the Dollar', *ABC News*, 10 May 2019, https://www.abc.net.au/news/2019-05-10/foodora-owes-millions-unpaid-workers/11100380; 'Failed Food Delivery Platform Coughs Up $2.3m for Former Riders', *Workplace Express*, 10 May 2019. See also Alison Griswold, 'Food-Delivery Giant Deliveroo Is Pulling out of Germany', *Quartz*, 12 August 2019, https://qz.com/1685962/food-delivery-startup-deliveroo-exits-germany/; David Doorey, 'Thoughts on the Foodora Fiasco: Have Labour Laws Been Violated?', *Canadian Law of Work Forum*, 28 April 2020, http://lawofwork.ca/thoughts-on-the-foodora-fiasco-have-labour-laws-been-violated/.

8 See, for example, Thomas Haipeter, Dominik Owczarek, Michele Faioli and Feliciano Iudicone (eds), *Don't Gig Up: Final Report* (Rome: Fondazione Giacomo Brodolini and Partners, 2020).

9 Trebor Scholz, *Uberworked and Underpaid: How Workers Are Disrupting the Digital Economy* (Cambridge: Polity Press, 2017), 45.

10 See, for example, Veena Dubal, 'A Brief History of the Gig', *Logic* 10 (4 May 2020) https://logicmag.io/security/a-brief-history-of-the-gig/; Alex Rosenblat, *Uberland: How Algorithms Are Rewriting the Rules of Work* (Oakland: University of California Press, 2018); Sarah Kessler, *Gigged: The Gig Economy, the End of the Job and the Future of Work* (London: Random House Business Books, 2018); James Bloodworth, *Hired: Six Months Undercover in Low-Wage Britain* (London: Atlantic Books, 2018).

11 On the approach to worker categorisation under Australian common law, see Andrew Stewart and Shae McCrystal, 'Labour Regulation and the Great Divide: Does the Gig Economy Require a New Category of Worker?', *Australian Journal of Labour Law Review* 32, no. 1 (2019): 4–22 (6–8).

12 In Australia see, for example, TWU, *Rideshare Driver Survey* (October 2018); Paula McDonald, Penny Williams, Andrew Stewart, Damian Oliver and Robyn Mayes, *Digital Platform Work in Australia: Preliminary Findings from a National Survey* (Victoria: Victorian Department of Premier and Cabinet, 18 June 2019), 18–19.

13 In five out of six decisions to date, Australia's Fair Work Commission has upheld the designation of platform workers as independent contractors who cannot pursue an unfair dismissal claim under the *Fair Work Act 2009*: *Kaseris v. Rasier Pacific V.O.F.* [2017] FWC 6610; *Pallage v. Rasier Pacific Pty Ltd* [2018] FWC 2579; *Suliman v. Rasier Pacific Pty Ltd* [2019] FWC 4807; *Gupta v. Portier Pacific Pty Ltd; Uber Australia Pty Ltd T/A Uber Eats* [2019] FWC 5008; *Gupta v. Portier Pacific Pty Ltd; Uber Australia Pty Ltd T/A Uber Eats* [2020] FWCFB 1698. Compare *Klooger v. Foodora Australia Pty Ltd* [2018] FWC 6836. For analysis of these cases, see Anthony Forsyth, 'Playing Catch-Up but Falling Short: Regulating Work in the Gig Economy in Australia', *King's Law Journal* 31, no. 2 (2020): 287–300.

14 Jennifer Duke, '"New Set of Problems": Gig Economy a Curve Ball for Retirement System', *Sydney Morning Herald*, 13 February 2020, https://www.smh.com.au/politics/federal/new-set-of-problems-gig-economy-a-curve-ball-for-retirement-system-20200211-p53zpy.html.

15 McDonald et al., *Digital Platform Work in Australia*, 22–23.

16 This issue has not yet arisen for determination in Australia. In the United Kingdom, the ability of Deliveroo food delivery riders to access the statutory procedure for union recognition (the first step towards bargaining for a collective agreement) was successfully contested by the company: *R (on the application of the Independent Workers Union of*

Great Britain) v. Central Arbitration Committee and Roofoods Ltd T/A Deliveroo [2018] EWHC 3342 (Admin); see Joe Atkinson and Hitesh Dhorajiwala, '*IWGB v. RooFoods*: Status, Rights and Substitution', *Industrial Law Journal* 48, no. 2 (2019): 278–95. In Canada, a union established collective bargaining rights in a case involving Foodora, which (soon after) exited the Canadian market: see Ryan White, 'How the Ontario Labour Board Ruled Foodora Workers Are Employees and Not Independent Contractors', *Canadian Law of Work Forum*, 5 March 2020, http://lawofwork.ca/how-the-ontario-labour-board-ruled-foodora-workers-are-employees/; Doorey, 'Thoughts on the Foodora Fiasco'.

17 See note 16 above.

18 Alice Uribe, 'Gig Economy Workers Don't Need a Union: Airtasker Chief', *Australian Financial Review*, 15 August 2017; see also Ewin Hannan, 'How the New Economy Is Disrupting Unions: No Holiday Pay, Sick Leave or Super', *Australian Financial Review*, 8 April 2016, https://www.afr.com/work-and-careers/management/how-the-new-economy-is-disrupting-unions-20160309-gne986, including similar comments from Airtasker CEO Tim Fung.

19 World Economic Forum, *Charter of Principles for Good Platform Work* (2020), 3.

20 Uber, *Submission*, 11–12.

21 See, for example, John Pencavel, 'Company Unions, Wages and Work Hours', *Advances in Industrial and Labor Relations* 12 (2003): 7–38.

22 Shirin Ghaffary, 'New York City Has Set the Nation's First Minimum Pay Rate for Uber and Lyft Drivers', *Vox*, 4 December 2018, https://www.vox.com/2018/12/4/18125789/uber-lyft-drivers-wage-minimum-new-york.

23 'Campaigns', Independent Drivers Guild, 2019, https://drivingguild.org/current-campaigns/; and 'News', Independent Drivers Guild, 2019, https://drivingguild.org/news/.

24 Veena Dubal, 'Gig Worker Organizing for Solidarity Unions', *Law and Political Economy Blog*, 19 June 2019, https://lpeblog.org/2019/06/19/gig-worker-organizing-for-solidarity-unions/. See also Steven Greenhouse, *Beaten Down, Worked Up: The Past, Present, and Future of American Labor* (New York: Alfred A. Knopf, 2019), 229–31.

25 Noam Scheiber, 'Uber Has a Union of Sorts, but Faces Doubts on Its Autonomy', *The New York Times*, 12 May 2017, https://www.nytimes.com/2017/05/12/business/economy/uber-drivers-union.html.

26 Dubal, 'Gig Worker Organizing for Solidarity Unions'; see also Hannah Johnston and Chris Land-Kazlauskas, 'Organizing On-Demand: Representation, Voice and Collective Bargaining in the Gig Economy', ILO Conditions of Work and Employment Series No. 94 (International Labour Organization, Geneva, 2018), 11–12.

27 See generally Kurt Vandaele, 'Will Trade Unions Survive in the Platform Economy? Emerging Patterns of Platform Workers' Collective Voice and Representation in Europe' (Working Paper No. 2018.05, European Trade Union Institute, Brussels, 2018); Jeremias Prassl, *Collective Voice in the Platform Economy: Challenges, Opportunities, Solutions* (Brussels: European Trade Union Confederation, September 2018); Johnston and Land-Kazlauskas, *Organizing On-Demand.*

28 See, for example, notes 3 and 4 above; the last two decisions mentioned in note 13; and note 16.

29 Kate Minter, 'Negotiating Labour Standards in the Gig Economy: Airtasker and Unions New South Wales', *The Economic and Labour Relations Review* 28, no. 3 (2017): 438–54.

30 Sarah O'Connor, 'Gig Economy Agreements Promise a Brighter Future for Trade Unions', *Financial Times*, 26 February 2019, https://www.ft.com/content/25271b48-38eb-11e9-b856-5404d3811663.

31 See, for example, Unions NSW, *Innovation or Exploitation? Busting the Airtasker Myth*, 2016, https://www.unionsnsw.org.au/wp-content/uploads/2019/06/Airtasker-report.pdf; TWU, *Rideshare Driver Survey*; VTHC, YWC/TWU, *Snapshot*.

32 See, for example, Australian Associated Press, 'Uber Drivers Log Off in Australia-Wide Protest against Low Fares', *Guardian*, 6 August 2018, https://www.theguardian.com/australia-news/2018/aug/06/uber-drivers-log-off-in-australia-wide-protest-against-low-fares; Simon Thomsen, 'Uber Drivers Are Holding Another Nationwide Strike in Australia Today', *Business Insider*, 22 August 2018, https://www.businessinsider.com.au/uber-drivers-are-holding-another-nationwide-strike-in-australia-today-2018-8.

33 Kate Conger, Vicky Xiuzhong Xu and Zach Wichter, 'Uber Drivers' Day of Strikes Circles the Globe Before the Company's I.P.O.', *New York Times*, 8 May 2019, https://www.nytimes.com/2019/05/08/technology/uber-strike.html.

34 Arianna Tassinari and Vincenzo Maccarrone, 'Striking the Startups', *Jacobin* (January 2017), https://www.jacobinmag.com/2017/01/foodora-strike-turin-gig-economy-startups-uber/; Lorenzo Zamponi, 'Bargaining with the Algorithm', *Jacobin* (June 2018), https://www.jacobinmag.com/2018/06/deliveroo-riders-strike-italy-labor-organizing; Arianna Tassinari and Vincenzo Maccarrone, 'Riders on the Storm: Workplace Solidarity among Gig Economy Couriers in Italy and the UK', *Work, Employment and Society* 34, no. 1 (2020): 35–54.

35 Arianna Tassinari and Vincenzo Maccarrone, 'The Mobilisation of Gig Economy Couriers in Italy: Some Lessons for the Trade Union Movement', *Transfer* 23, no. 3 (2017): 353–57; James Politi, 'Di Maio Takes Aim at Italy's Gig Economy', *Financial Times*, 19 June 2018, https://www.ft.com/content/04b6d97c-7305-11e8-aa31-31da4279a601.

36 Callum Cant, 'I'm a Deliveroo Rider. Collective Action Is the Only Way We'll Get a Fair Deal', *Guardian*, 31 March 2017, https://www.theguardian.com/commentisfree/2017/mar/31/deliveroo-organising-wages-conditions-gig-economy; Paul Shanks, 'Resisting Exploitation and Building Power: the Deliveroo Workers Fighting Back', *Bright Green*, 12 February 2019, http://bright-green.org/2019/02/12/resisting-exploitation-and-building-power-the-deliveroo-workers-fighting-back/; Tassinari and Maccarrone, 'Riders on the Storm'.

37 Independent Workers' Union of Great Britain, 'About Us', https://iwgb.org.uk/en/page/about-us.

38 See also the discussion of barriers to union organising in the context of precarious work more broadly, in Chapter 6 by Iain Campbell herein, 'Trade Unions and Precarious Work: In Search of Effective Strategies' .

39 Valerio De Stefano and Antonio Aloisi, *Digital Age: Employment and Working Conditions of Selected Types of Platform Work – National Context Analysis, Italy* (Dublin: European Foundation for the Improvement of Living and Working Conditions, 2018), 20; Tassinari and Maccarrone, 'Riders on the Storm', 38, 40 (see also 43 et seq. on overcoming the obstacles to building solidarity among food delivery riders).

40 Kurt Vandaele, Agnieszka Piasna and Jan Drahokoupil, '"Algorithm Breakers" Are Not a Different "Species": Attitudes Towards Trade Unions of Deliveroo Riders in Belgium' (Working Paper No. 2019.06, European Trade Union Institute, Brussels, 2019), 4, 14, 19–21, 30–32.

41 Sarah Kaine and Emmanuel Josserand, 'The Organisation and Experience of Work in the Gig Economy', *Journal of Industrial Relations* 61, no. 4 (2019): 479–501 (487).

42 Dara Khosrowshahi, Logan Green and John Zimmer, 'Open Forum: Uber, Lyft Ready to Do Our Part for Drivers', *San Francisco Chronicle*, 12 June 2019, https://www.sfchronicle.com/opinion/openforum/article/Open-Forum-Uber-Lyft-ready-to-do-our-part-for-13969843.php. See also Shannon Bond, 'Uber and Lyft Set Aside Rivalry in Driver Status Fight', *Financial Times*, 12 June 2019, https://www.ft.com/content/ecafd04c-8d46-11e9-a1c1-51bf8f989972.

43 California Legislative Information, *AB-5 Worker Status: Employees and Independent Contractors* (Assembly Bill No 5, Introduced by Assembly Member Gonzalez, 3 December 2018), https://leginfo.legislature.ca.gov/faces/billNavClient.xhtml?bill_id=201920200AB5. On the background to AB5, see Lorena Gonzalez, 'Commentary: Why Workers Need State Protections', *San Diego Union-Tribune*, 21 August 2019, https://www.sandiegouniontribune.com/opinion/story/2019-08-21/commentary-why-workers-need-state-protections.

44 *Dynamex Operations West, Inc v. Superior Court of Los Angeles* ('*Dynamex*'), 416 P.3d 1, 36 (Cal. 2018).

45 Although some form of the ABC test is already on the statute books of 17 US states: Robert Sprague, 'Using the ABC Test to Classify Workers: End of the Platform-Based Business Model or Status Quo Ante?', *SSRN*, 22 February 2020, https://papers.ssrn.com/sol3/papers.cfm?abstract_id=3526353, 11; Robert Sprague, *William and Mary Business Law Review* (forthcoming).

46 *Dynamex*, 416 P.3d 1, 36 (Cal. 2018). The three elements of the ABC test are explored closely in Sprague, *Using the ABC Test to Classify Workers*, 12–19.

47 According to a University of California Berkeley report, around 64 per cent of independent contractors in the state would be presumed to be employees under AB5 including cleaners, truck drivers and child care workers: Jaclyn Diaz and Andrew Wallender, 'Gig Worker Law Ripples Across California as Court Fights Pile Up', *Daily Labor Report (Bloomberg)*, 24 December 2019, https://news.bloomberglaw.com/daily-labor-report/california-unions-companies-gear-up-for-new-gig-worker-law.

48 Carolyn Said and Dustin Gardner, 'Gig-Work Bill Passes Senate Committee as Crowds Rally for and against It', *San Francisco Chronicle*, 10 July 2019, https://www.sfchronicle.com/business/article/Gig-work-bill-passes-Senate-committee-as-crowds-14085950.php.

49 John Logan, 'The Union Avoidance Industry in the United States', *British Journal of Industrial Relations* 44, no. 4 (2006): 651–75.

50 Johana Bhuiyan, 'Uber and Lyft Drivers Were Paid up to $100 to Demonstrate against Bill', *San Diego Union-Tribune*, 15 July 2019, https://www.sandiegouniontribune.com/business/technology/story/2019-07-15/la-fi-tn-ab5-uber-lyft-rally-sacramento-pay-20190715.

51 Shirin Ghaffary, 'Some Uber and Lyft Drivers Say They Were Misled into Petitioning against Their Own Worker Rights', *Vox*, 27 June 2019, https://www.vox.com/recode/2019/6/27/18759387/uber-lyft-drivers-misled-companies-political-campaign.

52 Noam Scheiber, 'Debate Over Uber and Lyft Drivers' Rights in California Has Split Labor', *New York Times*, 29 June 2019, https://www.nytimes.com/2019/06/29/business/economy/uber-lyft-drivers-unions.html. See also Sam Harnett, 'Uber and Lyft Drivers Ramp Up Organizing Efforts, but Question Big Unions' Motives', *KQED*, 3 March 2020, https://www.kqed.org/news/11804507/uber-and-lyft-drivers-are-organizing-but-worry-big-unions-will-sell-them-out.

53 Scheiber, 'Debate Over Uber and Lyft Drivers' Rights'.

54 Alexia Fernandez Campbell, 'California Just Passed a Landmark Law to Regulate Uber and Lyft', *Vox*, 18 September 2019, https://www.vox.com/2019/9/11/20850878/california-passes-ab5-bill-uber-lyft.

55 Said and Gardiner, 'Gig-Work Bill Passes Senate Committee'; Kari Paul, 'California Uber and Lyft Drivers Rally for Bill Granting Rights to Contract Workers', *Guardian*, 27 August 2019, https://www.theguardian.com/us-news/2019/aug/27/california-uber-and-lyft-drivers-rally-for-bill-granting-rights-to-contract-workers.

56 Kate Conger and Noam Scheiber, 'California Bill Makes App-Based Companies Treat Workers as Employees', *New York Times*, 11 September 2019, https://www.nytimes.com/2019/09/11/technology/california-gig-economy-bill.html.

57 Veena Dubal, 'An Uber Ambivalence: Employee Status, Worker Perspectives, and Regulation in the Gig Economy', UC Hastings Research Paper No. 381, *SSRN*, 1 December 2019, https://papers.ssrn.com/sol3/papers.cfm?abstract_id=3488009, 19.

58 Levi Sumagaysay, 'Uber Sues California Over the Gig-Worker Law. Now What?', *Los Angeles Daily News*, 31 December, 2019, https://www.dailynews.com/2019/12/31/uber-sues-california-over-the-gig-worker-law-now-what/.

59 *Olsen, et al. v. State of California, et al.*, CV 19-10956-DMG (RAOx), 10 February 2020.

60 Ibid., 11.

61 Ibid., 8–13; this included consideration of AB5's many exemptions (for other industries or types of work, for example, direct salespersons) from the application of the ABC test propounded in *Dynamex*.

62 Ibid., 24.

63 Kate Conger, 'California Sues Uber and Lyft, Claiming Workers Are Misclassified', *New York Times*, 5 May 2020, https://www.nytimes.com/2020/05/05/technology/california-uber-lyft-lawsuit.html.

64 Dara Kerr, 'Uber, Lyft, DoorDash's Gig Worker Ballot Initiative Heads to Voters in November', *cnet.com*, 27 February 2020, https://www.cnet.com/news/uber-lyft-doordashs-gig-worker-ballot-initiative-heads-to-voters-in-november/.

65 Alexia Fernandez Campbell, 'Uber and Lyft Have Launched a Campaign to Avoid Government Regulation in California', *Vox*, 29 October 2019, https://www.vox.com/identities/2019/10/29/20938109/ab5-uber-lyft-ballot-initiative-referendum.

66 Andrew Hawkins, 'Uber and Lyft Had an Edge in the Prop 22 Fight: Their Apps', *The Verge*, 4 November 2020.

67 Suhauna Hussain, Johana Bhuiyan and Ryan Menezes, 'How Uber and Lyft Persuaded California to Vote Their Way', *Los Angeles Times*, 13 November 2020.

68 Ibid.

69 See, for example, Alexander Sammon, 'Prop 22 Is Here, and It's Already Worse Than Expected', *American Prospect*, 15 January 2021.

70 See, for example, Deliveroo, *Submission to the Victorian Government Inquiry*, 9: 'Companies should not be forced, as they effectively are now, to choose between offering workers a relationship with a great deal of flexibility and fewer benefits or a relationship with much less flexibility and more benefits. […] Were the law more accommodating, we would seek to give our riders greater security without sacrificing their flexible supplier agreements.'

71 On the legal and regulatory responses to the COVID-19 pandemic in more than 60 nations, see the special issue 'Covid-19 and Labour Law: A Global Review', *Italian Labour Law e-Journal* 13, no. 1S (2020).

72 Ariel Bogle, 'Gig Economy Workers Fear Livelihoods, Customers at Risk During Coronavirus Outbreak', *ABC News (Science)*, 6 March 2020, https://www.abc.net.au/news/science/2020-03-06/gig-economy-workers-uber-deliveroo-ola-coronavirus-outbreak/12022072.

73 Ibid.

74 'Financial Cover for Sick, Quarantined Gig Workers', *Workplace Express*, 10 March 2020; see also 'Looking After Gig Workers Is Good Sense', *The Age (Editorial)*, 11 March 2020.

75 Mridula Amin, 'Food Delivery Riders Say Employers Not Doing Enough to Protect Them from Coronavirus', *ABC News*, 4 April 2020, https://www.abc.net.au/news/2020-04-04/food-delivery-riders-not-being-supported-in-coronavirus-response/12120480.

76 'Ola Pro Terms and Conditions for Drivers', Ola, https://ola.com.au/ola-pro-terms-and-conditions/.

77 Jack Derwin, 'Ola Is Now Offering "Super-Sanitised" Rides in the Most Confusing Coronavirus Feature Yet', *Business Insider Australia*, 30 April 2020. Another feature of Ola Pro is the requirement that drivers must log onto the app for a minimum of 50 hours each week and have a driver participation rate of at least 75 per cent while engaged in the programme; this (along with the safety conditions drivers must comply with) increases the prospect of drivers being found at law to be employees rather than contractors: Nick Bonyhady, 'Safety Measures May Put Gig Economy Contractor Status at Risk', *Sydney Morning Herald*, 4 May 2020, https://www.smh.com.au/politics/federal/safety-measures-may-put-gig-economy-contractor-status-at-risk-20200504-p54pm3.html.

78 Australian Government, *JobKeeper Payment: Frequently Asked Questions* (9 April 2020).

79 Notionally 'self-employed' workers have also been excluded from the COVID-19 income support schemes introduced in many other countries: Nicola Countouris, Valerio De Stefano, Keith Ewing and Mark Freedland, 'Covid-19 Crisis Makes Clear a New Concept of "Worker" Is Overdue', *Social Europe*, 9 April 2020, https://www.socialeurope.eu/covid-19-crisis-makes-clear-a-new-concept-of-worker-is-overdue.

80 Steven Hamilton, Anthony Forsyth and David Peetz, 'Australia's $130 billion JobKeeper Payment: What the Experts Think', *The Conversation*, 30 March 2020, https://theconversation.com/australias-130-billion-jobkeeper-payment-what-the-experts-think-135043.

81 Unless they are from New Zealand: see further Joo-Cheong Tham, 'Why Temporary Migrants Need JobKeeper', *The Conversation*, 7 April 2020, https://theconversation.com/why-temporary-migrants-need-jobkeeper-135688.

82 McDonald et al., *Digital Platform Work in Australia*, 12–13; VTHC, YWC/TWU, *Snapshot*.

83 See, for example, on the European Union, Leila Chaibi, 'Pandemic Is Time to Recognise Gig Workers' Rights', *EU Observer*, 30 March 2020, https://euobserver.com/opinion/147902; and on the United Kingdom, Mattha Busby, '"The Government Has Abandoned Us": Gig Economy Workers Struggle to Cope', *Guardian*, 17 March 2020, https://www.theguardian.com/business/2020/mar/17/the-government-has-abandoned-us-gig-economy-workers-struggle-to-cope.

84 Andrew Woodcock and John Stone, 'Coronavirus: UK Government's Failure to Protect Self-Employed and Gig Economy to be Legally Challenged by Union', *Independent*, 23 March 2020, https://www.independent.co.uk/news/uk/politics/coronavirus-uk-news-self-employed-gig-economy-union-a9418421.html. On the wider impact of

the pandemic on work and workers in the United Kingdom and the limitations of the government's response, see Chapter 11 by K. D. Ewing in this volume, 'Trade Unions, Labour Law and Democratic Socialism: The COVID-19 Crisis in the United Kingdom' .

85 Kari Paul, 'Coronavirus Forces Companies Like Uber and Lyft to Reckon with Workers' Rights', *Guardian*, 11 March 2020, https://www.theguardian.com/business/2020/mar/11/coronavirus-outbreak-uber-lyft-workers-ab5.

86 Veena Dubal and Meredith Whittaker, 'Uber Drivers Are Being Forced to Choose Between Risking Covid-19 and Starvation', *Guardian*, 25 March 2020, https://www.theguardian.com/technology/2020/mar/25/uber-lyft-gig-economy-coronavirus.

87 Jiayang Fan, 'The Uncertain Life of New York City's Immigrant Uber Drivers During the Pandemic', *New Yorker*, 29 April 2020, https://www.newyorker.com/news/daily-comment/the-uncertain-life-of-new-york-citys-immigrant-uber-drivers-during-the-pandemic.

88 Ibid.; Annie Correal and Andrew Jacobs, '"A Tragedy Is Unfolding": Inside New York's Virus Epicenter', *New York Times*, 9 April 2020, https://www.nytimes.com/2020/04/09/nyregion/coronavirus-queens-corona-jackson-heights-elmhurst.html.

89 Megan Cassella and Rebecca Rainey, 'Gig Workers Struggle to Claim Unemployment Relief', *Politico*, 15 April 2020, https://www.politico.com/news/2020/04/15/workers-struggle-to-claim-unemployment-relief-188814, noting that platform worker groups in other US states had to take similar action.

90 See, for example, Lisa Herzog, 'What Does the Corona Crisis Teach Us About the Value of Work?', *New Statesman*, 1 April 2020, https://www.newstatesman.com/politics/economy/2020/04/what-does-corona-crisis-teach-us-about-value-work.

91 See, for example, 'Adapting How We Organise' in 'Our Covid-19 Response', Independent Workers Union Great Britain, https://iwgb.org.uk/covid-19.

92 In another context, see Vincent Pasquier and Alex Wood, 'The Power of Social Media as a Labour Campaigning Tool: Lessons from OUR Walmart and the Fight for 15' (Policy Brief No. 10, European Trade Union Institute, Brussels, 2018).

93 See, for example, David Marin-Guzman, 'How "Young Tech Dudes" are Decentralising Unions with Blockchain, AI', *Australian Financial Review*, 28 December 2017, https://www.afr.com/policy/economy/how-young-tech-dudes-are-decentralising-unions-with-blockchain-ai-20171214-h04bfq.

94 For example, very soon after reports emerged of employer abuses of workers' rights under the JobKeeper program, the VTHC established its 'JobScammer' website (https://www.jobscammer.com.au/) to enable the reporting of 'dodgy bosses'. This was an important measure to demonstrate (particularly to young, highly vulnerable and/or casual workers) the value of collective action amidst the crisis.

95 Patty, "It's Not Fair. It's Not Right".

96 Stewart et al., *Creighton and Stewart's Labour Law*, 698 (see further 697–99).

97 *Owner Drivers and Forestry Contractors Amendment Act 2019* (Vic).

98 For example, potential liability for price-fixing or reducing competition in a market under the *Competition and Consumer Act 2010* (Cth). A recent Australian Competition and Consumer Commission (ACCC) class exemption for small businesses offers some potential for platform workers to bargain collectively, although without the ability to engage in boycott activity or other means of ensuring bargaining occurs: see 'Bargaining Go-Ahead a "Big Step Forward" for Gig Workers', *Workplace Express*, 23 October 2020.

99 This includes the majority support determination mechanism under ss 236–37, which can be used to compel a reluctant employer to bargain.

100 Although it must be noted that the case law on these provisions has significantly watered down their capacity to protect industrial activists against adverse treatment by employers: see, for example, *Barclay v. Board of Bendigo Regional Institute of Technical and Further Education* (2012) 290 ALR 647; *Construction, Forestry, Mining and Energy Union v. BHP Coal Pty Ltd* (2014) 253 CLR 243.

101 See generally Stewart et al., *Creighton and Stewart's Labour Law*, 564–75.

102 'TWU Seeks SafeWork Intervention at Deliveroo', *Workplace Express*, 27 February 2020.

103 Ibid.; note also that Deliveroo had previously sought to establish its own rider group to consider safety issues, see David Marin-Guzman, 'Deliveroo Sets up Gig Economy's First Rider Advisory Panel', *Australian Financial Review*, 15 October 2019, https://www.afr.com/work-and-careers/workplace/deliveroo-sets-up-gig-economy-s-first-rider-advisory-panel-20191014-p530hb.

104 David Marin-Guzman, 'Deliveroo Riders Elect Safety Reps in Industry "Milestone" ', *Australian Financial Review*, 4 January 2021. This was a particularly significant development in the wake of the deaths of five food delivery riders in late 2020, highlighting further the dangers encountered by these workers (amplified by the platforms' imposition of contractor status): see, for example, Isabelle Lane, 'With Five Food Delivery Riders Killed in Two Months, Australia's Gig Economy Faces a Reckoning', *New Daily*, 26 November 2020.

105 See, for example, *Change the Rules – Campaign Kit*, ACTU, https://psa.asn.au/wp-content/uploads/2017/12/ctr_delegate-campaign-meeting-kit.pdf; Shae McCrystal, Breen Creighton and Anthony Forsyth (eds), *Collective Bargaining Under the Fair Work Act* (Annandale, NSW: Federation Press, 2018).

106 See again the Introduction to this volume by Joo-Cheong Tham and Caroline Kelly.

Chapter 8

TEMPORARY MIGRANT WORKERS AND TRADE UNIONS IN AUSTRALIA: A COMPLEX RELATIONSHIP

Joanna Howe

Both globally and within Australia, there has been an acute transformation of labour markets characterised by the fragmentation of work and organisations and the growth in non-standard employment arrangements.[1] This is evidenced in the segmentation of labour markets, the casualisation of workforces and the triangulation of work arrangements. Temporary labour migration is now an embedded feature of many labour markets, and Australia is no exception, with visa holders constituting at least one-tenth of the Australian labour force. This chapter highlights these changes and challenges, through examining the complex relationship between trade unionism and temporary labour migration in Australia. It shows how trade unions that have been traditionally most active in the regulation of standard employment now have to adapt to representing the interests of a more flexible and less homogeneous group of workers, and they have to do so without straining relationships with their traditional rank-and-file membership in traditional jobs and industries. In this context, there is an urgent need for unions to engage with temporary migrant workers. This group of workers has been shown to be particularly vulnerable to precarious work and the wages and conditions received by this group of workers has far-reaching effects on all workers in the labour market.

This chapter begins by examining the complex relationship between trade unionism and temporary labour migration in Australia. It exposes a concerning paradox: although temporary migrant workers *need* unions more than most other cohorts of workers and face far greater barriers in joining them and accessing their help, Australian unions, with a few notable exceptions, have been largely unsuccessful in recruiting temporary migrants as members and representing their interests. This chapter then turns to a case study of the role of unions in the Australian horticulture industry and focuses on unions' new approaches under changed conditions in this industry. Temporary migrant workers on a range of visas are the mainstay of the horticulture industry's workforce, and unions have adopted new approaches to organising these workers and advocating for changes to government policy and regulation to better suit their interests.

Labour laws and policies, through recognising and supporting the work of trade unions, are vital for remedying the unequal footing of workers when negotiating with employers. This is particularly the case for temporary migrant workers who typically have far less power, resources and control over their presence and future in the Australian labour market. It is for this reason that trade unions are critical to temporary migrant workers to ensure their interests are protected in an Australian democracy where this critical workforce is rarely consulted about changes to their interests and cannot exercise voting rights. Conversely, as a growing proportion of the labour market, temporary migrant workers are critical to the future of the Australian trade union movement. Thus, there is a symbiotic and co-dependent relationship between temporary labour migration and trade unionism in Australia.

The Context

The rapid expansion of Australia's temporary labour migration programme has posed significant challenges for the trade union movement. There are close to 900,000 temporary visa holders with work rights (not including New Zealand citizens) in Australia through a cacophony of visa schemes,[2] some of which provide 'dedicated' entry channels into the labour market, such as the Temporary Skill Shortage visa and the Seasonal Worker Program (SWP), and others which provide 'de-facto' entry through visas for Working Holiday Makers and international students.[3] There are also an unknown number of undocumented migrant workers in the Australian labour market, who likely entered Australia on tourist visas, are visa 'over-stayers' or are in breach of a work condition in their visa.[4] For trade unions, the sheer number and complexity of visa arrangements in Australia poses enormous challenges in recruiting and organising temporary migrant workers. Language barriers, different cultural norms, limited community networks, geographical dispersion and the temporary nature of visa holders' employment in Australia all present as substantial barriers for union organisers in recruiting temporary migrants as union members. These barriers, combined with an increasingly segmented labour market, mean trade unions are often faced with organising different cohorts of workers performing the same work but with different levels of commodification by the employer.[5]

There is also an inherent dilemma in the relationship between temporary labour migration and trade unionism: should unions resist or embrace the advent of temporary labour migration as a feature of the Australian labour market?[6] In times gone by, Australian unions have been viewed as 'xenophobic' and 'racist' for their resistance to temporary migrant workers. More recently there has been a shift in the union movement's approach, with unions often arguing for limits on temporary labour migration at a macro level to protect job opportunities for local workers, exemplified in the debate over the labour provisions in the China-Australia Free Trade Agreement. However, increasingly unions are advocating for additional protections for temporary migrant workers once they arrive in Australia and are employed in the labour market.

It is hard to deny that temporary migrant workers are in need of additional protection in the labour market. As an established category of precarious work (see further Chapter 6 by Iain Campbell in this volume), many temporary migrants and in particular those in de-facto and undocumented visa arrangements experience widespread wage underpayments, substandard and exploitative working conditions as well as substantial barriers in accessing legal remedies. The demand-driven design of Australia's temporary labour migration programme means that employers are able to bolster their power over a temporary migrant workforce through wearing many 'hats' such as that of employer, immigration sponsor and, in some cases, accommodation provider.[7] Temporary migrant workers, therefore, have an even greater need for trade unions to be a countervailing force in the face of considerable employer power (see further Chapter 1 by Joo-Cheong Tham and Caroline Kelly in this volume).

Equal rights at work – regardless of migrant status – is a key principle of the *Universal Declaration of Human Rights*; the *International Covenant on Economic and Social Rights*; the International Labour Organization standards on labour migration; and the *International Convention on the Protection of the Rights of All Migrant Workers and Members of Their Families*. This principle is adopted by the *Fair Work Act 2009* (Cth) which does not exclude migrant workers from its scope. Nonetheless, equal rights under the law does not equate with temporary migrant workers being able to access those rights and exercise them in practice. A study of temporary migrants accessing unfair dismissal protection in Australia found that these workers faced (almost) insurmountable barriers in receiving either reinstatement or compensation for arbitrary dismissal.[8] Conversely, the importance of unions and community organisations in assisting workers to rectify wage theft was indicated in a recent study of temporary migrants' ability to access legal remedies in Australia, which found that workers who relied on unions or community organisations were far more successful in achieving some rectification of underpayments.[9]

Paradoxically, despite their need for additional labour protection, temporary migrant workers are typically less likely to proactively seek trade union assistance. A national survey conducted in 2017 found that only 4 per cent of temporary migrant workers stated that they were trade union members,[10] compared with approximately 10 per cent in the private sector.[11] There are notable exceptions, however, as trade unions in industries such as meat packing, horticulture and commercial cleaning have recruited and represented temporary migrant workers with considerable success.

There is an inconsistent approach to managing the involvement of trade unions in Australia's temporary labour migration programme. Two visa programmes specifically conceive of a role for trade unions. First, the SWP, a visa scheme designed to import foreign workers from Pacific nations to work on a seasonal basis in the Australian horticulture industry, provides a role for trade unions in its visa design. Second, the formation of labour agreements, which are formal arrangements negotiated between an employer and the Australian government to enable an employer to recruit skilled migrant workers, requires consultation with trade unions. Nonetheless, most of the other visa pathways do not conceive of a special role for unions in either addressing the vulnerability of a temporary migrant workforce or protecting local job opportunities. The government's own Ministerial Advisory Council for Skilled Migration (MACSM) which was established in 2012 by a Labor government as a tripartite body comprising industry, union and government representatives was reconstituted in 2015 by the Coalition government, with its composition unfairly weighed in favour of employers, leading to the resignation of the sole union representative.[12] Since then, MACSM has been dormant as an advisory body to the federal government.

There is also a democratic deficit facing temporary migrant workers in Australia which can be ameliorated through trade unions. The management of Australia's labour migration programme is characterised by a high degree of executive decision making which has led to deficiencies in public accountability and transparency.[13] Tham has identified that temporary migrant workers tend to be excluded from consultation around how their interests are affected by regulatory changes as these workers are typically never consulted on the impact of proposed regulatory changes.[14] This is despite the fact that changes in the rules of visa schemes have a profound impact upon visa applicants and visa holders. More recently, the decision to deny the JobKeeper payment during the COVID-19 outbreak provides another example of a failure to recognise temporary migrants as members of the Australian community,[15] a point underscored by the hostility of some regional communities towards temporary migrant workers and their request that these workers return to their countries of origin.[16] Notably, unions were vocal in advocating for the

JobKeeper payment to be extended to visa holders,[17] illustrating the fact that trade unions are now being 'called upon to address issues well beyond labour claims and labour equality, increasingly involving the social and legal status of migrants'.[18] In this way, the position of trade unions is not just in representing temporary migrants in the workplace but in a more comprehensive way, including their institutional power resources and ability to form coalitions to argue for their interests in changes to Australia's labour migration law and policy. The multidimensional role of trade unions in representing temporary migrant workers is particularly reflected in the horticulture industry, a topic to which we now turn.

Temporary Migrant Workers and Trade Unions in the Horticulture Industry

The horticulture labour market in Australia is a highly relevant site for developing this focus on the complex relationship between temporary migrant workers and trade unions because temporary migrant workers are the mainstay of the harvest workforce employed in picking, packing and grading fresh fruit and vegetables. Several studies have identified extensive reliance among growers on temporary visa holders.[19] There are seasonal workers from the Pacific under the dedicated Temporary Work (International Relations) (subclass 403) visa. These workers are employed through the SWP. There are also Working Holiday Makers (WHMs) under the Working Holiday (subclass 417) and Work and Holiday (subclass 462) visas. International students who reside in Australia on one of a range of study visas (subclasses 570–76) also make a contribution to the horticulture workforce. Of these four types of temporary migrants, WHMs are by far the most common source of harvest labour used in Australia; however, their engagement varies regionally. In 2017–18, 36,617 WHMs were granted a second year extension on their visa, with a likely 90 per cent of these earning this extension through working for 88 days in the horticulture industry. In contrast, in that same year, only 8,459 workers from the Pacific on the SWP were employed in horticulture.

Undocumented workers are also prevalent in the horticulture industry, although it is impossible to determine the extent and nature of their involvement. 'Undocumented workers' is a catch-all phrase to refer to temporary migrant workers in a range of situations such as: 'visa overstayers', when a visa is no longer valid because it has expired; visa holders without a right to work, which are typically migrants on tourist visas that do not contain a right to work in Australia; and visa holders in breach of a visa condition allowing a limited right to work. This last category tends to be international students in breach of the restriction preventing them from working for more than 40 hours a fortnight during semester. In each of these situations, the worker is considered to be 'undocumented' because they are in breach of the law and liable for deportation under the *Migration Act 1968* (Cth). Evidence suggests that the numbers of undocumented workers also vary from region to region, with virtually no presence in some regions, and in others, amounting to almost all the harvest workforce.[20]

It is not just the sheer number of temporary migrant workers in the Australian horticulture industry which makes this industry a relevant site for an examination of the relationship between trade unions and temporary migrant workers, but the particular vulnerability of this workforce, which means the need for trade unions is even stronger. There is now considerable evidence of the precarity of temporary migrant workers employed in the Australian horticulture industry.[21] A Fair Work Ombudsman (FWO) report found that 39 per cent of horticulture employers were non-compliant with labour standards.[22] The FWO's Harvest Trail Inquiry recovered over a million dollars in wages but its report indicated the FWO's belief 'that the full extent of wage underpayments is significantly higher than this'.[23] In 2016, another FWO report, following a two-year inquiry into the performance of work by WHMs, found that more than one-third of WHMs surveyed were paid less than the minimum wage, 14 per cent had to pay to secure regional work and 6 per cent had to pay an employer to 'sign off' on their regional work requirement.[24] In 2017, an online survey found that the worst paid jobs were in fruit and vegetable picking, where 15 per cent of respondents said they had earned $5 an hour or less and 31 per cent had earned $10 an hour or less.[25] A three-year study investigating the conditions of work in the Australian horticulture industry found that 'non-compliance is endemic and multi-faceted' and that the employment of WHMs typically involved substantial wage underpayments, with the lowest wage reported being $1 an hour.[26] Thus, there appears to be a particularly strong need for trade unions in the horticulture industry to enforce labour standards and to represent temporary migrant workers in situations of exploitation such as wage underpayments.

There are two main unions involved in horticulture: the Australian Workers Union (AWU) and the United Workers Union (UWU). Although the AWU has low membership coverage in the horticulture industry, the UWU has increased its membership through innovative and extensive efforts to organise and recruit temporary migrant farm workers in certain regions in South Australia and Victoria. The UWU's involvement in the horticulture industry increased significantly following the airing of the ABC *Four Corners* programme in May 2015 exposing poor working conditions in the industry in which some South Australian and Victorian growers were prominently featured.[27] This saw the UWU launch a national Fair Food Campaign. One of the goals of this campaign is to educate consumers about the origins of the fresh produce they purchase and to improve wages and conditions in the industry. In a report investigating labour standards in the horticulture industry, a union official from the UWU argued that the acceptance of unions being in the industry would ameliorate over time and lead to a gradual lifting of labour standards:[28]

> Three-quarters of the industry have been getting away with non-compliance and brazen award breaches for 30 years, and so there is of course a hostility towards the union. In other industries there has been some historical experience with unions being present, so there is more tolerance for unions.

Within the horticulture industry's temporary migrant workforce, unions have had to engage different strategies to recruit different groups of visa holders. Both the UWU and AWU are active in the SWP, recruiting temporary migrant workers from the Pacific as union members. Established in 2008, the SWP creates a pathway for workers from select Pacific island nations to work in Australia. Although the SWP accounts for a relatively small proportion of the horticulture labour force in Australia, the numbers in the SWP have grown steadily since its inception.[29] From its inception, the SWP was developed according to a tripartite model, involving unions, industry and government. This led to its design specifically incorporating a role for unions in inducting workers from the Pacific shortly after their arrival. Approved employers under the SWP are required to complete an arrival form for each batch of seasonal workers. This form requires the employer to confirm that the on-arrival briefing has included a presentation by the FWO and the unions. Nonetheless, despite the requirement that worker induction provides seasonal workers with access to unions, a report in 2019 found that worker inductions occur in a sporadic and inconsistent manner.[30] Although the relevant union and the FWO are notified via an automatic email from the Department of Jobs whenever an approved employer has had their request to sponsor a group of SWP visa holders approved, this does not specify the details of the workers' induction. There is no mandatory process to be followed that compels the approved employer to guarantee that unions, the FWO and other relevant parties are involved in the induction process. The report found evidence that some employers reported that unions never 'bothered to turn up' to worker inductions, whereas UWU and AWU officials reported that invitations to inductions were highly unusual, often did not provide details or the time or location and did not give sufficient notice to enable them to attend.[31] Another concern of unions officials was that when they were present at an induction, employers often stayed in the room and gave them insufficient time to present their role to seasonal workers. While there appear to be some deficiencies in the enforcement of the worker induction requirement in the SWP, it is an important mechanism for ensuring that temporary migrant workers are provided with contacts, information and support from unions upon arrival in Australia.

Although there are inherent challenges to recruiting temporary migrant farm workers who hold Working Holiday Maker visas, the UWU has had some success in recruiting this group as union members. For example, midway through 2016 it was revealed that the UWU had successfully forced the Costa group to the bargaining table at its Guyra, Victoria, site after 200 of its workers (mainly Working Holiday visa holders) had signed a petition indicating their support for enterprise bargaining.[32]

In addition, the UWU has been highly active in recruiting and organising undocumented migrant farm workers. This is a group which has traditionally never been unionised in Australia. To overcome the reluctance of this group to unionise, the UWU has employed union organisers from the same ethnic background and language of the main source countries of undocumented workers and developed key contacts over a long period of time within certain horticultural regions. The UWU has also employed in-house migration lawyers to assist undocumented farm workers to apply for other visas so that they can regularise their immigration status. The role of the UWU in helping enforce labour standards in the horticulture industry for undocumented migrant farm workers was recognised by the Fair Work Commission in November 2016.[33] The Commission exercised a rarely used power to allow the UWU access to the employment records of every worker employed on a vegetable farm in Victoria because of clear evidence of widespread wage underpayments.

The UWU has also been innovative in its research and advocacy work on behalf of undocumented migrant farm workers. It has commissioned research on their role and presence in the industry and formed coalitions with industry to argue for an amnesty for undocumented migrant workers to resolve their irregular immigration status.[34] This advocacy work goes beyond the traditional role of unions in advocating for labour law changes by recognising the importance of visa conditions and migration law in framing the vulnerability of temporary migrant workers (see further the discussion of the decommodification function of trade unions in Chapter 1 by Joo-Cheong Tham and Caroline Kelly in this volume).

Beyond their traditional representative and advocacy role on behalf of temporary migrant farm workers, in recent years unions in the Australian horticulture industry have made considerable inroads in using the supply chain to improve labour standards on farms. Before turning to the specific initiatives of both the UWU and the AWU to regulate the supply chain, it is important to understand the dynamics of the supply chain in the Australian horticulture industry.

Supply chains mediate the sale of produce harvested by fruit and vegetable growers. Before reaching consumers, this produce is purchased from growers by supermarkets, food retailers, food processers, wholesalers or sold through growers' markets. Produce sold to consumers overseas may require the involvement of export, import and other trading agents. Transportation and distribution companies will typically be involved in moving produce from farms to these other actors in the supply chain. Traders and other companies may be involved between these stages.

Each stage of the supply chain requires a commercial transaction in which the bargaining power of the grower to negotiate a fair price may be constrained. The often large and commercially powerful nature of 'lead firms' at the consumer end of supply chains, for example, supermarkets, wholesalers, transportation and distribution companies, accounts for why growers are often in a weak bargaining position.[35] Many of these lead firms have increased their commercial presence as a result of market concentration and business consolidation through mergers and acquisitions, which have been driven by financial pressures for increased short-term shareholder returns.[36]

These features have come to characterise agro-food industries in many countries. They have shifted power dynamics within supply chains from growers and other firms located at the producer end to lead firms closer to the consumer end.[37] This size means that lead firms often purchase produce from a large number of growers to both serve their consumer base and spread their risk. This can enable these entities to dictate the price and other standards to individual growers who must comply to complete the transaction and maintain the commercial relationship.

Generally speaking, the bargaining power of buyers of horticulture produce in the Australian market has increased in recent years while the bargaining power of the sellers of this produce has diminished. In particular, many large buyers of produce, such as supermarkets and large food brands, have been able to use their commercial power to dictate prices or make changes in delivery orders at short notice. This is evident in the 'price wars' between the major Australian supermarkets which have resulted in pressure on growers to reduce the costs of production.

Supply chain and labour issues in horticulture were a focus of the final report of the 2017 inquiry by a joint committee of the Australian Parliament into the establishment of a *Modern Slavery Act*.[38] The report noted that evidence to the committee:

> highlighted that the long-standing challenges faced by the horticultural industry to secure a reliable and efficient labour force have been compounded by recent changes to the relationship between supermarkets and suppliers [...] The Committee heard that the low prices set by supermarkets for produce is putting increasing pressures on farmers and growers to reduce labour costs to ensure farms are economically viable.[39]

Despite mounting evidence to the contrary, the major retailers have consistently maintained that responsibility for breaches of workplace laws in the horticulture industry is the sole responsibility of the FWO. Although major retailers encourage individuals or organisations that have evidence of a breach to take it to the FWO, the retailers do not largely get involved in investigating breaches themselves.[40]

Even following the 2015 ABC *Four Corners* investigation into exploitation of workers in the horticulture industry, in which certain grocery chains were implicated, the major retailers did not introduce more stringent auditing of the workforces of their suppliers.[41] At a subsequent Senate inquiry, a representative from Woolworths stated that it would not conduct an audit as this would place extra costs on suppliers.[42]

Despite the revelation of widespread exploitation particularly of temporary migrant workers, the major retailers consider Australia to be 'low risk' because of its robust workplace laws and mechanisms for monitoring compliance.[43] In her analysis of retailers' response to the ABC *Four Corners* investigation, Australian labour law scholar Rosemary Owens concludes that 'when confronted with the evidence of exploitation, the [retailers] frequently resorted to platitudes defending the values of their organisation and restating their commitment to ethical behaviour by all in the supply line'.[44]

To combat the reluctance of the major retailers to take responsibility for labour standards in the horticulture supply chain, unions have turned to leveraging shareholder power. Working with the Australian Centre for Corporate Responsibility (ACCR) and with a superannuation company with a large shareholding in Woolworths, the UWU was part of an innovative initiative to file shareholder resolutions at Woolworths annual general meetings in 2017 and 2018. The 2017 shareholder resolution was withdrawn prior to the annual general meeting after Woolworths agreed to implementing a process by which the union could vet labour hire providers working in the supply chain.[45] This led to Woolworths developing its Responsible Sourcing Standards which restricted its suppliers to labour hire providers which were registered under a state licensing scheme, were approved under the SWP or certified via a third party scheme. The following year, ACCR initiated another shareholder resolution because of union dissatisfaction with Woolworths' Responsible Sourcing Standards which did not engage with unions to vet labour hire providers and instead relied on a labour hire accreditation programme developed by the labour hire industry's peak body. The UWU argued that this industry-led programme did not sufficiently vet labour hire contractors and used its 2018 shareholder resolution to compel Woolworths to implement stricter reporting on labour conditions and for the retailer to involve the union in workplace education and grievance resolution procedures.[46] Following the 2018 shareholder resolution, Woolworths agreed to enter a memorandum of understanding with the UWU to meet regularly to discuss workers' rights. This is consistent with the UWU's long-term objective which is to compel Woolworths and other lead retailers in the horticulture supply chain to develop an industry agreement that would ensure the rights of workers in the supply chain are protected.[47]

Following the UWU's lead, the AWU has also sought to use supply chain pressures to improve labour standards in the horticulture industry. In 2019, the AWU, in conjunction with the Shop, Distributive and Allied Employees Association (SDA) and the Transport Workers Union (TWU) struck a new deal with Coles to promote ethical practices across the company's supply chain. This agreement came after the ACCR filed a shareholder resolution pushing Coles to embed a union voice within its supply chain.[48] The Coles agreement with the AWU, SDA and TWU includes provision to commission research into the benefits of ethical sourcing, along with exploring regulatory and legislative reform on labour hire use in supply chains. Workers will also receive more education on their rights, including information on freedom of association and migrant worker training.[49]

These types of multi-stakeholder arrangements being introduced by Woolworths and Coles have a longer pedigree in the United States. In that jurisdiction, tripartite agreements between supermarkets, food manufacturers, growers, industry associations and unions have been used to provide guarantees of individual and collective rights and wage standards to workers, assurances to growers that they will receive prices high enough to remain financially viable and dispute resolution procedures to enable continuity of production.

One type of multi-stakeholder initiative in the United States involves agreements that guarantee specific production volumes by growers in return for lead firms providing payments into an industry fund, which provides wage supplementations to workers. Agreements along these lines have been established between the Coalition of Immokalee Workers and major lead firms such as McDonald's, Burger King and Taco Bell.[50] Under the Equitable Food Initiative (EFI), certified growers agree to pay higher wages to workers, develop worker participation and development programmes as well as implement ethical recruitment practices as the basis for high-quality and more efficient production. Supermarkets and food retailers who participate in the programme require their fruit and vegetable suppliers to be certified and in return pay higher prices for certified produce to assist growers' compliance. The EFI's design is thus 'wholly built around the principle of shared responsibility and shared benefit within the supply chain'.[51] According to David Weil, a leading US academic and former head of the Department of Labor's Wage and Hour Division, these multi-stakeholder models of supply chain regulation can:

> address the distributional tension underlying fissured decisions [associated with commercial pressures from lead firms onto their horticulture suppliers] by making the lead food organization […] adjust the price it pays (and therefore the return it receives) to accommodate better conditions for workers at the base of the supply chain.[52]

Conclusion

The increasing reliance on temporary labour migration in Australia poses challenges and opportunities for the trade union movement. Traditional strategies of advocacy and representation require adaption to meet the needs of temporary migrant workers who are vulnerable because of their dual identities as workers and temporary migrants. As the case study attests, unions have been adopting new approaches to address the precarious migration status of migrant farm workers in Australia, advocating for changes to migration law and leveraging shareholder power to regulate the supply chain in the horticulture industry. Although these approaches are time consuming and resource intensive, they have the potential to bear fruit through the creation of industry agreements which lift labour standards across all farms supplying produce to the main supermarket retailers and provide unions with access to farms to monitor and inspect that there is compliance with the agreements. These new strategies have the potential to provide temporary migrant workers with greater voice to overcome democratic deficits given that this critical workforce is rarely consulted about changes to their interests and cannot exercise voting rights in Australia. It is clear that in the future unions will have to adapt and, in some cases, disregard traditional strategies because of new challenges in organising and representing a temporary migrant workforce. The precarious migration status of this workforce, their temporary nature and concentration in industries with structural non-compliance with labour standards means that unions will need to build broad coalitions across media, the public, labour, industry and government in order to address systemic disadvantage.[53]

Notes

1 See generally, Judy Fudge, 'Fragmenting Work and Fragmenting Organizations: The Contract of Employment and the Scope of Labour Regulation', *Osgoode Hall Law Journal* 44, no. 4 (2006): 609–48; Katherine V. W. Stone, *From Widgets to Digits: Employment Regulation for the Changing Workplace* (New York: Cambridge University Press, 2004), 67–83; Guy Standing, *Global Labour Flexibility: Seeking Distributive Justice* (Basingstoke: Palgrave Macmillan, 1999), 29–289. See also Chapter 6 by Iain Campbell in this volume and, in particular, his discussion of 'fragmentation' which he sees as stemming from 'multiple workforce groups, stretched out on a continuum of socio-economic inequality' [.

2 Australian Government, *Report of the Migrant Workers Taskforce*, 20 March 2019, https://www.ag.gov.au/sites/default/files/2020-03/mwt_final_report.pdf. See also Chapter 10 by Patricia Ranald in this volume and, in particular, her discussion of temporary overseas workers and labour rights.

3 Joo-Cheong Tham, Iain Campbell and Martina Boese, 'Why Is Labour Protection for Temporary Migrant Workers So Fraught?: A Perspective from Australia', in *Temporary Labour Migration in the Global Era: The Regulatory Challenges*, ed. Joanna Howe and Rosemary Owens (Oxford: Hart Publishing, 2016).

4 Joanna Howe, Stephen Clibborn, Diane van den Broek, Alex Reilly and Chris F. Wright, *Towards a Durable Future: Tackling Labour Challenges in the Australian Horticulture Industry* (Sydney: The University of Sydney, January 2019), https://www.sydney.edu.au/content/dam/corporate/documents/business-school/research/work-and-organisational-studies/towards-a-durable-future-report.pdf.

5 Joanna Howe, Stephen Clibborn, Diane van den Broek, Alex Reilly and Chris F. Wright, 'Slicing and Dicing Work in the Australian Horticulture Industry: Labour Market Segmentation within the Temporary Migrant Workforce', *Federal Law Review* 48, no.2 (2020): 247-271.

6 For a look at this dilemma in the European context, see Stefania Marino, Judith Roosblad and Rinus Penninx, *Trade Unions and Migrant Workers: New Contexts and Challenges in Europe* (Cheltenham: ILERA and Elgar Publishing, 2017).

7 Joanna Howe, 'Contesting the Demand-Driven Orthodoxy', in Howe and Owens, *Temporary Labour Migration in the Global Era.*

8 Joanna Howe, Laurie Berg and Bassina Farbenblum, 'Unfair Dismissal Law and Temporary Migrant Labour in Australia', *Federal Law Review* 46, no. 1 (2018): 19–47.

9 Laurie Berg and Bassina Farbenblum, *Wage Theft in Australia: Findings of the National Temporary Migrant Worker Survey* (Migrant Worker Justice Initiative: n.p., 2017), 30, https://apo.org.au/sites/default/files/resource-files/2017-11/apo-nid120406.pdf.

10 Bassina Farbenblum and Laurie Berg, Migrant Worker Justice Initiative, 'Wage Theft in Silence' (Migrant Worker Justice Initiative: n.p., October 2018), 14, https://www.mwji.org/highlights/wage-theft-in-silence.

11 Bradley Bowden, 'Three Charts On: The Changing Face of Australian Union Members', *The Conversation*, 5 July 2017, https://theconversation.com/three-charts-on-the-changing-face-of-australian-union-members-80141.

12 Paul Karp, 'Ged Kearney Quits Advisory Role after Being Bypassed by 457 Visa Changes', *Guardian Australia*, 21 April 2017, https://www.theguardian.com/australia-news/2017/apr/21/ged-kearney-quits-advisory-role-after-being-bypassed-on-457-visa-changes.

13 Joo-Cheong Tham, 'Work and Employment: Law-Making and Temporary Migrant Labour Schemes: Accountability and the 457 Visa Scheme', *Australian Journal of Administrative Law* 17, no. 1 (2009): 18–20.

14 Ibid.

15 Steven Hamilton, Anthony Forsyth and David Peetz, 'Australia's $130 billion Jobseeker Payment: What the Experts Think', *The Conversation,* 30 March 2020, https://theconversation.com/australias-130-billion-jobkeeper-payment-what-the-experts-think-135043.

16 Jessica Schremmer and Samantha Dawes, 'Backpackers Face Abuse and Job Losses in Regional South Australia as Communities Fear Coronavirus Spread', *ABC News,* 21 April 2020, https://www.abc.net.au/news/2020-04-21/backpackers-slammed-with-go-home-notes-amid-coronavirus-pandemic/12166012.

17 For example, see, 'Key Points on the JobKeeper payment', Australian Council of Trade Unions, https://www.actu.org.au/media/1449028/cv04-41-jobkeeper_factsheet.pdf.

18 Marino et al., *Trade Unions and Migrant Workers.*

19 Joanna Howe, Stephen Clibborn, Diane van den Broek, Alex Reilly and Chris F. Wright, *Sustainable Solutions: The Future of Labour Supply in the Australian Vegetable Industry* (Sydney: Horticulture Innovation Australia, 2017). Similarly, a 2016 study conducted by the Australian Bureau of Agricultural and Resource Economics and Sciences found that close to 70 per cent of seasonal horticultural workers were visa holders: *Horticulture Fact Sheet*, Department of Agriculture and Water Resources, Australian Government, Canberra, 2016, http://www.agriculture.gov.au/ag-farm-food/hort-policy/horticulture_fact_sheet#trade-statistics.

20 Howe et al., *Towards a Durable Future.*

21 See, generally, Caro Meldrum-Hanna and Kerry O'Brien, 'Slaving Away: The Dirty Secrets behind Australia's Fresh Food', *Four Corners*, 4 May 2015; Fair Work Ombudsman, *Harvest Trail Inquiry: A Report on Workplace Arrangements along the Harvest Trail* (Canberra: Commonwealth of Australia, November 2018); Ben Doherty, 'Hungry, Poor, Exploited: Alarm over Australia's Import of Farm Workers', *Guardian,* 3 August 2017, https://www.theguardian.com/global-development/2017/aug/03/hungry-poor-exploited-alarm-over-australias-import-of-farm-workers; Nick McKenzie and Richard Baker, 'Fruits of Their Labour: Investigation into Exploitation of Migrant Fruit Picking Workers in Australia', *Sydney Morning Herald*, November 2016, https://www.smh.com.au/interactive/2016/fruit-picking-investigation/; Elsa Underhill and Malcolm Rimmer, 'Layered Vulnerability: Temporary Migrants in Australian Horticulture', *Journal of Industrial Relations* 58, no. 5 (2015): 608–26; Senate Education and Employment References Committee, *A National Disgrace: The Exploitation of Temporary Work Visa Holders* (Canberra: Parliament of Australia, 17 March 2016); Joint Standing Committee on Foreign Affairs, Defence and Trade, *Hidden in Plain Sight: An Inquiry into Establishing a Modern Slavery Act in Australia* (Canberra: Parliament of Australia, December 2017); and Fair Work Ombudsman, *Inquiry into the Wages and Conditions of People Working under the 417 Working Holiday Visa Program* (Canberra: Commonwealth of Australia, October 2016).

22 Fair Work Ombudsman, *Horticulture Industry Shared Compliance Program 2010* (Canberra: Commonwealth of Australia, November 2010), 1.

23 Fair Work Ombudsman, *Harvest Trail Inquiry: A Report on Workplace Arrangements Along the Harvest Trail* (Canberra: Commonwealth of Australia, 2018), 4.

24 Fair Work Ombudsman, *Inquiry into Wages and Conditions*, 4.

25 Berg and Farbenblum, *Wage Theft in Australia*, 30.
26 Howe et al., *Towards a Durable Future.*
27 Meldrum-Hanna and Russell, 'Slaving Away'.
28 Howe et al., *Sustainable Solutions.*
29 The Fair Work Ombudsman estimates that there are approximately 130,000 workers employed annually in the industry: Fair Work Ombudsman, *Horticulture Industry Shared Compliance Program 2010.*
30 Howe et al., *Sustainable Solutions*, 124.
31 Howe et al., *Towards a Durable Future.*
32 Ben Schneiders, 'Historic Win for Low-Paid Farmers at Supermarket Supplier', *Sydney Morning Herald*, 30 July 2016, http://www.smh.com.au/national/investigations/historic-win-for-lowpaid-farm-workers-at-supermarket-supplier-20160729-gqgenh.html.
33 Richard Baker, Nick McKenzie and Ben Schneiders, 'Another Supermarket Fruit Supplier Caught Allegedly Underpaying Migrants', *Sydney Morning Herald*, 15 November 2016, http://www.smh.com.au/business/workplace-relations/another-supermarket-fruit-supplier-caught-allegedly-underpaying-migrants-20161115-gspu0v.html.
34 Joanna Howe and Ankur Singh, *Covid-19 and Undocumented Workers in the Australian Horticulture Industry* (Victoria: United Workers Union, 20 May 2020).
35 Jimmy Donaghey, Juliane Reinecke, Christina Nifourou and Benn Lawson., 'From Employment Relations to Consumption Relations: Balancing Labor Governance in Global Supply Chains', *Human Resource Management* 53 (2014): 229–52.
36 Peter Dicken, *Global Shift: Mapping the Changing Contours of the World Economy*, 7th ed. (New York: Guilford Press, 2015), chapter 13.
37 Bill Vorley, *Food, Inc: Corporate Concentration from Farm to Consumer* (Middlesex: UK Food Group, 2003).
38 The committee adopted a 'a non-legal umbrella definition' of modern slavery that included 'slavery, servitude, forced labour, trafficking in persons, forced marriage, child trafficking, debt bondage and other slavery-like practices': Joint Standing Committee on Foreign Affairs, Defence and Trade, *Hidden in Plain Sight: An Inquiry into Establishing a Modern Slavery Act in Australia* (Canberra: Parliament of Australia, December 2017), 47.
39 Senate Education and Employment References Committee, *A National Disgrace: The Exploitation of Temporary Work Visa Holders* (Canberra: Parliament of Australia, 17 March 2016), 282–83.
40 Ibid.
41 Meldrum-Hanna and Russell, 'Slaving Away'.
42 Senate Education and Employment References Committee, *A National Disgrace.*
43 Ibid., 283–87.
44 Rosemary Owens, 'The Global Challenge of Temporary Labour Migration: Regulatory Responses and Possibilities', in Howe and Owens, *Temporary Labour Migration in the Global Era*, 396.
45 Patrick Hatch, 'Woolies to be Grilled on Farm Exploitation at AGM', *Sydney Morning Herald*, 21 November 2018, https://www.smh.com.au/business/companies/woolies-to-be-grilled-on-farm-exploitation-at-agm-20181120-p50h76.html.
46 Ibid.
47 Brooke Littlewood, 'Farm Workers Rally for Better Pay, Conditions', *Sunraysia Daily*, 4 November 2019, https://www.sunraysiadaily.com.au/news/895201/farm-workers-rally-for-better-pay-conditions.

48 Dominic Powell, 'Coles under Pressure over Potential Worker Exploitation in Supply Chains', *Sydney Morning Herald,* 11 September 2019, https://www.smh.com.au/business/companies/coles-under-pressure-over-potential-worker-exploitation-in-supply-chains-20190910-p52ptv.html.

49 Dominic Powell, 'Coles Strikes Deal with Unions to Quell Worker Exploitation Concerns', *Sydney Morning Herald,* 5 November 2019, https://www.smh.com.au/business/companies/coles-strikes-deal-with-unions-to-quell-worker-exploitation-concerns-20191105-p537kz.html.

50 James Brudney, 'Decent Labour Standards in Corporate Supply Chains: The Immokalee Workers Model', in Howe and Owens, *Temporary Labour Migration in the Global Era*, 351; David Weil, *The Fissured Workplace* (Cambridge, MA: Harvard University Press, 2014).

51 Jennifer Gordon, 'Roles for Workers and Unions in Regulating Labour: Recruitment in Mexico', in Howe and Owens, *Temporary Labour Migration in the Global Era*, 329.

52 Weil, *The Fissured Workplace*, 262.

53 For a successful international example of this type of campaign, see the successful 'Ya Basta' campaign in California in 2016, organised by the Service Employees International Union United Service Workers West in California, which stands out as a success story of a trade union mobilising temporary migrant women and collectively fighting against sexual harassment. See further: B. Yeung, 'A Group of Janitors Started a Movement to Stop Sexual Abuse', *PBS*, 16 January 2020, www.pbs.org/wgbh/frontline/article/a-group-of-janitors-started-a-movement-to-stop-sexual-abuse (accessed 26 July 2020).

Chapter 9

UNIONS, FOSSIL FUEL EXPORTS AND A JUST TRANSITION

Jeremy Moss

A climate transition needs to make deep cuts to our emissions in a very short amount of time. Though the timeframe to achieve cuts sufficient to avoid harmful impacts is contracting rapidly, a transition must nevertheless aim to ensure that whatever policies are adopted achieve a just outcome, especially for the disadvantaged. Tax increases, lifestyle restrictions or the closing of whole fossil fuel industries must be managed in a way that does not place unfair burdens on those who are least able to bear them. The need to combine mitigation with justice is captured in just transition discussions that typically position a climate transition as part of a broader social renewal, such as the Green New Deal.[1]

The role of the union movement in this process will be vital. Unions can play a key role in arguing for and achieving a just transition given their representative position for the many workers who stand to be affected by a climate transition and in virtue of their substantial public advocacy capacity. Moreover, as Joo-Cheong Tham and Caroline Kelly argue in Chapter 1 to this volume, social justice is central to trade unions. This is reflected in their direct advocacy on behalf of their members and in their ability to achieve broader social change. Yet, the role of unions will not always be straightforward. While their potential for increasing the likelihood of a just transition is great, their choices will involve short-term disadvantage for some union members and significant readjustments for some unions as a whole, especially mining unions. Bringing about a just transition will involve job losses for workers employed in the fossil fuel industry – a small but significant subset of union members in countries such as Australia. Identifying what positive role the union movement can play as well as identifying potential 'flashpoints' deserves attention. This will be particularly true in Australia where the fossil fuel industry exerts such a huge influence on responses to climate change.

There will be many kinds of issues facing the union movement as a whole in relation to climate change, from protecting workers in industries that are acutely affected by climate change (aged care workers, firefighters and so on) to articulating the larger framework that a just transition needs to follow. These issues will be addressed in different ways by the different parts of the union movement which consists of individual unions as well as state, national and international organisations such as the International Labour Organization (ILO).

This chapter will focus on some of the more general moral reasons why questions of justice have to be at the forefront of a response to climate change, followed by an analysis of the issues that will affect those in the fossil fuel production and export sector and the role of the union movement in this process. This sector is of course not alone in encountering climate challenges, but it faces one of the most difficult adjustments. The reasons why the fossil fuel export industry is so critical to the union movement are several. Perhaps most obviously, it covers industries that have strong union representation. As we will see, the sector is also by far the largest cause of global greenhouse gas (GHG) emissions of any industry in Australia. Yet, the significance of those emissions is sometimes questioned because, among other reasons, they occur in other countries, leading to the misguided idea that Australia's focus ought to be solely on reducing the emissions that occur within our borders.[2] I will focus here on the key arguments that are often put forward for why this is a mistaken idea and how it ought to change the focus of the union movement's response to climate change. While there are many such arguments, those which are key turn on moral claims about who is responsible for climate harms. Before discussing these arguments and the role of unions in detail, we need to understand why pursuing a just transition – not merely mitigation – is so important. A focus on these more general arguments will hopefully strengthen the connection between ideas of justice, democracy and the union movement.

Motivating a Just Climate Transition

Why are questions of justice central to a climate transition and what kind of justice goals ought a transition adopt? The first point to note is that questions of justice are unavoidable. No matter what technologies are chosen or policy mechanisms adopted to achieve a climate transition, each will produce benefits and burdens which will have to be paid for and shared among individuals or groups within society. Sharing benefits and burdens within (and between) societies is a question of distributive justice. In this sense, justice is inescapable: we cannot avoid distributing the financial and other costs within society. The transformation of the stationary energy sector is a case in point. As some

Australian states transition to a greater reliance on renewable energy, debate concerning the impacts on power prices (particularly for poorer households) has intensified. Also controversial are questions of whether energy companies are profiting excessively and whether a switch to renewables will allow reliable and secure electricity supply. Add in the issue of whether there should be more 'distributed' energy (in part allowing for greater independence), and we have a complex set of justice-related goals that are (rightly) being considered as part of the switch to renewables. Failure to take these kinds of consideration into account will plausibly make the acceptance of an ambitious climate transition, and thus the associated potential benefits, less likely.[3]

A more instrumental reason for focusing on a just transition is that without it we risk alienating people who might feel they are taking on too many of the costs or not getting enough of the benefits. It is at least possible that perceptions of unfairness could lead to a backlash and Australia's own Trump/Brexit type reaction to a transition. Workers who feel they are not getting a fair deal might not support a transition and make a transition less likely to succeed. Unions could potentially play a major role in avoiding this kind of outcome.

Such considerations are, of course, not unique to climate transitions. Various industries and professions regularly face closures, mass redundancies and disruption due to international relocation, frequently with devastating effects on the economic, material and psychological well-being of large numbers of people. The current COVID-19 pandemic is a good example. Up until 2021, over $137 billion in spending commitments have been made in Australia to address the crisis. Some of the measures include 'JobKeeper' payments of $101 billion, and the increase of 'JobSeeker' unemployment payments by $550 a fortnight to $1,100 a fortnight for six months.[4] Other measures include free childcare ($1.6 billion), a range of tax write-offs for businesses and direct assistance to specific industries such as aviation. Given inevitable changes to people's lifestyles as well as costly new infrastructure, a climate transition will potentially involve a significant and longer-term societal adjustment. Yet the transition out of the COVID-19 pandemic and the climate transition must both attend to the way in which responses incorporate principles of justice.

One justice-related constraint on a just transition is that we ought not to cause wrongful harm to others where we can avoid it. This is especially true of Australia's impact on people in other countries. For the purposes of this chapter, it will be assumed that causing wrongful harm should provide a powerful and important constraint on our actions. It gives us a prima facie reason to restrain our actions and/or to be liable for the consequences.[5] One reason for invoking the injunction not to harm is its ability to be endorsed by a variety of foundational ethical theories and positions. For example, even if someone is a nationalist, it seems implausible to argue that there are no constraints on what one can do to foreigners, and the harm principle is a good way of capturing such a constraint. Not wrongfully harming others whether it is overseas or domestically should be a key part of any just transition.

But a climate transition also offers a more profound opportunity to achieve justice-related goals, namely, the opportunity to create a *more equal* society. Through improved transportation, cleaner energy or changes in the ownership structure of resources, a *just* climate transition should make society substantially better off. Thus, incorporating robust principles of justice into a climate transition has the potential to help avoid the worst of climate change while offering the possibility of social transformation.

One might worry that bringing some of these broader justice-based goals into our planning for a climate transition decision-making framework will overcomplicate an already difficult task. Further, trying to accommodate into the planning process an array of complex disagreements over which justice-based goals a society must pursue may even hamper progress. For example, requiring that a climate transition address health or education goals might invite the objection that such an expanded set of goals is excessively ambitious, too controversial and not focused solely on addressing climate change. This is an important point.

Yet much will depend on what kind of values or goals are at stake. What Simon Caney calls a 'maximal' approach to justice will have very specific and perhaps controversial commitments; for example, it might entail a radical political programme.[6] No doubt some maximal ideas of distributive justice are like this and would drastically complicate the climate transition process. In contrast, we can find elements of distributive justice that are more minimal and less controversial, where disagreement would not be so great, such as ensuring that workers and communities are no worse off.

A further point we need to consider in relation to a just transition concerns its scope. There are two related points here. As we saw above, the first is that a climate transition ought to at least focus on removing the risks of harm to others. One way in which we do that is by cutting our domestic emissions. But the other way in which we do that is by phasing out our exports of fossil fuels. Australia is not only a heavy domestic emissions producer, we also export a huge quantity of coal and gas, contributing significantly to global emissions. As the world's largest exporter of coal and liquefied natural gas (LNG), the amount of emissions produced from Australia's exports of fossil fuels is double our domestic emissions.[7] As we will see below, we are partly morally responsible for those further emissions, though they do not currently count in our domestic emissions budget.[8]

Given that our emissions have contributed to harming others, should we direct some of our efforts and resources toward the climate transitions of other countries? Or should we focus on making our own reductions as significant as possible? If Australia were to further reduce its domestic emissions, this would lessen the burden on other countries to cut their emissions. This might allow other countries to make a smoother climate transition. But a more important reason to think that Australia ought to focus on assisting other countries to transition pertains to the distribution of benefits. Transitioning in Australia will reduce our emissions, but it will also deliver benefits – cleaner environment and so on – to Australia and not to those countries who have been harmed by Australia's contribution to climate change.

All of these motivations for a just transition ought to mean that considerations of justice must be the focal point of a transition strategy, not a cursory 'co-benefit' or as a mere afterthought.

The Role of Unions

The union movement as a whole is clearly closely aligned with justice goals. The role of unions is to secure equitable conditions for their members and for working people more generally. In relation to the movement's response to climate change, unions have three major roles in ensuring a just transition. The first and most obvious is as direct advocates for those affected, particularly those whose jobs will be lost or badly impacted by climate change. By working to give those affected a voice and meaningful future options, unions can try to ensure affected workers are treated fairly. Unions typically perform these vital functions for any sector facing disruption, and climate disruption is no different. Indeed, much of the discussion from unions themselves focuses on these kinds of direct outcomes for affected workers. Unions typically demand that those who lose their jobs, coal workers for instance, have access to new jobs with equivalent conditions or which have generous severance packages.

But I'd like to note two more general functions that unions can – and should – play. The first is to advocate for all workers – not just those whose industries must close, such as coal mining. What happens to directly affected workers is a significant element of a just transition, but still only a part; there are more than *12 million* employed people in Australia, of which coal workers make up around 34,000.[9] Given many of these other jobs will also be affected by climate change and a transition, the role of unions should extend to include advocating for all those affected, whether directly or indirectly.

The second point to note about the scope of unions' role is the potential to act as 'norm changers'. In addition to advocating for those directly affected, unions have the potential to have a positive impact on the public debate concerning climate change. Those who oppose significant action on climate change often do so on the grounds of it being too costly or likely to risk energy or economic security. Because of the links that unions have with their members, they can act as a counterweight to these kinds of arguments. But, more importantly, unions have to be able to assist in promoting a progressive agenda on climate change, that, for instance, includes a discussion of the benefits and opportunities for social change offered by climate action.

The 'maximal' view mentioned above – highlighting the possibilities offered by a climate transition to make society a more equal place – is the kind of view that ought to be championed by unions. Unions' valuable role derives from being able to articulate the benefits that could flow from a transition, which, as we have seen, is important if we are to avoid a backlash against climate transition.

Yet achieving these goals will involve different commitments from the movement, and we need to be clear about who these goals apply to and in what way. The degree to which any part of the union movement could achieve any of these goals will depend on its resources, how it is affected and what impact it can have. National peak bodies are better placed to do much of what is required. The same might be true of state-level organisations. Individual unions might naturally focus on representing members whose jobs are directly affected. But even here, given the size of many unions, norm-changing activities are both desirable and possible.

Unions, Coal and Exports

Unions advocating for the benefits of a transition have the potential to have a positive effect on how a transition is perceived and hence its likelihood of success. However, such advocacy may conflict with the perceived short-term interests of some unions. If fossil fuel industries shut down, then workers in those industries will lose their jobs. Unless they are able to get new jobs in similar industries, this will obviously cause a decline in union membership. This is indeed the situation of unions who represent workers who are employed directly in fossil fuel industries such as coal-fired power generation or, more significantly, in the fossil fuel export industry. I want to focus on the latter, particularly the thermal coal export industry as it represents what I take to be the largest challenge to Australia's climate transition and is a source of contention for some unions. Unions representing coal or gas workers may stand in opposition to, or seek to delay action on, for instance, phasing out coal mines or hinder efforts by resisting opposition to the development of new mines.

To appreciate the significance of the challenge, it is useful to have some idea of the scale of the fossil fuel export industry. The value of Australia's overall export trade in fossil fuels is huge. In 2018–19, the value of the export of coal and gas was A$120 billion (metallurgical coal A$44 billion, thermal coal A$26 billion, LNG A$50 billion, with oil another A$9 billion).[10] These three exports alone make up about half of Australia's mining exports. The total mining sector (including iron, gold etc.) represents about 8.5 per cent of Australian GDP. To put that it in perspective, the combined total of Australia's fossil fuel exports dwarf other exports (iron ore A$64 billion, education A$35 billion).[11]

Yet the number of people employed in the coal industry is very small and declining. According to the Australian Bureau of Statistics, in 2019 there were around 34,000 people directly employed in the coal industry and 64,300 in the combined coal, oil and gas industry. Whereas there are around 12.5 million people employed in Australia overall. Coal jobs in particular are also declining. In 1995, there were about 107 jobs per 1Mt of coal, and in 2017 there were about 73.5 jobs per 1Mt.[12] It is worth pointing out that this jobs decline has happened during the long boom following the Global Financial Crisis (GFC). So even in good economic times the trend for coal employment is poor. This is not a growing industry.

Moreover, the industry is heavily subsidised by the Australian taxpayer. Estimates of the amount of subsidies vary between $12–47 billion per year for the energy sector as a whole. One estimate by researchers at the International Monetary Fund (IMF) estimates the subsidies for fossil fuels in Australia to be US$29 billion per annum: 2.3 per cent of GDP. That's around A$47 billion per year at today's exchange rate, which equates to every Australian paying A$1,867 per year compared to around A$78 as a one-off for bushfire relief.[13]

The huge volume of emissions that are produced from Australia's exported emissions (roughly double Australia's domestic emissions)[14] are clearly incompatible with addressing climate change. Yet, despite the size and significance of the fossil fuel export industry, it is often thought to be of less concern to unions and just transitions than industries that produce emissions in Australia. Typically this is for two reasons: the emissions are produced elsewhere and have an impact elsewhere so not our concern. Second, Australia ceasing its fossil fuel exports makes no difference as some other country will export fossil fuels and cripple industries here in Australia. I want to analyse these common arguments for why unions ought not to support the rapid phase out of the Australian fossil fuel export industry.

The first claim, that emissions produced from Australian fossil fuel exports are not Australia's concern, is based on an outdated 'territorial' model of responsibility. The argument is roughly the following. Why should we hold Australia responsible for the emissions that result from the consumption of our products that occur in other countries? After all, except for the emissions produced during extraction (which for gas can be very high), Australia does not directly produce these emissions. For the most part we contribute by being *producers* and *suppliers* of fossil fuels. Other countries – those that operate the power plants and steelworks – do the bulk of the actual emitting.

For this reason, countries such as Australia are often seen as only having responsibility for emissions that they have produced *directly* through their extraction and processing operations (their 'Scope 1 and 2' emissions in the language of the UN). So, when a coal company such as BHP sells coal, the emissions produced extracting the coal (Scope 1 and 2) are the responsibility of the country where it was mined, but the Scope 3 emissions are the responsibility of the country or company who consumes them.[15] This is what we called the 'territorial model' of responsibility. It is widely used as a model for how their responsibility for emissions and the harms that they cause should be counted.

Yet the responsibility of exporters such as Australia is much greater than the territorial model suggests. There is a powerful case for claiming that Australia has *a high degree* of responsibility for *at least part* of the harms resulting from their exported emissions (Scope 3), with implications for how the union movement ought to see its role. To see how this might be the case, let's bracket climate issues for a moment and consider the following analogies. Suppose a company produces and exports large amounts of tobacco to a developing country without health warnings for smoking. Given what we know about the links between smoking and death and disease, the exporting company is implicated in the harm caused, and, plausibly morally responsible for at least part of the resulting harm.

The same might be true for hazardous waste. Where one company knowingly ships its dangerous medical or industrial waste to a country that has low or no standards for its safe disposal, we might say that the exporter is liable for the at least some of the harms that result when the waste is not properly disposed of. This is still likely to be the case even though there is consent from the importer to take the waste.

More obvious still is the case of uranium exports. There are good reasons why many countries place restrictions on where companies can sell their uranium. The risks of weapons proliferation, accidents at reactors, storage issues, and so on are, in many cases, just too great to permit export. If a company were knowingly to export uranium to another country where safety is lax, we could rightly accuse it of acting irresponsibly and having a share in the blame if an accident were to happen. We could make similar analogies with the exports of other products, such as live animals or dangerous industries that use asbestos.

The harms caused by tobacco exporting and waste disposal are similar to climate harms in the morally relevant respects; fossil fuel exporters knowingly contribute to harming the significant interests of others in ways that could be avoided. In wealthy countries such as Australia, the export of fossil fuels is not the only means to maintain a high standard of living.

Common to all the above cases is the fact that harm is caused in a morally significant and blameworthy way and the exporting company is contributing something vital to the eventual harm. If it is the case that fossil fuels are exported in the knowledge that they cause significant harm or risk causing harm to significant human interests and the practice can be avoided, then Australian carbon majors are prima facie responsible for the harms resulting from the export of fossil fuels.

What this tells us is that the harm caused by Australia's exported fossil fuels ought also to be part of the response to climate change and not just Australia's domestic climate transition. If the union movement ought to be guided by not harming others, then this must extend to the harms caused by exports. What matters also is the impact of actions of Australia on the well-being of people – including union members in other countries – in other countries as well. Such a concern ought also to resonate with the commitments of those parts of the union movement that have an international focus such as the ILO. Part of the remit of the ILO is to promote social justice and 'internationally recognise human and labour rights'.[16] So many important rights will be threatened by the continued level of emissions from Australian exported fossil fuels as these represent a threat to the interests of workers not just in Australia but everywhere, given the huge volume of emissions Australia exports produce.

Is it really a harm?

Some might object that even though we ought to avoid causing wrongful harm, we might question whether the harm created by being a producer or exporter of fossil fuels really is like the more clear-cut cases of exporting medical waste or uranium. While we might agree that harming per se is to be avoided, how it is applied in this case is not appropriate. For instance, someone might object to my claim along the following lines. They might argue that while there are clear climate harms caused by exports, overall these harms are balanced out by the *benefits* that generating, say, power from coal brings. Coal-fired power plants have allowed developing countries in particular to produce cheap reliable electricity that has driven their economic growth and, at least initially, helped lift millions out of poverty. Coal is 'good for humanity' as a former Prime Minister of Australia claimed. Evaluations of emission levels should not be made in isolation from these broader considerations of justice: such decisions must be taken *all things considered*.[17]

But even if it is true that coal brings benefits within the country in which it is consumed, this does not account for an important feature of climate harms.

To see how this is the case, think about a common case of harm involving a worker in a dangerous industry. In the case where workers who knowingly accept dangerous jobs for high pay, while there is certainly a harm or a high risk of harm involved for the person performing the job, the benefits might in some circumstances (unfortunately) outweigh the risks because there is no other work, they have a family to support and so on. But the harm of climate change is not like this. Exporting fossil fuels may have produced benefits and harms in the country where the fuel is consumed. Using coal to generate electricity helps those who consume the electricity by allowing them to heat their homes or gain access to jobs, though it also increases local air pollution and associated negative health impacts. However, the harm of climate change potentially falls on everyone on earth to varying degrees because the effects of a change in the climate are diffused throughout the world. Producing emissions in one place does not just alter the climate in that place alone but also elsewhere on the planet. So the kind of response that claims that the benefits outweigh the harms ignores the *non-isomorphic* nature of the benefits and burdens in the case of climate change. There could, of course, be some trickle-down benefits from increased global trade or technological development, but by their nature these benefits are only a small fraction of the those created and probably not likely to compensate for increased exposure to extreme weather events, sea-level rises, reduced rainfall or bushfires. The burdens created by burning coal do not just fall within the borders of the country that consumes it.

Difference making

As we have seen, there are compelling arguments for why the phase out of fossil fuel exports ought to be advocated by unions. Yet one common response to this claim is that even if this is the case, stopping fossil fuel production is unlikely to make any difference. The major exporters and the governments who support them typically make this kind of claim. What are called 'no difference arguments' are familiar enough from a range of everyday problems. Take the example of polluting the oceans with plastic waste. The Great Pacific garbage patch, made up of millions of tonnes of plastic waste, covers an area larger than Texas.[18] Surely my throwing one bag in the sea will make only an insignificant difference to the problem?[19] The same argument is often made in relation to GHG emissions: if there are millions of tonnes of emissions released into the atmosphere each year, how could one person's emissions make any difference? This is the *insignificant difference* argument. Important though it is, it should not concern us here for the simple reason that we are here talking about the contribution of an entire country's export industry with huge emissions and not just one individual. In the case of Australia, there is little reason to doubt that the huge volume of fossil fuels exported every year makes more than an insignificant difference to the problem of climate change.

But there is another version of the no difference problem. This version of the argument claims that my action makes no difference because if I don't do it someone else will. Again, this is a familiar enough argument. Countries often claim that selling arms to a regime known for its human rights abuses is justified because if they don't sell the arms then some other country will and the abuses will go on just the same. As Tony Maher, national president of the Construction, Forestry, Maritime, Mining and Energy Union (CFMMEU), put it when commenting on whether Australia's trading partners will give up coal if Australia stop exporting, 'but they will not do so simply because Australia refuses to export to them. If one source dries up, they will turn to another.'[20]

This type of argument is also often made in connection to GHG emissions and especially with fossil fuel exports. Governments and corporations claim that if we don't sell coal or oil, some other country will, and why should we send 'our' (surprisingly few) jobs overseas when the coal or oil will be bought and consumed anyway?

One of our key criteria for whether an act is indeed harmful is that it contributes to the harm or risk of harm. In everyday language, this idea is captured by something having made a difference – without the provision of ammunition the bombardment would not have been possible. The claim at issue here is that the actions of, say, a coal exporter do not contribute to the harm of climate change as they do not make a difference because the exports and harms will happen anyway. Turning again to how this idea is applied in moral and legal theory, a commonly applied standard of something having made a difference in many legal systems is the 'But for' condition. But for the action of the shooter, the person would not have been injured. The idea here is that the action of, in this case the principal actor, was *necessary* for the harm to occur.[21] There may of course be other actions that were necessary as well.

Yet, requiring that a contribution be necessary in this sense – without it the harm would not have occurred – is a very strong sense of contribution. The context here is important. The kind of cases in which we are interested are forward looking – they are concerned with what a coal exporting country *should do* when confronted with alternatives. We don't know for certain what effect their actions will have. In many contexts the question that is asked is, 'might the action have made a difference and how much?'[22] If the action of the gun seller might have contributed to the murder, and they went ahead and sold the gun anyway, then we must hold them responsible to some degree. Thus a more plausible basis on which to determine whether actions contribute to liability for harm is to ask how probable it is that the agent's actions, when combined with other actions, will bring about the harm in question. That means that we are assessing their actions in terms of what we could reasonably expect to result from what they do given available information. If an agent knows that they might be about to harm some other agent, they have strong reasons not to do it.

In the case of the Australia exporting coal this would mean that without the supply of fossil fuels or lobbying on behalf of enormous level of subsidies we noted above, it is possible that the power plants would not have emitted as they did or as much as they did. So, are the actions of the Australian fossil fuel industry in producing fossil fuels likely to be done by others? Would they have happened anyway?

One problem with this way of justifying contributing to harm via exports is that of course that is not the way that exporters really think. It is implausible to suppose that Australian exporters spend literally billions of dollars on the exploration, development and then export of coal and gas simply in order to save another country from being an accessory to a harm. Relying on this argument as a justification for exporting fossil fuels is no defence at all if that is obviously not the real reason for exporting.[23]

A further reason to be sceptical of this argument is the difficulty and cost of fossil fuel exploration and production. To become a major supplier producing accessible products on a scale that is cost competitive is not something just any company or country can do. There's only a small cohort of companies that have the expertise and capital to become a major producer. In an environment where access to finance for fossil fuel production and insurance is becoming increasingly constrained, a major producer ceasing its production means that others may not immediately be able to increase their supply to fill the gap. Moreover, Australian producers have reliable resources, are close to the major markets, operate in a stable political and social environment that provides them huge subsidies as well as provide a product at a competitive price. These attributes may not be available to other producers. That is, after all, why other companies buy coal, oil and gas from Australia in the first place. Thus in deciding whether their actions in developing, financing and finally selling fossil fuels might be decisive in leading to harm, the answer is that it is likely. Recall that what we are interested in here is the actions that the exporters are faced with now, and not just a retrospective analysis. The question is: what should they do now? Will their actions simply be done by someone else?

Phasing Out Fossil Fuel Exports

In closing, I'd like to return to the question of how the union movement ought to advocate for the workers and communities that will be affected by the phase out of the fossil fuel export industry. Unions such as the CFMMEU who represent workers in the coal industry should of course negotiate the best severance or assistance packages for those affected. While this has to be one of the key roles that unions play, it is important to bear in mind broader justice considerations here as well.

For instance, one obvious source of funding for the payout of communities is a fossil fuel company selling their coal mines or gas deposits to fund some of the costs of assistance packages. Lest this be taken as a kind of back door policy for business as usual, it is important to be clear that phasing out has to be a real and urgent goal. Adopting phase-out targets that stretch far into the future and relegate closures to far off dates likely reflect dubious commitment.

Yet if the interests of all workers are to be protected, this source of funding is not desirable. Recent developments in the Australian coal industry provide a good example. In 2017, Rio Tinto sold its Coal & Allied Industries Limited to Yancoal, and in 2018 completed the sale of its final Australian coal assets, with the divestment raising a total of $5.39 billion.[24] On the face of it, this seems like to the right thing to do as Rio is no longer, as far as coal goes, contributing to the risk of climate harms. Yet if a fossil fuel company sells its fossil fuel assets to another company who will continue to exploit those assets, the risk of climate change is not diminished for the simple reason that the contribution will simply continue via another company.

Retiring assets in a safe and sustainable way, on the other hand, does not contribute substantially to climate harms. For this reason, unions must necessarily advocate for fossil fuel companies to retire their assets sustainably and fund transitions from non-fossil fuel assets. Yet not all (or any) companies are likely to fund the kind of packages that will provide enough assistance to affected communities or employees. This makes it more likely that any assistance will come from governments and not the fossil fuel companies themselves.[25]

Yet if government assistance is a possible way to ease a transition away from exports, this does not remove the need for hard choices within the union movement. I have argued that justice considerations must play a central role in shaping a climate transition. Justice goals not only determine how quickly we ought to transition, they can also be used to guide how the benefits and burdens of a climate transition should be distributed. The role of the union movement in this process as advocates and norm changes is significant. Yet if we are to achieve a transition that is just for all workers, then unions must focus on broader justice goals and not simply the interests of some sectors. This means making difficult decisions as a movement in recognition of the significant harm that Australian coal exports are inflicting on people all over the world.

Notes

1 The author would like to acknowledge the support of the Australian Research Council through their Discovery Grants programme through a grant entitled *Ethics, Responsibility and the Carbon Budget* (DP180100355). A grant from the UNSW Digital Grid Futures Institute A Just Energy and Climate Transition, provided funding for the research. The author would also like to thank Kitty-Jean Laginha for editorial assistance, the three anonymous reviewers, Caroline Kelly for helpful comments and the organisers of the *Symposium on the Centenary of the International Labour Organisation: Democracy, Labour Law and the Role of Trade Unions (July 18–19, 2019)*, Joo-Cheong Tham and Julian A. Sempill.

House of Representatives Concurrent Resolution 109, 116th Congress (2019). *Recognizing the Duty of the Federal Government to Create a Green New Deal*, https://www.congress.gov/116/bills/hres109/BILLS-116hres109ih.pdf.

2 Nicholas Stern famously estimates the overall costs of 'business as usual' on climate change at the equivalent of 5–20 per cent of global GDP, each year, for the foreseeable future. Several studies have concluded that climate change poses a severe threat to the survival of many species of plants and animals, largely through the elimination of suitable habitats, and the inability of species to adapt to changing conditions (IPCC, *Climate Change 2014: Impacts, Adaptation, and Vulnerability. Part A: Global and Sectorial Aspects. Contribution of Working Group II to the Fifth Assessment Report of the Intergovernmental Panel on Climate Change* (Cambridge: Cambridge University Press, 2014), 300–1). See also Nicholas Stern, *The Economics of Climate Change: The Stern Review* (Cambridge: Cambridge University Press, 2006). The damage done by Australia's exported emissions is in proportion to its contribution to this overall damage. For a comparison of Australia's domestic emissions with its exported emissions, see Climate Justice Protect, 'Climate Justice', https://climatejustice.co.

3 For further discussion of economic democracy in the context of achieving a just climate transition, see Chapters 2 and 3 by David Peetz and Julian Sempill respectively in this volume.

4 Parliament of Australia, 'Australian Government Expenditure', https://www.aph.gov.au/About_Parliament/Parliamentary_Departments/Parliamentary_Library/pubs/rp/BudgetReview202021/; Australian Government, Expenditure: Government of Australia, 'Budget 2020–21', https://budget.gov.au/2020-21/content/covid-19.htm.

5 There are numerous different accounts of the harm principle that might fit this context. For other similar discussions, see Elizabeth Cripps, 'Climate Change, Collective Harm and Legitimate Coercion', *Critical Review of International Social and Political Philosophy* 14, no. 2 (2011): 171–93; Joel Feinberg, *Harm to Others: The Moral Limits of the Criminal Law* (Oxford: Oxford University Press, 1984); and Henry Shue, 'Exporting Hazards', *Ethics* 91, no. 4 (1981): 579–606.

6 Simon Caney, 'Just Emissions', *Philosophy and Public Affairs* 40, no. 4 (2012): 255–300.

7 For a comparison of Australia's domestic emissions with its exported emissions, see Climate Justice Protect, 'Climate Justice', https://climatejustice.co.

8 Jeremy Moss, 'Mining and Morality', *Australian Journal of Political Science* 51, no. 3 (2016): 496–511.

9 Australian Bureau of Statistics, 'Labour Account Australia, Annual Balanced: Subdivision, Division and Total All Industries', 2019, http://stat.data.abs.gov.au/Index.aspx?DataSetCode=ABS_LABOUR_ACCT.

10 Office of Chief Economist, *Resources and Energy Quarterly December 2019* (Canberra: Australian Government, Department of Industry, Science, Energy and Resources, December 2019), https://www.industry.gov.au/data-and-publications/resources-and-energy-quarterly-december-2019.
11 Department of Foreign Affairs, *Australia's Top 10 Goods and Services Imports and Exports*, Australian Government, https://www.dfat.gov.au/trade/resources/trade-at-a-glance/Documents/top-goods-services.html.
12 Michelle Cunningham, Luke Van Uffelen and Mark Chambers, *The Changing Global Market for Australian Coal, Reserve Bank of Australia* (Sydney: Reserve Bank of Australia, September 2019), https://www.rba.gov.au/publications/bulletin/2019/sep/pdf/the-changing-global-market-for-australian-coal.pdf.
13 David Coady, Ian Parry, Nghia-Piotr Le and Baoping Shang, 'Global Fossil Fuel Subsidies Remain Large: An Update Based on Country-Level Estimates' (International Monetary Fund Working Paper, Fiscal Affairs Department, Washington, DC, May 2019), 35.
14 Climate Justice Protect, 'Climate Justice', https://climatejustice.co.
15 Simon Eggleston, Leandro Buendia, Kyoko Miwa, Todd Ngara and Kiyoto Tanabe, *2006 IPCC Guidelines for National Greenhouse Gas Inventories* (Japan: Intergovernmental Panel on Climate Change, IPCC National Greenhour Gas Inventories Programme, 2006).
16 International Labour Organisation, 'Mission and Impact of the ILO', https://www.ilo.org/global/about-the-ilo/mission-and-objectives/lang—en/index.htm.
17 Caney, 'Just Emissions'.
18 Laura Parker, 'The Great Pacific Garbage Patch Isn't What You Think It Is', *National Geographic*, 22 March 2018, https://www.nationalgeographic.com/news/2018/03/great-pacific-garbage-patch-plastics-environment.
19 Walter Sinnott-Armstrong, 'It's Not My Fault: Global Warming and Individual Moral Obligations', *Perspectives on Climate Change: Science, Economics, Politics, Ethics: Advances in the Economics of Environmental Resources Vol 5,* ed. Walter Sinnott-Armstrong and Richard Howarth (Amsterdam and London: Elsevier JAI, 2005), 293–315.
20 Tony Maher, 'Energy, Mining and Climate – Fact and Fiction' (Speech to the Sydney Institute, 27 November 2019), https://me.cfmeu.org.au/sites/me.cfmeu.org.au/files/uploads/ResearchSubs/Sydney_Institute_Maher_FINAL4.pdf.
21 See for instance, Herbert L. Hart and Tony Honoré, *Causation in the Law* (Oxford: Oxford University Press, 1985).
22 Sanford Kadish, 'Complicity, Cause, and Blame: A Study in the Interpretation of Doctrine', *California Law Review* 73, no. 2 (1985): 329–410 (360).
23 See John Gardiner, 'Complicity and Causality', *Criminal Law and Morality* 1, no. 2 (2007): 127–141.
24 Stephanie Chalmers, 'Rio Tinto Completes Its Exit from Coal with Sale of Queensland Mine', *ABC News*, 28 March 2018, https://www.abc.net.au/news/2018-03-28/rio-tinto-sells-last-coal-mine-kestrel/9597352#:~:text=Mining%20giant%20Rio%20Tinto%20has,Adaro%20Energy%20for%20%242.9%20billion.
25 For a discussion of the role and duties of the major fossil fuel companies or 'carbon majors', see Jeremy Moss, 'Carbon Majors and Corporate Responsibility for Climate Change', in *Climate Justice and Non-State Actors*, ed. Jeremy Moss and Lachlan Umbers (London: Routledge, 2020).

Chapter 10

TRADE AGREEMENTS, LABOUR RIGHTS AND DEMOCRACY

Patricia Ranald

Any discussion of trade agreements, labour rights and democracy must begin with an account of current trade policy. The dominant version of trade policy, part of a suite of economic policies known as neoliberalism or the Washington consensus[1] practised by successive Australian governments, has been brought into question from critics on both the right and left of the political spectrum, and most recently by the COVID-19 pandemic.

Neoliberal trade policy argues that a one-size-fits-all elimination of tariffs and other trade barriers by all countries will increase trade and investment and reduce prices for consumers in a globalised competitive market that will eventually raise living standards for all. Each country should specialise in exporting its lowest cost products or services, import everything else at the lowest possible prices as well as have zero tariffs, no active industry policies and minimal government regulation. This results in global production chains in which national economies are narrowly specialised and governments compete for global investment, leading to what some have called a race-to-the-bottom on labour and environmental standards. This model has been increasingly criticised by economists dealing with real-world outcomes, and by unions concerned with both workers' rights and social and environmental justice.

Critics of neoliberal trade policies point to the limitations of the basic assumptions of early-nineteenth-century neoclassical comparative advantage theory (e.g. that all resources are used in production, that capital is immobile) most of which do not apply to real-world twenty-first century economies.[2] Historical studies question whether the application of neoliberal trade policies have delivered promised economic development in many low-income countries, or whether they have instead contributed to global inequality. They argue that the established industrialised countries, and most successful developing economies, achieved their own industrial development through selective tariffs and active industry policies, before negotiating lower tariffs and other barriers. The imposition of strict neoliberal policies on low-income countries amounts to 'kicking away the ladder' to economic development.[3] Studies of more recent regional and bilateral trade agreements criticise their expansion into non-tariff areas of law and policy normally decided through national democratic processes.[4]

Right wing populists like Donald Trump have tapped into resentment of the failures of neoliberal trade policies, which have not always delivered on promises of jobs and growth for all. There are always both winners and losers from trade deals. But unions have rejected the simplistic responses of high tariffs on imports, trade wars, building walls and discriminatory immigration policies that will not restore lost jobs nor improve peoples' lives. They have advocated for alternative policies consistent with the principles of democracy, social justice, equality and solidarity outlined in Chapter 1 of this volume by Joo-Cheong Tham and Caroline Kelly.

The COVID-19 pandemic has also exposed flaws in neoliberal trade policies. These range from lack of local manufacturing capacity to produce essential health products like facemasks,[5] to trade rules that reinforce and extend 20-year monopolies on medicines, delaying access to cheaper versions of those medicines. Government interventions which are needed to save lives but which contradict neoliberal trade policy have opened up more discussion of alternative policies.[6]

This chapter explores the progressive critique by unions of the impact of neoliberal trade policies on labour rights, social justice and democracy, and the need for alternative trade policies that can ensure that trade policy will not undermine labour rights and be consistent with democratic processes. Neoliberal trade theory ignores the power imbalance between global corporations and business organisations, and unions and community groups which defend the interests of the less powerful. Global corporations pressure governments for trade rules that suit their interests, often at the expense of workers and communities which resist such rules.[7]

The 164 government members of the World Trade Organization (WTO) have legally binding agreements which include trade in goods, agriculture, trade-related intellectual property rights and trade-related investment measures. Since the 1990s, there has also been a growth in numbers of preferential bilateral and regional agreements which include only some countries and are not mainly about reducing tariffs. They have expanded to include complex forms of regulation in many areas which seek to maximise free flows of trade and investment for global corporations, and which can restrain governments from regulating in the public interest.[8] All trade agreements are legally enforceable through government-to-government dispute processes and, ultimately, trade sanctions.

The legal enforceability of trade agreements contrasts with United Nations (UN) and International Labour Organization (ILO) conventions which have complaints processes but no adverse consequences except ‘naming and shaming’. Adverse findings against governments for violations of conventions are often ignored by governments, including by the Australian government. For example, in 1998, following the passage of the Howard government’s *Workplace Relations Act 1996* (Cth), Australia was asked to appear before the Conference Committee on the Application of Conventions and Recommendations to explain its non-compliance with the obligations under the *Right to Organise and Collective Bargaining Convention* but the government ignored the ILO body’s concerns.[9]

This chapter analyses four of impacts of neoliberal trade policy on labour rights, social justice and democracy, and union responses to them. The first is the impact on the global race-to-the-bottom on labour rights in the absence of effective government commitments to enforceable labour rights. The second is the influence of transnational corporations like pharmaceutical companies in achieving other types of international trade rules which suit their interests, like stronger medicine monopolies that delay the availability of cheaper medicines. The third is the inclusion in trade agreements of additional legal rights for transnational investors that enable them to claim compensation of millions and, in some cases, billions of dollars in international tribunals over changes in domestic legislation, including health, environmental and labour regulation. The fourth is the secrecy and lack of democratic process in trade negotiations themselves.

Unions, as key democratic mass organisations, have been among the most consistent critics of neoliberal trade policies and have made proposals for alternative policies that are summarised in the conclusion.

Labour Rights

The neoliberal trade model of global production chains encourages competition to provide the lowest labour and other costs for exports, which can erode workers’ rights, especially in low-income countries. This often occurs in export processing zones or export industries where the workers have no effective labour rights to join a union or engage in collective bargaining.

One study done for Oxfam in 2004 summarised the impacts on workers in these industries:

> Supermarkets and clothing stores source the products that they sell from farms and factories worldwide. At the end of their supply chains, the majority of workers – picking and packing fruit, sewing garments, cutting flowers – are women. Their work is fuelling valuable national export growth. And their jobs could be providing the income, security, and support needed to lift them and their families out of poverty. Instead, women workers are systematically being denied their fair share of the benefits brought by globalisation. Commonly hired on short-term contracts – or with no contract at all – women are working at high speed for low wages in unhealthy conditions. They are forced to put in long hours to earn enough to get by. Most have no sick leave or maternity leave, few are enrolled in health or unemployment schemes, and fewer still have savings for the future. Instead of supporting long-term development, trade is reinforcing insecurity and vulnerability for millions of women workers.[10]

A 2019 study commented on declining labour standards in the global clothing industry:

> The apparel sector has long been associated with the worst end of labour standards. However, these conditions have deteriorated further with the emergence of the fast fashion and super-fast fashion models. These changes have prompted an increased 'disposability' approach to clothing where the business model is based upon cheap goods with ever-shorter product life cycles and profits generated through volumes of goods sold.[11]

Such competition encourages investors to move production from one low-income country to another where costs are lower. For example, a 2019 study reported that after Chinese labour costs increased as the result of the labour law introduced in 2008, some international companies relocated production to Vietnam, saving them a third of labour costs.[12] There are similar reports of companies moving to Cambodia and Bangladesh.[13]

A notorious example of lack of workers' rights in export processing industries is the collapse in 2013 of the Bangladeshi Rana Plaza garment factory building. Workers left a dangerous building when cracks appeared, but had no effective rights to refuse when they were ordered back into the building. The building then collapsed, killing 1,200 people, mostly women and children. Those factories were supplying garments to retail stores in Australia.[14]

More recently there have been allegations of forced labour in Western China contributing to production chains for exports of clothing to Australia.[15] The China-Australia Free Trade Agreement gives preferential zero tariff access for Chinese imports to Australia but has no commitments by either government about labour rights.[16] If these allegations were proven to be accurate, there would be no means for the Australian government to raise the issue of whether such products should have preferential access to Australia, and there is no obligation on the Chinese government to take action to end forced labour.

Unions have responded to the erosion of labour rights in export industries by advocating that governments entering into trade agreements should make legally enforceable commitments to abide by ILO conventions on labour rights, including freedom of association, the right to organise and bargain collectively, safe hours of work, health and safety standards, no child labour, no forced labour and no discrimination in the workplace.[17]

The Australian Council of Trade Unions (ACTU) has also supported calls from environmental organisations that governments should make enforceable commitments to UN environmental agreements, including agreements to reduce carbon emissions and combat climate change. The ACTU advocates that both labour and environment chapters in trade agreements should be enforced through the same government-to-government dispute process as other chapters, whereby failure to implement commitments can result in trade penalties.[18] But WTO agreements and most other bilateral and regional trade agreements still do not include such enforceable labour rights commitments[19] despite the promise of them in the original post-Second World War proposal for an international trade organisation.[20]

Australia's bilateral agreements with Malaysia, Japan, China, Hong Kong and Indonesia do not include any reference to labour rights or environmental standards.[21] Nor does the Australia-New Zealand-ASEAN regional Free Trade Agreement.[22] The giant Regional Comprehensive Economic Partnership (RCEP) text signed in November 2020 between Australia, New Zealand, China, Japan, South Korea and the 10 ASEAN countries does not include any chapters on labour rights or environmental standards.[23]

There are some examples of labour rights chapters in Australia's trade agreements but they vary in enforceability. Australia's agreements with the United States and South Korea have labour rights and environment chapters which are aspirational only and have no disputes processes to enforce them.[24] The Comprehensive and Progressive Trans-Pacific Partnership (CPTPP), also known as the TPP-11,[25] which Australia has ratified, does have labour and environment chapters with their own specific disputes processes. The CPTPP labour chapter is modelled on some US agreements with Central and South American countries. Labour chapters have been part of US trade agreements since unions succeeded in pressuring the Democrat majority in Congress to support them in the North American Free Trade Agreement.[26]

However, the International Trade Union Confederation (ITUC) has argued that the range of labour rights commitments in the CPTPP is limited.

Examples include that its rules apply only to trade-related sectors of the economy, there is no commitment to ban the imports of forced and child labour, and that they only 'discourage' such imports. The disputes process is specific to the chapter and is very lengthy and convoluted, compared with the government-to-government dispute process that applies to other chapters in the agreement.[27] Environment organisations have made similar criticisms of the TPP-11 environment chapter.[28]

The European Union (EU) includes a social or sustainable development chapter dealing with labour and environmental standards, and other social issues in its agreements, but the government-to-government dispute process does not apply to that chapter. The EU prefers to use persuasion rather than trade penalties on these issues, and this is the approach being taken in its current negotiations for a free trade agreement with Australia.[29] European trade unions have called for greater legal enforceability.[30]

In summary, trade agreements made through the WTO, and most regional and bilateral trade agreements made by Australia, do not have legally binding commitments to implement labour rights or environmental standards. Union advocacy has resulted in some labour rights chapters that are aspirational, and others that have lengthy and convoluted disputes processes compared with the government-to-government dispute process that applies to other chapters in the agreements. Despite some progress, union advocacy has not yet met its goals of preventing downward pressure on labour rights, especially in developing countries.

Temporary Overseas Workers and Labour Rights

Some aspects of trade agreements have also had impacts on labour rights in Australia. The inclusion in trade agreements of clauses which increase the numbers of temporary overseas workers has been driven by employer demands and has contributed to downward pressure on labour rights for those workers in Australia. The vulnerability of these workers, which had been exposed in recent years by a series of studies, has been spotlighted by the COVID-19 pandemic, since the government has excluded them from payments available to permanent Australian residents and citizens.[31]

Australia is a nation built on immigration and has a permanent migration scheme which has created a vibrant multicultural society. Permanent migrants have the same rights at work as other Australians. Their employment is not dependent on the sponsorship of one employer, and they cannot be deported if they lose their employment.

Temporary work visas for overseas workers were originally designed to address specific skills shortages identified by employers and were subject to local labour market testing to establish whether there was a skills shortage. However, their use has expanded since the 1990s, and there are now many different forms of temporary work visas, including the Temporary Skill Shortage visa, training visas, Working Holiday visas, Seasonal Work visas and student visas (the latter permit a limited number of working hours). The number of temporary workers utilising these visas has greatly increased. The Migrant Workers' Task Force established by the federal government reported that there were over 800,000 temporary visa workers in Australia in 2018.[32] Temporary workers are in a weaker bargaining position than permanent migrants because they are often sponsored by a single employer, or dependent on the employer for extension of their visa, and loss of their employment can lead to deportation. This leaves them vulnerable to exploitation.

Increases in numbers of temporary overseas workers are now being included as legally binding commitments in trade agreements. The removal of the requirement for labour market testing and/or increases in the numbers of specific categories of temporary workers are found in the China-Australia Free Trade Agreement,[33] the Korea-Australia Free Trade Agreement,[34] the CPTPP with 10 other countries[35] and the Indonesia Free Trade Agreement.[36] The PACER-Plus agreement with Pacific Island countries has a parallel government-to-government agreement for temporary seasonal workers in the horticultural and tourism industries.[37]

Academic studies comparing various recent trade agreements have demonstrated that governments are using temporary work visas as a means of deregulating labour markets. Such arrangements create groups of workers with less bargaining power who are more vulnerable to exploitation because loss of their employment can lead to deportation.[38] A survey of temporary overseas workers in Australia published in 2017 by University of New South Wales academics found temporary overseas workers experienced widespread wage theft.[39] Similar evidence was provided in 2017 to the Joint Parliamentary Committee Inquiry into a *Modern Slavery Act*[40] and by a 2019 study of the horticultural industry.[41] The evidence from these studies shows gross violations of Australian minimum work standards including failure to pay even minimum wages, long hours of work, and lack of health and safety training leading to workplace injuries, as well as lack of effective freedom of association and collective bargaining rights. Chapter 8 by Joanna Howe in this volume documents the efforts by unions to organise temporary workers in the horticultural industry and recover lost wages.

Since the COVID-19 pandemic, thousands of temporary workers and overseas students have lost their jobs but are not eligible for government payments. The government has abandoned responsibility and told them to return to their home countries, but many lack the means to do so.[42] The ACTU has advocated for these workers to be included in the pandemic wage subsidy schemes and to receive unemployment payments.[43]

In summary, the inclusion of arrangements for temporary workers driven by employer demands in trade agreements without effective protection of their labour rights treats these workers as commodities, creating a pool of workers vulnerable to extreme exploitation. They have also been excluded from payments and social supports available to other workers. Unions have exposed these conditions, won back-payment of wages for some workers, and advocated for them to have access to the same social supports as other workers.

Stronger Monopolies on Medicines

In addition to their impact on labour rights, trade agreements have expanded into many other social policy areas previously regarded as the domain of more transparent democratic national parliamentary processes, and for which unions have advocated as part of their broader commitment to social justice.

One of the most controversial examples is the achievement of global pharmaceutical companies in influencing US, European and Japanese governments to use various means in bilateral and regional trade agreements to achieve longer monopolies on medicines. Pharmaceutical companies are among the most profitable companies in the world.[44] Yet they have persuaded governments they need more than the 20-year patent monopoly that was achieved in the WTO Agreement on Trade-Related Aspects of Intellectual Property Rights of 1995. This process of extending monopolies has been documented by public health scholars, as well as the Productivity Commission.[45] Australian unions have consistently supported affordable access to medicines since the beginnings of the Pharmaceutical Benefits Scheme under the Chifley Labor government.[46] They have supported access to health care more generally in the form of Medicare established as part of the social wage component of the Accord between the ACTU and the Labor government in 1983.[47]

Delays in the availability of cheaper medicines can increase public health costs by hundreds of millions each year in Australia and other high-income countries where governments subsidise medicine prices[48] and can make medicines simply unaffordable in low-income countries.[49]

The extension of data protection rules for biologic medicines, which are the most expensive medicines used to treat cancer and other life-threatening diseases, was included at the insistence of the United States in the original TPP-12 agreement. These provisions were opposed by unions, community organisations and most other governments, and they were suspended (not removed) when the United States left the agreement, pending a possible return of the United States to the agreement.[50]

During the pandemic, WTO 20 year patent monopolies mean that pharmaceutical companies control global vaccine production. Governments have to negotiate with them about both quantities and price of COVID-19 vaccines, despite the fact that most were developed with public investment. High-income countries are first in line while the majority in low-income countries will not have access to vaccines until 2022 or 2023.[51] Unions have supported the proposal from South Africa and India, and over 100 other low-income countries out of 164 WTO members and the World Health Organization for a temporary waiver to WTO patent rules during the pandemic, arguing the waiver would enable faster and fairer access to vaccines in low-income countries.[52]

In summary, the use of trade agreements to strengthen monopolies on medicines exemplifies the extent of corporate influence in the trade agreement process. Delays in the availability of cheaper medicines disadvantage workers and communities, with the worst impacts in developing countries. In the context of the COVID-19 epidemic, public health advocates are debating how to move outside the monopoly patent model to develop vaccines that will be accessible to all.[53] Australian and international unions, public health and other community organisations have supported demands by low-income countries for changes to WTO rules to enable more equitable access to COVID-19 vaccines.

Legal Rights for Global Corporations to Sue Governments

The third example of the disproportionate influence of global corporations on trade agreements and negative impacts on workers and communities that have been resisted by unions is the use of trade agreements to give additional legal rights to global corporations that already have enormous market power. As explained above, all trade agreements are enforced by government-to-government dispute processes, and this is the only disputes mechanism available in the WTO. However global corporations have succeeded in persuading governments to include in older bilateral investment agreements and more recent bilateral and regional trade agreements a process known as Investor-State Dispute Settlement (ISDS). This gives individual foreign (but not local) investors the right to bypass national courts and sue governments for millions in compensation in a non-WTO international investment tribunal if they can claim that a change in law or policy has harmed their investment, even if the change is in the public interest.[54] Unions have argued that this undermines the democratic process and hard-won social policies and labour rights.

Legal experts like former Australian High Court Chief Justice Robert French and international investment law expert George Kahale have argued that ISDS tribunals are not independent and lack the legal safeguards of national systems. The tribunals consist of investment law experts who can continue to be practising advocates, and there are no precedents or appeals.[55] As of April 2020 there were over 1,000 known ISDS cases, many against public interest legislation or policy.[56] Cases against health, environment, Indigenous land rights and labour laws show the scope of ISDS challenges to democratic regulation.

The Philip Morris Tobacco company used ISDS to claim billions of dollars from the Australian government after the tobacco companies lost their bid for compensation in Australia's High Court for the 2012 plain packaging law and had to pay all of the Australian government's costs. Philip Morris, a US-based company, could not use ISDS in the United States-Australia free trade agreement because union and community opposition pressured the Howard government to refuse to include ISDS in that agreement. Philip Morris found an obscure Hong Kong-Australia investment agreement that contained ISDS, shifted some assets to Hong Kong, claimed to be a Hong Kong company and launched a case that claimed billions in compensation.[57]

It took almost five years for the ISDS tribunal to decide that Philip Morris was not a Hong Kong company and that the case was an abuse of process. It took a further four years and two Freedom of Information cases to discover that the arbitration and legal costs to the Australian government were A$24 million and that the Australian government only recovered half of them.[58] Even when governments win cases, they can lose tens of millions defending them.

The US Bilcon mining company did succeed in winning millions of dollars of compensation from Canada because a quarry development was refused by a provincial government for environmental reasons.[59] The US Westmoreland Coal Company is suing Canada over Alberta's decision to phase out coal-powered energy,[60] and other cases against government actions to reduce emissions are predicted.[61]

The Canadian Bear Creek mining company won US$36 million in compensation and costs from Peru because Peru cancelled a mining contract after the company failed to obtain free, prior and informed consent from Indigenous people about the mine.[62] The company was compensated despite the fact it had ignored both Peruvian and international law on informed consent from Indigenous people.

The French Veolia company sued Egypt for compensation for a rise in the minimum wage as part of a dispute over a local government contract. The case took seven years and was lost by the company, but there is no public information about the costs to the Egyptian government.[63]

ISDS clauses are included in Australian agreements already in force. These include the China-Australia Free Trade Agreement; the Korea, Indonesia and

Hong Kong agreements; the Australia-NZ agreement with ASEAN; and the CPTPP or TPP-11.[64]

Unions and other community organisations have strongly opposed ISDS,[65] and governments have been influenced by these social movements. Most ISDS cases are lodged against developing countries, and damages of billions have been awarded against them. Brazil, South Africa, India and Indonesia have not ratified or have withdrawn from bilateral investment agreements that contain ISDS.[66]

There have been increasing numbers of cases against industrialised countries. In January 2019, the 28 EU member states decided to terminate ISDS arrangements between themselves, after several notorious cases against environmental and health regulation and a decision by the European Court of Justice.[67] The EU is not including ISDS in its current negotiations for an EU-Australia free trade agreement.[68] In the longer term, Europe is pursuing a controversial proposal for a permanent Multilateral Investment Court, which would still allow foreign investors to sue governments but would attempt to address procedural concerns about temporary tribunals and lack of precedents and appeals.[69]

The United States and Canada have excluded ISDS from application to each other in the revised North America Free Trade Agreement and the United States-Mexico-Canada Agreement.[70] The two institutions that oversee ISDS cases, the United Nations Commission on International Trade Law and the World Bank International Centre for Settlement of Investment Disputes, are conducting reviews of the ISDS system.[71]

The COVID-19 pandemic has also exposed the dangers of ISDS. Law firms specialising in ISDS cases are already advising corporations of possible ISDS cases against government actions taken to address the pandemic. An international arbitration law firm Aceris Law LLC has told its clients thus:

> While the future remains uncertain, the response to the COVID-19 pandemic is likely to violate various protections provided in bilateral investment treaties and may bring rise to claims in the future by foreign investors […] While States may invoke *force majeure* and a state of necessity to justify their actions, as observed in previous crises that were economic in nature, these defences may not always succeed. [72]

Legal scholars critical of ISDS cite more examples of such advice from law firms. Based on the experience of ISDS cases against government actions taken in previous crises, they estimate that governments could face many possible ISDS cases after the pandemic is over.[73]

Unions and other community organisations have responded to these threats by urging governments to suspend ISDS clauses in trade agreements for pandemic-related cases, and to remove ISDS from trade agreements in the longer term.[74]

In summary, unions have opposed ISDS because it gives additional legal rights to global corporations at the expense of workers and communities, and it has resulted in cases against health, environmental and labour laws as well as against pandemic-related regulation. Opposition from unions and other social movements and damages of billions awarded against some governments have resulted in exclusion of ISDS from some trade agreements.

The Trade Agreement Process and Democratic Rights

The fourth impact of trade agreements is on the democratic rights of workers and communities. Trade agreements enable decisions about workers' rights, temporary workers, stronger monopolies on medicines and corporate rights to sue governments described above to be made in secret, only to become public after agreements are signed.

The current Australian process is a Cabinet process which excludes Parliament as well as the public. Cabinet makes the decision to initiate trade negotiations and receives reports on the progress of negotiations, but the text remains secret until the negotiations are completed. Cabinet then makes the decision to sign the completed agreement. It is only after the agreement is signed that the text is tabled in Parliament and released to the public.[75]

However, the parliamentary process is extremely limited. The Joint Standing Committee on Treaties reviews the agreement but it cannot make changes to the text. Since the government has a majority on the committee, it usually endorses the agreement. Parliament does not vote on the text of the agreement, only on the implementing legislation, which is mostly confined to changes in tariffs.[76]

There are examples of more open processes. The WTO releases draft negotiating texts before they are signed,[77] as does the EU.[78] In the United States, Congress votes on the whole agreement, not just the implementing legislation.[79]

The Australian process was strongly criticised by a 2015 Senate Inquiry report aptly entitled *Blind Agreement* which recommended a more open process.[80] Suggested changes to the trade agreement process made by unions[81] and community organisations[82] include:

- Parliament, not Cabinet, should make the decision to enter trade negotiations;

- negotiating texts should be released and there should be regular consultation about them with unions and community groups as well as with business organisations;
- the completed text should be released and independent evaluations of its economic, health, gender and environmental impacts should be published before it is signed; and
- Parliament should vote on the whole text of the agreement not just the implementing legislation.

In summary, unions have opposed the secrecy and lack of accountability of the current Australian trade process and have proposed a more open and democratic process consistent with union principles.

Conclusion

The COVID-19 pandemic provides further opportunities for unions to promote alternatives to both current neoliberal trade policy and Trump-style unilateralism. Unions have participated in this debate as leading mass democratic organisations advocating for workers' rights and broader social justice goals. Trade can improve people's lives if it is part of an economic policy that delivers employment and higher living standards in an environmentally sustainable society that rejects discrimination and respects human rights and labour rights. This need not mean a return to high tariffs but can combine expanded trade with active industry policies that enable a more diverse economy capable of providing essential health products. Manufacturing, services, agriculture, sustainable energy and other sectors combined with high quality education, health and other essential services can support decent work based on labour rights.

Unions advocate[83] that trade rules should be negotiated openly and democratically in a system which includes all governments and provides for the specific needs of developing countries. Trade agreements should not prevent governments from regulating in the public interest. They should not strengthen monopolies, nor give additional legal rights like ISDS to global corporations which already have enormous market power. And trade agreements should be based on internationally agreed and fully enforceable labour rights and environmental standards, to counter the global race-to-the-bottom on these standards.

Notes

1 Joseph Stiglitz and Andrew Charlton, *Fair Trade for All* (Oxford: Oxford University Press, 2005), 2.

2 Graham Dunkley, *Free Trade, Myth, Reality and Alternatives* (London and New York: Zed Books, 2004), 18–62; Jim Stanford, *Economics for Everyone*, 2nd ed. (London: Pluto Press, 2015), 304–11.

3 Ha-Joon Chang, *Kicking Away the Ladder: Development Strategy in Historical Perspective* (London: Anthem Press, 2002).

4 Joseph Stiglitz, 'Don't Trade Away Health', *New York Times*, 30 January 2015, https://www.nytimes.com/2015/01/31/opinion/dont-trade-away-our-health.html; Patricia Ranald, 'The Trans-Pacific Partnership Agreement: Reaching Behind the Border, Challenging Democracy', *Economic and Labour Relations Review* 26, no. 2 (2015): 241–60.

5 Grace Tobin, 'Coronavirus Fires up Production at Australia's Only Medical Mask Factory', *ABC News*, 27 March 2020, https://www.abc.net.au/news/2020-03-27/inside-australias-only-medical-mask-factory/12093864.

6 Patricia Ranald, 'Corporations Prepare to Sue over Action to Save Lives as Pandemic Reveals Trade Flaws', *The Conversation*, 23 April 2020, https://theconversation.com/corporations-prepare-to-sue-over-action-to-save-lives-as-pandemic-reveals-trade-flaws-136604.

7 Robert Cox, 'Global Restructuring', in *Political Economy and the Changing Global Order*, ed. Richard Stubbs and Geoffrey Underhill (London: Macmillan, 1994), 45–59.

8 Ranald, 'The Trans-Pacific Partnership Agreement'.

9 Jane Romeyn, *The International Labour Organisation's Core Labour Standards and the Workplace Relations Act 1996* (Canberra: Commonwealth Parliamentary Research Services, 26 November 2007), https://www.aph.gov.au/About_Parliament/Parliamentary_Departments/Parliamentary_Library/pubs/rp/RP0708/08rp13.

10 Kate Raworth and Claire Hardy, *Trading Away Our Rights: Women Working in Global Supply Chains* (London: Oxfam International, 2004), 4, https://oxfamilibrary.openrepository.com/bitstream/handle/10546/112405/cr-trading-away-rights-women-global-supply-chains-10404-en.pdf;jsessionid=0B7351BAD0138619B21A146A3385884C?sequence=1.

11 Juliane Reinecke, Jimmy Donaghey, Nancy Bocken and Lucas Lauriano, *Business Models and Labour Standards* (London: Ethical Trading Initiative, Kings College London and Warwick University, 2019), 7, https://www.business-humanrights.org/sites/default/files/documents/Business%20models%20%26%20labour%20standards.pdf.

12 Dong Huang, 'Labour Standards in the Global Supply Chain: Workers' Agency and Reciprocal Exchange Perspective', *Societies* 9 (2019): 1–25 (3).

13 Marc Bain and Jenny Arvins, 'The Thing That Makes Bangladesh Such a Huge Success Also Makes It Deadly', *Quartz*, 25 April 2015, https://qz.com/389741/the-thing-that-makes-bangladeshs-garment-industry-such-a-huge-success-also-makes-it-deadly/.

14 Jim Yardly, 'Report on Deadly Factory Collapse in Bangladesh Finds Widespread Blame', *New York Times*, 22 May 2013, https://www.nytimes.com/2013/05/23/world/asia/report-on-bangladesh-building-collapse-finds-widespread-blame.html.

15 Sophie McNeil, Jeanavive McGregor, Meredith Griffiths, Michael Walsh, Echo Hui and Bang Xiao, 'Cotton on and Target Investigate Suppliers after Forced Labour of Uyghurs Exposed in China's Xinjiang', *ABC News*, 17 July 2019, https://www.abc.net.au/news/2019-07-15/uyghur-forced-labour-xinjiang-china/11298750?nw=0.

16 Text of the *China-Australia Free Trade Agreement* (Canberra: Department of Foreign Affairs and Trade, December 2015), https://www.dfat.gov.au/sites/default/files/chafta-agreement-text.pdf.

17 International Labour Organization, *Declaration on Fundamental Principles and Rights at Work* (Geneva: ILO, 18 June 1998), https://www.ilo.org/declaration/thedeclaration/textdeclaration/lang—en/index.htm).

18 Australian Council of Trade Unions, 'Trans-Pacific Partnership Agreement Inquiry', 9 November 2016, https://www.actu.org.au/our-work/policies-publications-submissions/2016/trans-pacific-partnership-tpp-agreement-inquiry.

19 Christian Häberli and Marion Janse, 'Regional Trade Agreements and Domestic Labour Market Regulation', in *Policy Priorities for International Trade and Jobs*, ed. Douglas Lippoldt (Paris: Organisation for Economic Cooperation and Development, 2011), https://www.oecd.org/site/tadicite/50288535.pdf.

20 'Havana Charter for an International Trade Organization', United Nations Conference on Trade and Employment, Havana, March 1948, art. 7, 17, https://www.wto.org/english/docs_e/legal_e/havana_e.pdf.

21 The text of all these agreements, which shows they have no labour chapters, can be found at https://www.dfat.gov.au/trade/agreements/in-force/Pages/free-trade-agreements-in-force.

22 *Australia-New Zealand-ASEAN Free Trade Agreement* (Canberra: Department of Foreign Affairs and Trade, 27 February 2009), https://www.dfat.gov.au/trade/agreements/in-force/aanzfta/official-documents/Pages/official-documents.

23 *Regional Comprehensive Economic Partnership* (Canberra: Department of Foreign Affairs and Trade, 15 November 2020), https://www.dfat.gov.au/trade/agreements/not-yet-in-force/rcep/rcep-text-and-associated-documents.

24 *Australia-United States Free Trade Agreement* (Canberra: Department of Foreign Affairs and Trade, 6 March 2004), chapter 18, https://www.dfat.gov.au/trade/agreements/in-force/ausfta/official-documents/Pages/official-documents; *Korea-Australia Free Trade Agreement* (Canberra: Department of Foreign Affairs and Trade, 12 December 2014), chapter 17, https://www.dfat.gov.au/trade/agreements/in-force/kafta/official-documents/Pages/full-text-of-kafta.

25 The United States withdrew in 2016, and the agreement now involves the 11 countries: Australia, New Zealand, Canada, Mexico, Peru, Chile, Japan, Malaysia, Singapore, Brunei and Vietnam.

26 Lori Wallach and Todd Tucker, 'US politics and the TPPA', in *No Ordinary Deal: Unmasking the Trans-Pacific Partnership Agreement,* ed. Jane Kelsey (Sydney: Allen and Unwin, 2010), 52–69.

27 International Trade Union Confederation, 'Trans-Pacific Partnership Labour Chapter Scorecard: Fundamental Issues Remain Unaddressed', 2015, https://www.ituc-csi.org/IMG/pdf/trans_pacific.pdf.

28 Sierra Club, 'TPP Text Analysis: Environment Chapter Fails to Protect the Environment', 2015, https://www.sierraclub.org/sites/www.sierraclub.org/files/uploads-wysiwig/tpp-analysis-updated.pdf.

29 European Union, 'Draft Text on Trade and Sustainability', 25 February 2019, https://trade.ec.europa.eu/doclib/docs/2019/april/tradoc_157865.pdf.

30 European Trade Union Confederation, 'ETUC Manifesto: 2019–23', 2019, 3, https://www.etuc.org/sites/default/files/publication/file/2019-06/CES-14e%20Congre%E2%95%A0%C3%87s-Manifesto%20EN.pdf.

31 Jane Gibson and Alexis Moran, 'As Coronavirus Spreads, "It's Time to Go Home" Scott Morrison Tells Visitors and International Students', *ABC News*, 3 April 2020, https://www.abc.net.au/news/2020-04-03/coronavirus-pm-tells-international-students-time-to-go-to-home/12119568.

32 Allan Fels and David Cousins, 'The Migrant Workers' Taskforce and the Australian Government's Response to Migrant Worker Wage Exploitation', *Journal of Australian Political Economy*, 84 (December 2019/January 2020): 13–45 (16), https://128f2a8c-7e2b-db29-c5ed-c863dde6f97c.filesusr.com/ugd/b629ee_e19802d05ca44b0ea1f58cbdce9b5c88.pdf.

33 *China-Australia Free Trade Agreement*, chapter 10, annex 10A. Two Memoranda of Understanding dealing with temporary visas are attached to the agreement: *Memorandum of Understanding on an Investment Facilitation Arrangement; Memorandum of Understanding on a Work and Holiday Visa Arrangement*, https://www.dfat.gov.au/trade/agreements/in-force/chafta/official-documents/Pages/official-documents.

34 *Korea-Australia Free Trade Agreement*, chapter 10, annex 10A.

35 *Trans-Pacific Partnership Agreement (incorporated into the Comprehensive Progressive Trans-Pacific Partnership Agreement)* (Canberra: Department of Foreign Affairs and Trade, 4 February 2016), chapter 12, annex 12A, https://www.dfat.gov.au/trade/agreements/not-yet-in-force/tpp/Pages/tpp-text-and-associated-documents.

36 *Indonesia-Australia Comprehensive Economic Partnership* (Canberra: Department of Foreign Affairs and Trade, 21 March 2019), chapter 12, art. 12.9. See also the following side letters dealing with temporary visas: *Indonesia-Australia Comprehensive Economic Partnership Side Letter on Work and Holiday Visas*; *Memorandum of Understanding on the Indonesia-Australia Skills Development Exchange Pilot* Project; and *Memorandum of Understanding on a Pilot Workplace-Based Training Visa Arrangement*, 2019, https://www.aph.gov.au/Parliamentary_Business/Committees/Joint/Treaties/Indonesia-AustraliaCEPA/Treaty_being_considered.

37 *Arrangement on Labour Mobility between Australia, New Zealand and Pacific Island Countries* (Canberra: Department of Foreign Affairs and Trade, 4 June 2017), https://www.dfat.gov.au/sites/default/files/arrangement-on-labour-mobility.pdf.

38 Stuart Rosewarne, 'Free Trade Agreements Driving Labour Market Reform by Stealth', *The Conversation*, 20 January 2015, http://theconversation.com/free-trade-agreements-driving-labour-market-reform-by-stealth-36124.

39 Laurie Berg and Bassina Farbenblum, *Wage Theft in Australia: Findings of the National Temporary Migrant Worker Survey* (Migrant Worker Justice Initiative, 2017), 30, https://apo.org.au/sites/default/files/resource-files/2017-11/apo-nid120406.pdf.

40 Joint Standing Committee on Foreign Affairs, Defence and Trade, *Hidden in Plain Sight: An Inquiry into Establishing a Modern Slavery Act in Australia* (Canberra: Parliament of Australia, December 2017), https://www.aph.gov.au/Parliamentary_Business/Committees/Joint/Foreign_Affairs_Defence_and_Trade/ModernSlavery/Final_report.

41 Joanna Howe, Stephen Clibborn, Diane van den Broek, Alex Reilly and Chris F. Wright, *Towards a Durable Future: Tackling Labour Challenges in the Australian Horticulture Industry* (Sydney: The University of Sydney, January 2019), https://www.sydney.edu.au/content/dam/corporate/documents/business-school/research/work-and-organisational-studies/towards-a-durable-future-report.pdf.

42 Gibson and Moran, 'As Coronavirus Spreads'.

43 Australian Council of Trade Unions, 'Submission to the Select Committee on COVID-19 Inquiry into the Australian Government's Response to the COVID-19 Pandemic', 28 May 2020, https://www.actu.org.au/media/1449161/d22-actu-submission-covid-19-response.pdf.

44 United States Government Accountability Office, 'Drug Industry Profits, Research and Development Spending, Merger and Acquisition Deals', November 2017, https://www.gao.gov/products/GAO-18-40.

45 Ruth Lopert and Deborah Gleeson, 'The High Price of "Free" Trade: US Trade Agreements and Access to Medicines', *Journal of Law, Medicine and Ethics* 41, no. 1 (2003): 199–223; Belinda Townsend, Deborah Gleeson and Ruth Lopert, 'Pharma's Next Frontier? New Threats to Public Health in the Regional Comprehensive Economic Partnership Agreement', *Australia and New Zealand Journal of Public Health* 40, no. 1 (2015): 5–6; *Bilateral and Regional Trade Agreements Final Report* (Canberra: Productivity Commission, 2010), 165–69, http://www.pc.gov.au/inquiries/completed/trade-agreements/report.

46 Commonwealth Parliamentary Library, 'The Pharmaceutical Benefits Scheme – An Overview', 2 January 2003, https://www.aph.gov.au/About_Parliament/Parliamentary_Departments/Parliamentary_Library/Publications_Archive/archive/pbs#:~:text=The%20Pharmaceutical%20Benefits%20Scheme%20as,72%201959.

47 Anne-Marie Boxall 'Medicare: The Making and Consolidation of an Australian Institution', in *Successful Public Policy Lessons from Australia and New Zealand*, ed. Joannah Luetjens, Michael Mintrom and Paul 't Hart (Canberra: ANU Press, 2019), 257–78.

48 Deborah Gleeson, Belinda Townsend, Ruth Lopert, Joel Lexchin, Hazel Moir, 'Financial Costs Associated with Monopolies on Biologic Medicines in Australia', *Australian Health Review* 43, no. 1 (2017): 36–42.

49 Hazel Moir, Brigitte Tenni, Deborah Gleeson and Ruth Lopert, 'The Trans Pacific Partnership Agreement and Access to HIV Treatment in Vietnam', *Global Public Health* 13, no. 4 (2016): 400–13.

50 Deborah Gleeson, Belinda Townsend, Kimberlee Weatherall, Patricia Ranald and Peter Robertson, 'The Trans-Pacific Partnership Is Back: Experts Respond', *The Conversation*, 14 November 2017, https://theconversation.com/the-trans-pacific-partnership-is-back-experts-respond-87432.

51 Deborah Gleeson, 'More Talk, No Action, Australia's Approach to Trade Rules Restraining Vaccine Production,' The Conversation, 23 March 2021, https://theconversation.com/more-talk-no-action-australias-approach-to-trade-rules-restraining-vaccine-production-156971.

52 ACTU et al., 'Open Letter to the Australian Prime Minister on the Waiver From Certain Provisions of the WTO TRIPss Agreement', 10 March 2021, http://aftinet.org.au/cms/sites/default/files/090321%20WTO%20TRIPS%20COVID-19%20waiver.pdf#overlay-context=node/1983.

53 Liam Mannix, 'Vaccine Development Is a Case of "Market Failure". Here's Why', *Sydney Morning Herald,* 13 April 2020, https://www.smh.com.au/national/vaccine-development-is-a-case-of-market-failure-here-s-why-20200413-p54jez.html.

54 Kyla Tienhaara, *The Expropriation of Environmental Governance: Protecting Foreign Investors at the Expense of Public Policy* (Cambridge: Cambridge University Press, 2009); Jonathan Bonnitcha, Lauge N. Skovgaard Poulsen and Michael Waibel, *The Political Economy of the Investment Treaty Regime* (Oxford: Oxford University Press, 2017).

55 The Honorable Justice Robert French, 'Investor-State Dispute Settlement – A Cut Above the Courts?', paper delivered at the Supreme and Federal Courts Judges Conference, Darwin, 9 July 2014, http://www.hcourt.gov.au/assets/publications/speeches/current-justices/frenchcj/frenchcj09jul14.pdf; George Kahale, 'Keynote

Address', speech delivered at the Eighth Juris Investment Arbitration Conference, Washington DC, 8 March 2014, http://www.curtis.com/siteFiles/Publications/8TH%20Annual%20Juris%20Investment%20Treaty%20Arbitration%20Conf.%20-%20March%2028%202014.pdf.

56 United Nations Committee on Trade and Development (UNCTAD), 'Investment Dispute Settlement Navigator', 2019, http://investmentpolicyhub.unctad.org/ISDS.

57 Patricia Ranald, 'Expropriating Public Health Policy: Tobacco Companies' Use of International Tribunals to Sue Governments over Public Health Regulation', *Journal of Australian Political Economy* 73 (2014): 76–102.

58 Patricia Ranald 'When Even Winning Is Losing. The Surprising Cost of Defeating Philip Morris over Plain Packaging', *The Conversation*, 27 March 2019, https://theconversation.com/when-even-winning-is-losing-the-surprising-cost-of-defeating-philip-morris-over-plain-packaging-114279.

59 *Clayton/Bilcon v. Canada* (2008), https://investmentpolicy.unctad.org/investment-dispute-settlement/cases/304/clayton-bilcon-v-canada.

60 *Westmoreland v. Canada* (2018), UNCTAD Investment Dispute Settlement Navigator, https://investmentpolicy.unctad.org/investment-dispute-settlement/cases/936/westmoreland-v-canada.

61 Kyla Tienhaara, 'The Fossil Fuel Era Is Coming to an End but the Lawsuits Are Just Beginning', *The Conversation*, 19 December 2018, https://theconversation.com/the-fossil-fuel-era-is-coming-to-an-end-but-the-lawsuits-are-just-beginning-107512.

62 *Bear Creek Mining Corporation v. Republic of Perú* (2017), International Centre for Settlement of Investment Disputes Case No. ARB/14/21, http://icsidfiles.worldbank.org/icsid/ICSIDBLOBS/OnlineAwards/C3745/DS10808_En.pdf.

63 *Veolia v. Egypt* (2012), UNCTAD Investment Dispute Settlement Navigator, https://investmentpolicy.unctad.org/investment-dispute-settlement/cases/458/veolia-v-egypt; Benoit Breville and Martine Bulard, 'The Injustice Industry and the TTIP', *Le Monde Diplomatique*, English edition, June 2014, http://www.bresserpereira.org.br/terceiros/2014/agosto/14.08.injustice-industry.pdf.

64 The text of all these agreements which shows they have ISDS provisions in their investment chapters can be found at https://www.dfat.gov.au/trade/agreements/in-force/Pages/free-trade-agreements-in-force.

65 Australian Council of Trade Unions , 'Trans-Pacific Partnership Agreement Inquiry'; European Trade Union Confederation, *ETUC Manifesto, 2019–23*.

66 Ranald, 'The Trans-Pacific Partnership Agreement'.

67 European Commission, 'Declaration of the Member States of 15 January 2019 on the Legal Consequences of the Achmea Judgement on Investment Protection', 17 January 2019, https://ec.europa.eu/info/publications/190117-bilateral-investment-treaties_en.

68 Office of the Prime Minister Malcolm Turnbull, 'Transcript of Press Conference with the Minister for Trade, Tourism and Investment and EU Trade Commissioner', 18 June 2018, https://www.malcolmturnbull.com.au/media/press-conference-on-eu-australia-free-trade-agreement.

69 Gus Van Harten, 'Key Flaws in the European Commission's Proposals for Foreign Investor Protection in TTIP', Osgoode Legal Studies Research Paper No. 16, SSRN, 2016, https://papers.ssrn.com/sol3/papers.cfm?abstract_id=2692122.

70 Nathalie Bernasconi-Osterwalder, 'USMCA Curbs How Much Investors Can Sue Countries – Sort of', International Institute on Sustainable Development, May, 2019, https://www.iisd.org/library/usmca-investors.

71 United Nations Commission on International Trade Law, 'Possible Reform of Investor-State Dispute Settlement (ISDS)', October 2019, https://uncitral.un.org/sites/uncitral.un.org/files/wp166.pdf.

72 Aceris Law, 'The COVID-19 Pandemic and Investment Arbitration', 26 March 2020, https://www.acerislaw.com/the-covid-19-pandemic-and-investment-arbitration/.

73 Nathalie Bernasconi-Osterwalder, Sarah Brewin and Nyaguthii Maina, 'Protecting against Investor-State Claims Amidst COVID-19: A Call to Action for Governments', International Institute for Sustainable Development, 14 April 2020, https://www.iisd.org/library/investor-state-claims-amidst-covid-19.

74 Civil Society Organisations, 'Open Letter to Governments on ISDS and COVID-19', Seattle to Brussels Network, Brussels, June 2020, http://s2bnetwork.org/wp-content/uploads/2020/06/OpenLetterOnISDSAndCOVID_June2020.pdf.

75 Department of Foreign Affairs and Trade, 'Australia's Treaty Making Process', 2013, https://www.dfat.gov.au/international-relations/treaties/treaty-making-process.

76 Patricia Ranald, 'Trade Agreements Need More Public and Parliamentary Scrutiny', *Sydney Morning Herald*, 1 May 2015, https://www.smh.com.au/opinion/trade-agreements-need-more-public-and-parliamentary-scrutiny-20150501-1mxqc9.html.

77 World Trade Organization, 'Proposals for the New Negotiations', https://www.wto.org/english/tratop_e/serv_e/s_propnewnegs_e.htm.

78 European Union, 'EU Negotiating Texts in TTIP', 14 February 2015, http://trade.ec.europa.eu/doclib/press/index.cfm?id=1230.

79 US Congressional Research Service, 'Trade Promotion Authority (TPA) and the Role of Congress in Trade Policy', Washington DC, 15 June 2015, https://fas.org/sgp/crs/misc/RL33743.pdf.

80 Senate Foreign Affairs, Defence and Trade References Committee, *Blind Agreement: Inquiry into the Commonwealth's Treaty-Making Process* (Canberra: Commonwealth of Australia, 2015), https://www.aph.gov.au/Parliamentary_Business/Committees/Senate/Foreign_Affairs_Defence_and_Trade/Treaty-making_process/Report.

81 Australian Council of Trade Unions, 'ACTU Submission to the Senate Foreign Affairs Defence and Trade References Committee Enquiry into the Commonwealth's Treaty-Making Process', 24 February 2015, https://www.aph.gov.au/Parliamentary_Business/Committees/Senate/Foreign_Affairs_Defence_and_Trade/Treaty-making_process/Submissions.

82 Australian Fair Trade and Investment Network, 'Submission to the Senate Foreign Affairs, Defence and Trade References Committee Inquiry into the Commonwealth's Treatymaking Process', February 2015, http://aftinet.org.au/cms/sites/default/files/AFTINET%20DFAT%20submission%20final%20edited%200215.pdf#overlay-context=node/954.

83 ACTU, *Trade Policy*, ACTU Congress, July 2018, https://www.actu.org.au/media/1034004/trade.pdf.

Chapter 11

TRADE UNIONS, LABOUR LAW AND DEMOCRATIC SOCIALISM: THE COVID-19 CRISIS IN THE UNITED KINGDOM

K. D. Ewing

The United Kingdom is a country where the Queen reigns but chaos governs. Chaos caused initially in recent years by the decisions of the Treasury to impose a 10-year programme of austerity with disproportionate burdens on the British population; followed by the distraction and self-immolation of Brexit on the back of a populist referendum in 2016; followed in turn by the domestic impact of the COVID-19 pandemic, which represents one of the greatest public administration failures in modern British history. It will be for consideration at some stage whether these failures were due in part to the programme of austerity and the distraction of Brexit by which they were preceded. Preliminary evidence suggests, however, that there was a state of neglect and unpreparedness before the crisis, as well as a lack of capacity to respond appropriately during it.

The United Kingdom has been a testing ground for neoliberalism and austerity, and their implications for workers' rights. The real test of any model, however, is how well it copes in a crisis. This would be true of labour law, as of any other area of law or any other institutional arrangements beyond the law. But in determining how well a system of labour law operates in a crisis, it is necessary to have a sense of the discipline's purpose, which is itself contentious. Every type of economy has a system of labour law, though the objectives are clearly very different. The neoliberal vision of labour law will be very different from a social democratic vision[1] – the former emphasising the virtues of flexible employment models and free labour markets, and the latter emphasising high labour standards, job security and different forms of worker involvement in decision making.[2]

The COVID-19 crisis has revealed the abject failure of the neoliberal vision. Correction. The COVID-19 crisis has revealed the spectacular success of the neoliberal vision through the lens of its authors. It has enabled employers to shed labour quickly and to cut pay with a minimum of formality and expense.[3] But with the shifting of responsibility in employment exclusively to the worker, COVID-19 also has serious implications for workers' communities, on a scale which is completely unsustainable even in the short term.[4] As a result, it has been necessary for the state to intervene, revealing the great contradiction of the neoliberal project, namely that it is the product of state engineering, and sustainable only because of a strong state as underwriter. This begs questions about a more benign economic model and a different use of state power once the current crisis has abated.

In this chapter, the concern is to explore some of these themes through the early experience of the British response to the ongoing COVID-19 crisis. The paper has its origins in a presentation at the Melbourne Law School Centre for Employment and Labour Relations Law on 18 July 2019, in very different circumstances. Informed in part by the experience of the global financial crisis,[5] the presentation was concerned with exploring the options for a different kind of labour law in the United Kingdom in place of that which had prevailed since the late 1970s.[6] In the event the project was rendered redundant for the time being by the general election later that year, with Britain (like Australia) electing another right-leaning Conservative administration. That said, however, COVID-19 and its consequences will represent for some the vindication of the need for transformative agenda which the Labour Party had been persuaded to adopt.[7] At the time of writing, the United Kingdom has the second highest excess death rate in the world.[8]

Before the Lockdown

Beginning with the capacity and resilience of the labour law system to deal with the crisis, we should begin with some context about the social conditions to which labour law has contributed. This context was laid bare in the withering report by the UN Special Rapporteur on Extreme Poverty and Human Rights following a visit to the United Kingdom in 2019. In the summary of his report, Professor Alston wrote thus:

> Although the United Kingdom is the world's 5th largest economy, one fifth of the population (14 million people) live in poverty, and 1.5 million of them experienced destitution in 2017. Policies of austerity introduced in 2010 continue largely unabated, despite the tragic social consequences. Close to 40% of children are predicted to be living in poverty by 2021. Food banks have

> proliferated, homelessness and rough sleeping have increased greatly; tens of thousands of poor families must live in accommodation far removed from their schools, jobs and community networks; life expectancy is falling for certain groups; and its legal aid system has been decimated.[9]

The foregoing suggests failures at multiple levels: tax, social welfare, housing and education. Also important, however, is the effect of falling labour standards and collapsing labour law protections, with the Coalition government of 2010 reacquainting itself with the policies of Thatcherism.

Standing at 82 per cent on the eve of Thatcher's election, collective bargaining coverage has fallen in a period of 40 years to 26.9 per cent of the workforce, and in the private sector to about 15.1 per cent.[10] The latter is in some respects the critical figure for present purposes, for to the extent that there are higher density levels in the public sector, this is a sector where pay bargaining is limited by pay restraints imposed by government. These are figures that bring the United Kingdom very close to US levels of density, and are one of the lowest in the developed world.[11] There are a number of explanations for this decline, not least being the new forms of macroeconomic government, economic restructuring away from extraction and manufacturing where unions were once dominant, and new styles of personnel management. To which we might add the decentralisation of collective bargaining, and the ineffectiveness of the decentralised legal model to assist unions secure bargaining rights with hostile employers, and to retain bargaining rights when under threat.[12]

Legislation to enable trade unions to secure bargaining rights was introduced in 2000 and has been in operation ever since. The fact that it survived for ten years of Conservative-led governments is a testament to its ineffectiveness. There is no demand from business for its removal or for any significant changes, having been wholly internalised and marginalised. Too many concessions were made to employers at the time the scheme was drafted, and although it was welcomed in some quarters as a significant improvement on statutory schemes operating in other countries, British experience has confirmed that the problem is not the trim but the model itself. It has not arrested the decline in collective bargaining density in the United Kingdom, which was higher when the collective bargaining legislation was introduced than it is at the time of writing some 20 years later. Indeed, it is doubtful to what extent if at all the legislation operated as a parachute to slow down the decline of collective bargaining density, as had been pessimistically suggested as its likely best effect.

In the absence of collective agreements, workers must fall back on minimum standards legislation for core protections. At least in the United Kingdom, these are now very low. It is true that there is a statutory minimum wage which has been increased annually. But despite cynically being rebranded as a national 'living' wage,[13] it is nothing of the kind, being set at a rate of only £8.72 an hour (for those 25 and over); £8.20 an hour (for those between 21 and 24); £4.45 an hour (for those between 18 and 20); and £4.55 an hour (for those under 18).[14] For those 25 or over able to secure full-time employment of 40 hours a week, this would provide a weekly income of £348.80; a monthly income of £1,395.20; and an annual income of £16,742.40. This in a country where the median weekly earnings a year earlier were £585,[15] giving an annual salary for a full-time worker of £30,420, which is about 80 per cent the Australian equivalent at the time of writing. To which we may add that the so-called living wage makes no provision for overtime or penalty rates.

Nor more importantly does the law guarantee to workers the right to a minimum number of hours to enable even this modest level of payment to be earned. As a result, it is misleading to refer to a minimum wage, when in fact all we have is a national minimum hourly rate, something altogether different (albeit a misrepresentation shared with a host of other jurisdictions). One effect is that workers in some sectors are now employed by the hour as and when needed,[16] in what is the ultimate form of commodification of labour. These so-called zero-hours contract arrangements are increasingly common in many sectors of the economy, and rekindle images of the casualisation of employment that were evident in the early phases of the industrial revolution, and more recently on the docks in the era pre-containerisation. According to the Office for National Statistics (ONS), 'there were 1.8 million contracts that did not guarantee a minimum number of hours, where work had actually been carried out under those contracts'.[17] For further discussion of the impact of casualisation of employment, see Chapter 6 by Iain Campbell in this volume.

But the problem is not just the rapid decline in collective bargaining coverage and its displacement by minimum standards of which the failings of the national minimum wage and working time regulation are symptomatic. Also important has been the emergence of largely unregulated work in the expanding so-called gig economy. Thus:

- in order to be eligible for even the most basic statutory rights the claimant must be a worker (minimum wage, paid holidays), or an employee (minimum wage, paid holidays, unfair dismissal, redundancy payments); and
- even if the individual is eligible as an employee, entitlement may depend on minimum periods of continuous service (two years in the case of unfair dismissal and redundancy payments).

Here we find employers creating and exploiting loopholes in an already fragile legal framework in order to deny access to these modest legal protections.

This is done by the insistence on contractual terms to create bogus forms of self-employment that bear no relationship to reality in which workers are wholly dependent on a particular 'customer' or 'client' for work. The favourite device in recent years has been to insist that the individual in question is free to arrange for a substitute to perform the work he or she has been contracted to do, thereby demonstrating that the contract is not for the personal provision of work or services. By these means all the risks associated with employment are transferred to the worker, who has no guaranteed income, no paid holidays, no secure employment, no protection from unfair dismissal and no access to admittedly wholly inadequate social insurance benefits. This is a form of employment relationship that is not only expanding (often alongside various forms of casualisation such as those referred to above), but is one that brings with it other advantages to the 'employer', not least in the form of reduced payroll tax liabilities. For further discussion of the challenges of the gig economy more generally, see Chapter 7 by Anthony Forsyth in this volume.

So the paradox of the United Kingdom is that before the pandemic it had a combination of high levels of employment but poor quality of jobs. Life for many workers was precarious and was characterised by the fragility of employment as well as an acute vulnerability to adverse events. There was little resilient capacity for many workers, in a country where poor conditions were underpinned by a brutal and coercive social security system. This is highlighted by Professor Alston's report, to which we return, a report notable for the observation that:

> the philosophy underpinning the British welfare system has changed radically since 2010. The initial rationales for reform were to reduce overall expenditures and to promote employment as the principal 'cure' for poverty. But when large-scale poverty persisted despite a booming economy and very high levels of employment, the Government chose not to adjust course. Instead, it doubled down on a parallel agenda to reduce benefits by every means available, including constant reductions in benefit levels, ever-more-demanding conditions, harsher penalties, depersonalisation, stigmatisation, and virtually eliminating the option of using the legal system to vindicate rights.[18]

Alston continued by saying that the 'basic message', 'delivered in the language of managerial efficiency and automation, is that almost any alternative will be more tolerable than seeking to obtain government benefits'.[19]

During the Lockdown

The British economy began to shut down on 23 March 2020. Schools were closed, except for vulnerable children and the children of critical workers – a term that included those employed in health and social care, education and childcare, key public services, local and national government, food and other essential items, public safety and national security, transport, and utilities, communications and financial services.[20] Public health regulations then required a number of other businesses to close; these were concerned mainly in the retail, leisure and hospitality sectors, while a number of other sectors voluntarily shut down.[21] It was not necessary to do so in the latter case, and indeed the regulations expressly listed going to work as a 'reasonable excuse' for leaving home during the lockdown.[22] Nevertheless, most businesses in manufacturing and construction chose to close, unable to comply with non-binding guidance on social distancing as fear stalked the nation.[23] International aviation did the same, and public transport began to reduce in capacity.[24]

All this exposed major weaknesses in the neoliberal restructuring of British labour law as described. First was the position of workers in key industries who were required to continue physically to be at work. Notable of course was the army of health and social care workers, as well as those engaged in food production, distribution and retail; mail and parcel deliveries as people shopped online; transport workers, including train and bus drivers providing the limited services still available, as well as taxi drivers; bank and post office staff; teachers in those schools providing services for critical workers and vulnerable children; and workers providing a host of local government services such as refuse collection. Although many – though not all – of these workers were engaged in what hitherto conveniently had been regarded as low skill jobs, they were also workers who because of the nature of their occupation were most at risk of contracting COVID-19 and of dying as a result.

Indeed, official data reveal that within a month of the lockdown:

- Compared with the rate among people of the same sex and age in England and Wales, men working in the lowest skilled occupations had the highest rate of death involving COVID-19, with 21.4 deaths per 100,000 males (225 deaths); and men working as security guards had one of the highest rates, with 45.7 deaths per 100,000 (63 deaths).
- Men and women working in social care, a group including care workers and home carers, both had significantly raised rates of death involving COVID-19, with rates of 23.4 deaths per 100,000 males (45 deaths) and 9.6 deaths per 100,000 females (86 deaths).

- Healthcare workers, including those with jobs such as doctors and nurses, were not found to have higher rates of death involving COVID-19 when compared with the rate among those whose death involved COVID-19 of the same age and sex in the general population.
- Among men, a number of other specific occupations were found to have raised rates of death involving COVID-19, including: taxi drivers and chauffeurs (36.4 deaths per 100,000); bus and coach drivers (26.4 deaths per 100,000); chefs (35.9 deaths per 100,000); and sales and retail assistants (19.8 deaths per 100,000).[25]

In providing these data the ONS was careful to point out that they 'do not prove conclusively that the observed rates of death involving COVID-19 are necessarily caused by differences in occupational exposure'.[26]

But the message is clear enough. Low paid and 'low skilled' workers unable to work from home were placed in danger – danger reinforced by the failure to provide adequate personal protection equipment. Although required by law,[27] Personal Protective Equipment (PPE) was in short supply and the government had no power – even in the emergency legislation introduced to deal with the crisis – to requisition property for that purpose or to direct manufacturers to use their equipment and resources.[28] And danger was compounded by the fact that workers with COVID-19 symptoms were expected to self-isolate for 7 or 14 days in a country where employers are not required to maintain wages during periods of ill health.[29] Those who did not have the benefit of an occupational sickness scheme were thus expected to self-isolate on statutory sick pay of £95.85 a week,[30] considerably less than the statutory minimum wage which would yield £348.80 for a 40-hour week.[31] It was not much of an incentive to take public health seriously.[32] Correction: it was an active incentive *not* to take public health seriously.

So much for those who were required to work. What about those who were unable to work or who were laid off because their businesses closed indefinitely? Here the future was grim, with only rudimentary procedures in place for workers in such a situation. Thus, for employees laid off or put on short-time working but not dismissed there is a statutory right to a guaranteed payment payable by the employer for the days in question.[33] According to the government website, the 'maximum you can get is £29 a day for 5 days in any 3 month period – so a maximum of £145'.[34] That would be an hourly rate of £3.62 for an eight-hour day, which is less than half of the hourly rate of the national minimum wage which at the time of writing is £8.72 an hour, or £69.76 for an eight-hour day. Nevertheless, the amount of the guaranteed payment greatly exceeds Job Seekers' Allowance, the partially insurance based benefit that replaced unemployment benefit. A worker who is dismissed rather than put on short-time working would be entitled to £74.35 a week, which might rise to £116 a week for a couple once any savings are largely depleted.[35]

The neoliberal inheritance was thus not fit for purpose. Faced with large-scale unemployment and destitution, the Treasury was compelled to intervene with a massive funding programme that turned neoliberal economics upside down. This involved securing from Parliament a budget of £260 billion for unspecified purposes to manage the COVID-19 crisis[36]: the measures taken for this purpose were to include a Coronavirus Job Retention Scheme (CJRS) and a similar scheme for the self-employed, as well as a host of other initiatives to protect income security during the early stages of the crisis. It is not without irony, however, that the former was based on similar initiatives taken in member states of the European Union (EU) (of which the United Kingdom ceased to be a member on 31 January 2020 on the eve of the pandemic's British arrival),[37] and was pressed on the government by trade unions (which had previously been largely ignored).[38] Old ideas, old friends and old ways it seems are sometimes the best after all.

It is true that the government was widely applauded for the CJRS which unconditionally paid for up to 80 per cent of the wages of workers whose employers chose to use it.[39] And it is true too that the CJRS was extended until October, with a number of variations to apply from July so that employers are gradually weaned off the scheme.[40] The scheme was nevertheless fraught with difficulty: it was introduced without any parliamentary approval under the blanket power giving the Treasury the authority to spend up to £260 billion from the government's contingencies fund;[41] and it was introduced in the form of a help to business from which workers would benefit vicariously as a result of the decisions of their employer.[42] But it was symptomatic of the nature of labour law that the scheme gave workers no enforceable rights. Apart from the fact that employers could choose to make workers redundant rather than go on what was referred to as 'furlough' under the scheme, workers had no right to be consulted about whether the employer went on the scheme, or whether they personally would be furloughed if the employer did so.[43]

In addition, there were a number of arbitrary exclusions causing significant hardship to the individuals concerned,[44] no obligation on the part of employers to retain staff once the state subsidy was discontinued, while the scheme applied only in respect of workers who were designated as employees for the purposes of income tax, thereby excluding the growing army of those engaged on self-employment arrangements, whether genuine or bogus.[45] But as the months rolled by, the government was becoming very concerned about the cost of underwriting wages of what had swelled to eight million workers, with another three million benefiting under the separate self-employed scheme subsequently announced.[46] The anxiety now extending beyond government was with a lack of preparation for the chaos to be restored as the schemes tapered to a close and employers decided that they are unable or unwilling to pay the wages of those who had been furloughed. In the absence of any job creation programme, the CJRS may end up being little more than a parachute into redundancy and unemployment for many if not most.

Emerging from Lockdown

On Sunday, 10 May 2020, the entire focus of concern changed in the United Kingdom, away from health towards the economy. In common with the new populist style of government which appears to have displaced parliamentary government, the change of tone was struck by the Prime Minister in a televised broadcast to the people from Downing Street.[47] Despite the mildest rebuke from the Speaker a few days earlier,[48] Parliament was not informed until Monday, 11 May, that the emphasis of government strategy was now to get people back to work. The new strategy was, however, confusing and led to uncertainty on the part of those to whom it was directed. Confusion was compounded by the announcement on Tuesday, 12 May, that the CJRS was to be continued for another four months until the end of October, albeit with modifications designed to allow for part-time working and to encourage employers to bear a bigger share of the cost.

The new message was designed to get the economy moving again, citizens being directed that if it is possible to do so they should continue to work at home. Where it was not possible to work at home, people should go to work, a message directed mainly at manufacturing and construction workers, who it was claimed were never expected to stay at home during the lockdown in the first place. This claim is consistent with the legislation authorising the lockdown whereby people were forbidden from leaving home unless they had a 'reasonable excuse'.[49] As already pointed out, one of the expressly permissible reasons was 'to travel for the purposes of work or to provide voluntary or charitable services, where it is not reasonably possible for that person to work, or to provide those services, from the place where they are living'.[50] That said, as also pointed out above, one reason why many workplaces did close nevertheless was to comply with (non-legally binding) government guidance on social distancing which would not be possible to observe in many workplaces. According to government's badly proofread guidelines produced on the day after Johnson's address to the nation:

These 'back to work' guidelines apply to those in essential retail like:

- Supermarkets
- Those in construction and manufacturing
- Those working in labs and research facilities
- Those administering takeaways and deliveries at restaurants and cafes
- Tradesmen, cleaners and others who work in people's homes
- Those who are facilitating trade or transport goods
- And so on[51]

The concern is that the back to work instruction would simply serve to reinforce the inequalities already exposed. In the first place there were logistical problems. How do workers with children comply with this instruction, when nurseries and schools are closed? Primary schools were only to reopen on 1 June but even then only for some year groups.[52] Second, how were workers to travel to work safely on public transport, with images of crowded buses and tube trains beginning to emerge? The government it seemed had abdicated all responsibility: workers were told to avoid public transport and drive, walk or cycle to work, taking advantage of a new £2 billion scheme designed to encourage cycling. They were also told to wear homemade face coverings (but not surgical masks required for healthcare workers), but 'there would be no policing of physical distancing on tubes, trains or buses, with the government instead relying on "gentle advice or exhortation" that people should avoid the busiest times and places'.[53]

So while people were being instructed to get back to work – at a time when the daily COVID-19 death toll still exceeded 600 – the transport minister not only suggested that 'he would not personally get on a crowded bus or tube',[54] but also conceded that the government was 'asking people to be very sensible and not flood back to public transport. Even with all the trains and buses back to running when they are, there will not be enough space. One in 10 people will be able to travel without overcrowding.'[55] Workers under pressure from their employers to return to work thus had no option but to put themselves in a position of danger that limousine driven ministers would refuse to contemplate, with government guidance about how to deal with unsympathetic employers far from reassuring. But of course it is not only those travelling to work who would be at risk of infection. Crowded public transport also exposes transport workers to greater danger, a matter of grave concern given the COVID-19 deaths and illness of transport workers during the period of the lockdown.

On the day the return to work was due to start, Government Guidance stated that 'we'll be setting out further guidance for passengers with more advice on how to stay safe during your journeys later this week'.[56] Let's hope it was not too late for anyone. Anxious workers were told that:

> Where work cannot be done at home, employers should take clear, practical steps to help protect workers and create safe places to work, such as shift working or staggering processes. To identify the precautions needed to manage risk, your employer should discuss the workplace risk assessment with you to identify the practical ways of managing those risks. If you remain concerned that your employer is not taking all practical steps to promote social distancing then you can report this to your local authority or the Health and Safety Executive who can take a range of action, including where appropriate requiring your employer to take additional steps.[57]

Workers even more anxious that they might lose their jobs if they did not overcome their fear and return to work were left with the irresponsible platitudes of a government washing its hands completely of worker concerns:

> We urge employers to take socially responsible decisions and listen to the concerns of their staff. Employers and employees should come to a pragmatic agreement about their working arrangements. If individuals need advice, they should approach ACAS where they can get impartial advice about work disputes.[58]

The same workers were directed to sector specific guidance for reassurance, the guidance welcomed remarkably by the Trades Union Congress (TUC).[59] This is despite continuing reservations by a number of individual trade unions, and despite the threat of legal action by the International Workers of Great Britain on behalf of gig workers who were concerned that health and safety obligations do not apply to them because of their false status as independent contractors.[60] These concerns are unlikely to have been assuaged by correspondence included in the following press report which appears to deflect responsibility for health and safety to gig workers themselves, in what seems to be symptomatic of the general approach of the government and public bodies. The report reads as follows:

> 'Health and safety has never been more critical than it is now', said Dr Jason Moyer-Lee, general secretary of the IWGB. 'Until the end of the transition phase [scheduled to be the end of 2020] EU law still applies in the UK.' 'We have written to the government and said [everyone] should be covered. Our members feel they have no protection. If they raise their concerns at work they

> fear they may be dismissed.' The letter was forwarded by the DWP to the Health and Safety Executive, which supervises and inspects workplaces. Its chief executive, Sarah Albon, wrote to the IWGB declaring: 'Under health and safety law, an employer has a general duty to manage workplace risks and should protect workers on non-standard contracts as they do their employees. This will include many temporary workers, agency workers and those who use IT platforms to access work, often referred to as the gig economy. As you will be aware, those working in the gig economy who are self-employed rather than workers have a general duty to manage risks to themselves and others that arise out of their work. We are confident that the health and safety framework provides the necessary protection for workers, including those on non-standard contracts, and have no plans to amend the legislation.'[61]

Otherwise, returning 'employees' were unlikely to have been impressed by the government's recommendations, one teaching union claiming that they were 'frankly unfathomable',[62] and a rail union threatening industrial action to protect its members and the travelling public. The prospect of industrial action in the public interest is deeply ironic in light of (1) malevolent legislation introduced to restrict strike action in important public services (including the railways) in 2016; and (2) proposals in the Conservative election manifesto in 2019 to require minimum service operations during transport strikes.[63] The former step was taken and the latter proposed in the 'public interest', which experience is beginning to show trade unions are better able to protect than the government. But apart from the logistics of getting to work, worker anxieties seem well placed if the feeble standards of government guidance are to be any indication of the standards to be expected.

Although the Health and Safety Executive is an 'arm's length' public body, its guidance on how to operate a 'Covid-secure' business would be risible were the matter not so grave. Its 'short guide' to employers on working safely during the coronavirus outbreak simply reminds employers of the need to carry out a risk assessment, and thereafter merely advises that the employer 'should think about' a host of different matters relating to safety.[64] The critical question of PPE is elided altogether with the instruction to 'continue providing the PPE that you normally use to protect yourself or workers, for example exposure to wood dust, flour, welding fume, silica dust'.[65] There is no mention of the situation of workers who now need PPE because of COVID-19, or of the legal obligation of the employer under the Provision of Personal Protective Equipment Regulations 1992.[66] More detailed 'non-statutory' government guidance is hardly more encouraging:

> Workplaces should not encourage the precautionary use of extra PPE to protect against COVID-19 outside clinical settings or when responding to a suspected or confirmed case of COVID-19.[67]

After the Lockdown

After the lockdown, what next? The talk now is of an economy shrinking by 14 per cent in 2020, which will be the biggest decline since 1706, bigger than the fall associated with the Great Depression, the Second World War and the Global Financial Crisis.[68] Although the impact on the United Kingdom may be greater than most, other countries in the developed and developing worlds will suffer comparable decline. That said, at the time of writing there are a number of countries – Australia and New Zealand among them – that appear to have managed the health crisis much more competently than the United Kingdom and the United States, while also minimising the impact on civil liberties.[69] But while Australia and New Zealand may talk of a travel bubble between countries that are COVID-19 free or COVID-19 lite,[70] it will be impossible not to be affected by the economic depression that seems likely to unfold elsewhere. The question for the wealthy countries that have been most badly affected is how to respond: will the model be 1934–45, or will it be 2008?[71]

In the case of the United Kingdom, the debate is already polarised. The left and centre-left write about not returning to the position that launched the virus, and to the need for international action to combat it. But no programme has emerged beyond the rhetoric and the hyperbole, the Labour Party under new leadership avoiding answers to all questions. The right and the hard-right are calling for the need to avoid tax increases to pay for the domestic cost of the pandemic, which is estimated to be £337 billion in 2020.[72] These are predictions made in May 2020, based on calculations that somehow the nightmare will be brought under control and the costs contained. But even at this level – which is more than A$500 billion – the impact on people's lives will be shattering, and the depth of the depression unprecedented: millions of workers in the private and public sectors will lose their jobs; the squeeze on wages will be profound as will the impact on public services; and the dependency on very basic welfare benefits which reflect the 'less eligibility' values of the poor law are unlikely to prevent destitution on a large scale.[73]

Perhaps the best analogy will be 'the 1930s on steroids'. Yet unlike the 1930s and the 1940s, we appear not to have the capacity to respond in an internationally coordinated way. Proposals were put forward at an early stage of the crisis by Gordon Brown, the former British Prime Minister, who is credited with playing a major part in the immediate response to the 2008 global financial crisis. On 26 March 2020, on the eve of a G20 meeting, he 'urged world leaders to create a temporary form of global government to tackle the twin medical and economic crises caused by the Covid-19 pandemic'.[74] While 'many countries have announced economic packages in the past two weeks', Brown was reported as proposing a global taskforce 'involving world leaders, health experts and the heads of the international organisations that would have executive powers to coordinate the response'.[75] Such a taskforce could 'make sure the efforts of central banks were coordinated; take steps to prevent the record flight of capital from emerging market economies; and agree a joint approach to the use of government spending to boost growth'.[76]

But however plausible this and other contributions from Brown might be, there is no evidence that anyone is listening, and certainly no evidence of any desire to use such proposed procedures for radical ends. The world lacks the leadership that was on display at the end of the Second World War when progressive politics if not progressive politicians were at the helm, and when polarised countries joined together albeit briefly in a shared endeavour to rebuild economies and redraw boundaries. In contrast, the prospect of a new world order based on the Social Bill of Rights in the *ILO Declaration of Philadelphia* of 1944 now seems remote.[77] Remote because there is little or no interest in the United States or its UK satellite in coordinated action, and remote because of the hostility and suspicion that now exists between the world's three great powers: China, the EU and the United States. Both the EU and the United States also have their own internal problems to contend with, while Brexit has sapped energy and strength from both the United Kingdom and the EU, which is struggling to rediscover a post-austerity social agenda.[78]

The governmental and corporate centre of gravity on social rights is now to be found in the *ILO Centenary Declaration for the Future of Work*, which makes for dismal reading for those still inclined to have a look.[79] Indeed, in its centenary year, the International Labour Organization (ILO) is moved not by the spirit of Philadelphia but the realpolitik of 'America First'. Thus, the *ILO Centenary Declaration for the Future of Work* reflects the values of global corporate wealth and contemporary US labour law. Although there is a nod in the direction of the *ILO Declaration of Philadelphia*, this is symbolic only.[80] Long gone is the commitment to 'further among the nations of the world programmes which will achieve' a 'just share of the fruits of progress to all'.[81] Long gone too is the commitment to 'further among the nations of the world programmes which will achieve' the 'effective recognition of the right of collective bargaining, the cooperation of management and labour in the continuous improvement of productive efficiency, and the collaboration of workers and employers in the preparation and application of social and economic measures'.[82]

In their place, we have a commitment to 'an adequate minimum wage, statutory or negotiated',[83] and to promoting workers' rights as a key element for the attainment of 'inclusive and sustainable growth, with a focus on freedom of association and the effective recognition of the right to collective bargaining as enabling rights'.[84] As indicated above, the ILO Centenary was also an opportunity to trumpet 'America First'. As I have explained elsewhere, the occasion of the ILO Centenary was marked by an extraordinary statement by Trump's Secretary of State, with Pompeo reminding us that the first international labour conference was held in the United States, that the *ILO Declaration of Philadelphia* was minted there, and that under US leadership the ILO won the Nobel Peace Prize in 1969. But the United States' commitment to 'advancing the rights of workers globally' rings hollow, the Trump administration more concerned to weaponize workers' rights for nakedly partisan purposes. Thus:

> We also recognize the suffering of the Venezuelan workers and employers who face severe limitations to their freedom of association and right to organize, and who have been systematically impoverished at the hands of the former Maduro regime.[85]

The inability of the ILO is not surprising. Whatever institutional desire there may or may not be among the secretariat in the International Labour Office, like any organisation it can be effective only to the extent that its members desire. And at the time of writing it does not look like the ILO's member states are willing to change course: 2020 is not 1944. At the national level, in contrast, the TUC has produced a valuable document on *A Better Recovery* to help get Britain out of the crisis and to avoid mass unemployment. Key recommendations include the following:

- **Decent work and a new way of doing business:** New business models based on fairer employment relationships. A fairer share for workers of the wealth they create, with a higher minimum wage and new collective bargaining rights.
- **Rebuilding public services:** Bringing our public services back to full strength, with decent pay for those who looked after us in the crisis, and a new focus on good jobs and direct employment in social care.[86]

The TUC proposals also contemplate a role for trade unions in government through a National Recovery Council, which would give workers 'a voice at the heart of government through a National Recovery Council bringing together workers and employers', in what would be a welcome return of tripartism.[87]

But again – no matter how plausible these proposals may be – there is no evidence that anyone is listening to the case for far-reaching change to address the underlying inequalities underpinning the COVID-19 crisis. Even on the centre-left we see a stunning lack of ambition and reinforcement of the COVID-19 inequalities in a report from the Resolution Foundation, the modern Labour Party's favourite economic think-tank.[88] In a 30-page briefing, we find proposals to raise the minimum wage to two-thirds the 'typical' wage over five years, alongside the better regulation of zero-hours contracts, and early-twentieth-century solutions in the form of trade boards in a small number of industries 'in clear need of improved standards'.[89] There was little of substance said about collective bargaining. Astonishingly, the authors claim defensively that many will say that 'these proposals go too far, rightly noting that our labour market already has many strengths'.[90] While also claiming that the midst of crisis is not the ideal time to be proposing 'labour market' [*sic*] reforms, the authors nevertheless boldly claim that their recommendations are 'balanced' and moderate.[91]

Conclusion

So although initially there was much talk about COVID-19 being a game changer, the international and domestic infrastructure necessary to make change does not appear to be present. What we see in the United Kingdom is a determination to return to 'normal' – normal being the status quo.[92] It is true that Johnson assumed an obligation to the voters in the so-called red wall seats to ameliorate the consequences of globalisation, and that he has publicly committed in the post-COVID-19 society to proceed with infrastructure spending plans.[93] So there is to be no austerity beyond that already suffered, partly because right wing think-tanks which inform government policy understand that austerity is no longer acceptable and are now necessarily relaxed about government borrowing and spending in the post-pandemic world.[94] The most dispiriting feature of what is likely to be the first phase of the COVID-19 crisis is the lack of any traction for countervailing proposals on how to replace neoliberalism and rebuild in the future. Some commentators appeal to the spirit of Beveridge and others to Keynes,[95] but for the most part the Labour Party under new leadership has fallen silent. While it is understandable that the nature of the crisis has placed political and industrial resources of the Labour movement under great pressure, it is nevertheless crucial that resources are set aside to develop a plan of action for the future. At a time when trade unions are being marginalised and vilified by governments, they are also being ignored by activists, as revealed in a statement to the press by a group of 6,000 academics from around the world.[96] Although at times incoherent and assertive, there were nevertheless well-placed demands for the decommodification of labour and the democratisation of enterprises. But unlike the manifesto appended to this chapter, there was no reference to the importance of trade unions as the means for this to happen.

So while it is important to will the ends, it is also important to provide the means. With this in mind, trade unions are essential, not only as intermediate organisations between the citizen and state to mobilise workers and their demands as agents of change, but also as important levers for the delivery of change. This is why a commitment to collective bargaining is important along with monetary and fiscal policy as a way of raising wages and redistributing income and wealth. In the absence of strong trade unions, it will be impossible to realise these goals, which cannot be met by alternative options such as a statutory minimum wage or a universal basic income as some are now calling for. But while the left fiddles as the virus burns, the government is quietly making preparations for a post-COVID-19 and post-Brexit society. It should be a concern to everyone that while COVID-19 is being bungled, Brexit negotiations with the EU have broken down precisely on the British refusal to accept common environmental and labour standards in a future trade agreement.[97]

Why is that a concern? The answer lies in the on-record comments of many senior members of the current government over many years, including those made by the Prime Minister himself. Although it is true that right wing populism is not necessarily incompatible with labour rights in principle, Johnson and his ministers have never disguised their contempt for workers' rights, and in some cases the role of the EU in creating these rights. A particularly notable example is the Prime Minister's own comments when, addressing a parliamentary committee, Johnson expressed the view that the EU Working Time Directive was not 'ideally tailored to the needs' of the British economy.[98] Having rejected the option of a progressive Labour government promising strong labour rights at the general election in 2019, British workers may yet have cause to regret that decision, as the full economic costs of the COVID-19 crisis come more clearly into view. British labour law no longer has – if it ever had – the institutional structures or the resilient capacity to absorb the shocks that are predicted to be on the way.

A POST-COVID-19 MANIFESTO

K. D. Ewing and Lord Hendy QC

1. There is a need for co-ordinated and progressive international action, as in the ILO Declaration of Philadelphia (1944).
2. EU institutions need to rediscover and recognise the principles set out in the EU Treaty, articles 2 and 3, and abandon their commitment to an 'open market economy'.
3. At domestic level, radical and transformative fiscal policies must be adopted to raise taxes, in order to increase public spending, in order to promote income equality and equality of wealth.
4. The State must be rebuilt as the expression of collective solidarity, not just in health, but also in employment, housing, education, transport, and income maintenance.
5. Participation in government must be expanded to give trade unions a voice in public policy development, while all public services must be delivered directly by public bodies.
6. The economic constitution must be to restored to recreate an open, robust, resilient and inclusive democracy based on entitlement through strong industrial citizenship.
7. As a result, sector-wide collective bargaining should be restored, as a key lever for redistribution and the promotion of equality.
8. Steps must be taken to ensure the dignity of **all** workers, and to end the various forms of exploitation through non-standard employment. Enough is enough.
9. We must re-assess the value of work and its rewards. Wage rates should be based on service to the community not market value, with much greater State intervention.
10. Steps must be taken to disempower global corporations and to democratise companies, as an integral part of the new economic constitution.

(First published in the *Morning Star*, 1 May 2020)

Notes

1 And both very different from anything in between. On the role of labour law on the threshold of the modern era, see Hugh Collins, 'Regulating the Employment Relation for Competitiveness', *Industrial Law Journal* 30, no. 1 (2001): 17–48.

2 For further discussion, see K. D. Ewing, 'The Unfinished Paper – A Tribute to Gordon Anderson', *Victoria University of Wellington Law Review* 50, no. 2 (2019): 173–92.

3 Joanna Partridge, 'Heathrow Airport Workers Threatened with Sack If They Reject "Voluntary" Pay Cuts', *The Guardian*, 8 April 2020, https://www.theguardian.com/uk-news/2020/apr/08/heathrow-workers-voluntary-pay-cuts-airport-coronavirus.

4 Anahita Hossein-Pour, 'Heathrow Airport Job Cuts Likely to Have a "Dramatic" Effect on Hounslow Says Council Leader', *MyLondon*, 25 May 2020, https://www.mylondon.news/news/west-london-news/heathrow-airport-job-cuts-likely-18256645.

5 See K. D. Ewing and J. Hendy QC, *Reconstruction after the Crisis: A Manifesto for Collective Bargaining* (Liverpool: Institute of Employment Rights, 2013).

6 An outline of that vision is to be seen in K. D. Ewing, John Hendy and Carolyn Jones (eds), *A Manifesto for Labour Law: Towards a Comprehensive Revision of Workers' Rights* (Liverpool: Institute of Employment Rights, 2016); K. D. Ewing, John Hendy and Carolyn Jones (eds), *Rolling Out the Manifesto for Labour Law* (Liverpool: Institute of Employment Rights, 2018).

7 See Labour Party, *For the Many Not the Few: The Labour Party Manifesto 2017* (London: Labour Party, 2017), 47–51. Similar commitments are to be found in the 2019 general election manifesto.

8 'UK Suffers Second-Highest Death Rate from Coronavirus', *Financial Times*, 29 May 2020, https://www.ft.com/content/6b4c784e-c259-4ca4-9a82-648ffde71bf0. There are just under 60,000 excess deaths.

9 *Visit to the United Kingdom of Great Britain and Northern Ireland: Report of the Special Rapporteur on Extreme Poverty and Human Rights* (New York: UN General Assembly, Human Rights Council, A/HRC/41/39/Add 1, 23 April 2019), https://undocs.org/A/HRC/41/39/Add.1.

10 *Trade Union Membership, UK 1995–2019: Statistical Bulletin* (London: Department for Business, Energy and Industrial Strategy, 27 May 2020), https://assets.publishing.service.gov.uk/government/uploads/system/uploads/attachment_data/file/887740/Trade-union-membership-2019-statistical-bulletin.pdf.

11 Ibid. Note, however, that other data cited by the statistical bulletin 'shows that around 39.2% of jobs had pay set by an agreement covering multiple employees (primarily through National or industry agreements, followed by organisational agreements). In the Public Sector around 91% of jobs had pay set by such agreements [...], compared to around 21% of jobs in the Private Sector.' Even so, that is about half of the level of coverage in 1979.

12 On the ineffectiveness of this model, see Alan Bogg, *The Democratic Aspects of Trade Union Recognition* (Oxford: Hart Publishing, 2009).

13 Nicholas Watt and Heather Stewart, 'George Osborne Introduces New "Living wage" but Cuts Working-Age Benefits', *Guardian*, 8 July 2015, https://www.theguardian.com/uk-news/2015/jul/08/budget-2015-uk-gdp-other-rich-nations-george-osborne.

14 These are the recently increased rates at the time of writing (31 May 2020).

15 *Employee Earnings in the UK: 2019* (Newport, UK: Office for National Statistics, 29 October 2019), https://www.ons.gov.uk/employmentandlabourmarket/peopleinwork/earningsandworkinghours/bulletins/annualsurveyofhoursandearnings/2019#:~:text=Main%20points,the%20year%20to%20April%202019.

16 Appropriately referred to as 'if and when' contracts in Ireland. See Caroline Murphy, Jonathan Lavelle, Thomas Turner, Lorraine Ryan, Juliet McMahon, Michelle O'Sullivan, Mike O'Brien and Patrick Gunnigle, 'Zero Hours Work in Ireland', in *Zero-Hours and On-call Work in Anglo Saxon Countries*, ed. Michelle O'Sullivan, Jonathan

Lavelle, Juliet McMahon, Lorraine Ryan, Caroline Murphy, Thomas Turner and Patrick Gunnigle (Singapore: Springer, 2019), 21–40.

17 *Contracts That Do Not Guarantee a Minimum Number of Hours: April 2018* (Newport, UK: Office for National Statistics, April 2018). According to the ONS report, 'people on "zero-hours contracts" are more likely to be young, part-time, women or in full-time education when compared with other people in employment. On average, someone on a "zero-hours contract" usually works 25.2 hours a week. Just over one-quarter of people (25.3%) on a "zero-hours contract" want more hours, with most wanting them in their current job, as opposed to a different job that offers more hours. In comparison, 7.3% of other people in employment wanted more hours.'

18 *Visit to the United Kingdom of Great Britain and Northern Ireland*, 95.

19 Ibid. This is the principle of the Victorian poor law of 1834, often referred to as 'less eligibility': Maurice Bruce, *The Coming of the Welfare State*, 4th ed. (London: B.T. Batsford, 1973 reprint), 96.

20 *Critical Workers Who Can Access Schools or Educational Settings* (London: Cabinet Office, Updated 14 May 2020).

21 The Health Protection (Coronavirus, Restrictions) (England) Regulations 2020, UK Statutory Instruments 2020, No. 350, r 4 and 5.

22 Ibid., r 6(2)(f).

23 *Guidance on Social Distancing for Everyone in the United Kingdom* (London: Public Health England, Updated 30 March 2020) (now withdrawn).

24 As reported by the *Guardian* on 15 March 2020.

25 *Coronavirus (Covid-19) Related Deaths by Occupation, England and Wales: Deaths Registered Up to and Including 20 April 2020* (Newport, UK: Office for National Statistics, 11 May 2020).

26 Ibid.

27 The Personal Protective Equipment at Work Regulations 1992, UK Statutory Instrument 1992, No. 2966.

28 This was an extraordinary omission from the emergency powers used or taken by the government under the Public Health Act 1984, and the Coronavirus Act 2020 respectively, and contrasted sharply with the emergency powers taken by governments in war time.

29 The right to sick pay is unlikely to be implied and would normally require an express term in the contract. Websites advise employers on how to minimise their liabilities.

30 Social Security Contributions and Benefits Act 1992, s 157.

31 See also text accompanying note 15 above.

32 This is despite the fact that the scheme was specifically extended during the lockdown 'to provide that a person who is isolating himself from others in accordance with advice on coronavirus disease is deemed to be incapable of work': The Statutory Sick Pay (General) (Coronavirus Amendment) Regulations 2020, UK Statutory Instrument 2020, No. 287, Explanatory Note. The other major change made was the relaxation of the three waiting days in such cases. But there was no extension to those on very low incomes, and no increase in the amount payable.

33 Employment Rights Act 1996, ss 28–35.

34 *Lay-offs and Short-Time Working: Guarantee Pay*, UK Government, https://www.gov.uk/lay-offs-short-timeworking.

35 *Jobseeker's Allowance (JSA)*, UK Government, https://www.gov.uk/jobseekers-allowance.

36 Contingencies Fund Act 2020.

37 See *Protecting Workers' Jobs and Livelihoods: The Economic Response to Coronavirus* (London: Trades Union Congress, 18 March 2020), https://www.tuc.org.uk/sites/default/files/2020-03/CoronavirusReportV1.pdf.

38 Ibid.

39 The Coronavirus Act 2020 Functions of Her Majesty's Revenue and Customs (Coronavirus Job Retention Scheme) Direction.

40 HM Treasury, 'Chancellor Extends Furlough Scheme Until October', 12 May 2020, https://www.gov.uk/government/news/chancellor-extends-furlough-scheme-until-october.

41 Contingencies Fund Act 2020. On the constitutional significance of this, see K. D. Ewing, 'Covid-19: Government by Decree', *King's Law Journal* 31, no. 1 (2020): 1–24.

42 For a critique, see ibid.

43 In cases where The Information and Consultation of Employees Regulations 2004, UK Statutory Instrument 2004, No. 3426, have been invoked, consultation ought to have taken place thereunder. Mainly for hubristic reasons, however, unions generally chose not to use these procedures.

44 Hilary Osborne, '"We're Heartbroken": New Starters Trapped by Furlough Loophole', *Guardian*, 18 April 2020, https://www.theguardian.com/money/2020/apr/18/new-starters-furlough-loophole-britain-coronavirus-support-newly-hired-staff-seasonal-workers.

45 The Coronavirus Act 2020 Functions of Her Majesty's Revenue and Customs (Coronavirus Job Retention Scheme) Direction, [13.1(e)].

46 As reported by the *Guardian*, 28 May 2020.

47 'Boris Johnson's Speech in Full: "First Careful Steps" to Ease Covid-19 Lockdown', *Guardian*, 10 May 2020, https://www.theguardian.com/world/2020/may/10/boris-johnson-details-first-careful-steps-to-ease-covid-19-lockdown.

48 House of Commons Debates, 5 May 2020, col. 492: 'It has been widely reported that the Government will make a major announcement about the review of lockdown this Sunday. I consider this a matter of regret. It is important that the press is kept informed, but it is the duty of this House to hold the Government to account, not the media. Major Government announcements should be made first in the House and this is more important than ever during this time of crisis.'

49 The Health Protection (Coronavirus, Restrictions) (England) Regulations 2020, r 6(1).

50 Ibid., r 6(2)(f).

51 This specific provision appears to have been taken down and replaced by more detailed guidance relating to each of the sectors in question.

52 According to Government Guidance, *Coronavirus Outbreak FAQ's: What You Can and Can't Do*: 'The government's ambition is for all primary school children to return to school before the summer for a month if feasible', 11 May 2020, https://www.gov.uk/government/publications/coronavirus-outbreak-faqs-what-you-can-and-cant-do/coronavirus-outbreak-faqs-what-you-can-and-cant-do accessed 13 May 2020. This ambition was not fulfilled.

53 Rowena Mason, 'Grant Shapps Says He Would Not Get on a Crowded Bus or Tube', *Guardian*, 13 May 2020, https://www.theguardian.com/uk-news/2020/may/13/grant-shapps-would-not-get-on-crowed-bus-tube-coronavirus-lockdown-eased.

54 Ibid.

55 Ibid.

56 *Coronavirus Outbreak FAQ's: What You Can and Can't Do*, 11 May 2020 ed., [5.1].
57 Ibid., [4.1].
58 Ibid., [4.2].
59 UK Government, 'New Guidance Issued to Help Get Brits Safely Back to Work', 11 May 2020, https://www.gov.uk/government/news/new-guidance-launched-to-help-get-brits-safely-back-to-work.
60 Owen Bowcott, 'UK Gig Economy Workers Exposed to Virus, Union Warns', *Guardian*, 12 May 2020, https://www.theguardian.com/business/2020/may/12/uk-gig-economy-workers-exposed-to-virus-union-warns.
61 Ibid. (emphasis added).
62 Ibid.
63 *Get Brexit Done. Unleash Britain's Potential: The Conservative and Unionist Party Manifesto 2019* (London: Conservative and Unionist Party, 2019), 27.
64 *Working Safely During the Coronavirus Outbreak* (London: Health and Safety Executive, 2020), https://www.hse.gov.uk/news/assets/docs/working-safely-guide.pdf.
65 Ibid., 7.
66 The Personal Protective Equipment at Work Regulations 1992.
67 *Working Safely During Covid-19 in Factories, Plants and Warehouses: Guidance for Employers, Employees and the Self-Employed* (London: HM Government, 11 March 2020), chapter6,https://assets.publishing.service.gov.uk/media/5eb965d5d3bf7f5d3c74a2dd/working-safely-during-covid-19-factories-plants-warehouses-200910.pdf.
68 Richard Partington, 'UK Unemployment to Double and Economy to Shrink by 14%, warns Banks of England', *Guardian*, 7 May 2020, https://www.theguardian.com/business/2020/may/07/uk-economy-to-shrink-by-25-percent-and-unemployment-to-double-warns-bank-of-england-coronavirus#:~:text=4%20months%20old-,UK%20unemployment%20to%20double%20and%20economy%20to,14%25%2C%20warns%20Bank%20of%20England&text=The%20Bank%20of%20England%20has,deepest%20recession%20in%20modern%20history.
69 On the impact on civil liberties in the United Kingdom, see Ewing, 'Covid-19: Government by Decree'.
70 Ben Doherty, 'Australia-New Zealand Travel Bubble Could Be in Place by September, Expert Group Says', *Guardian*, 27 May 2020, https://www.theguardian.com/world/2020/may/27/australia-new-zealand-travel-bubble-jacinda-ardern-says-plan-will-be-presented-in-june-coronavirus.
71 The austerity driven response to the 2008 financial crisis had a devastating effect on labour law, particularly in Europe.
72 Richard Partington and Heather Stewart, 'Chancellor Extends UK Furlough Scheme Until End of October', *Guardian*, 12 May 2020, https://www.theguardian.com/business/2020/may/12/uk-furlough-scheme-extended-rishi-sunak-coronavirus.
73 On which see Derek Fraser, *The Evolution of the British Welfare State* (London: Macmillan, 1973), 45–50.
74 Larry Elliott, 'Gordon Brown Calls for Global Government to Tackle Coronavirus', *Guardian*, 26 March 2020, https://www.theguardian.com/politics/2020/mar/26/gordon-brown-calls-for-global-government-to-tackle-coronavirus.
75 Ibid.
76 Ibid.
77 On the importance of the ILO Declaration, see Alain Supiot, *The Spirit of Philadelphia: Social Justice vs. the Total Market* (London: Verso, 2012).

78 For an upbeat account by way of balance and contrast, see Frank Hendrickx, 'The European Social Pillar: A First Evaluation', *European Labour Law Journal* 9, no. 1 (2018): 3–6, 3.

79 See K. D. Ewing, 'Reflections on the ILO Centenary', in *Papers from the Symposium on the Centenary of the ILO: Democracy, Labour Law and Trade Unions*, ed. Caroline Kelly, Joo-Cheong Tham and Julian Sempill (Melbourne: University of Melbourne, December 2019).

80 The nod is simply the recall and reaffirmation of the *ILO Declaration of Philadelphia* in the preamble to the Centenary Declaration.

81 *Constitution of the International Labour Organisation*, annex 'Declaration Concerning the Aims and Purposes of the International Labour Organisation (Declaration of Philadelphia)' (1944), part III(d).

82 Ibid., part III(e).

83 *ILO Centenary Declaration for the Future of Work* (2019), part III(B)(ii).

84 Ibid., part II(A)(iv).

85 Michael R. Pompeo, *On the Centenary of the Founding of the International Labour Organisation* (Geneva: US Mission to International Organisations in Geneva, 21 June 2019)

86 Janet Williamson, *A Better Recovery: Learning the Lessons of the Corona Crisis to Create a Stronger, Fairer Economy* (London: TUC, 20 May 2020).

87 Ibid., 3.

88 Torsten Bell, Nye Cominetti and Hannah Slaughter, *A New Settlement for the Low Paid: Beyond the Minimum Wage to Dignity and Respect* (London: Resolution Foundation, June 2020), https://www.resolutionfoundation.org/app/uploads/2020/06/A-new-settlement-for-the-low-paid.pdf.

89 Ibid., 6.

90 Ibid.

91 Ibid.

92 UK Government, 'Our Plan to Rebuild: The UK Government's Covid-19 Recovery Strategy' (Command Paper No. 239, Cabinet Office, London, 2020), https://www.gov.uk/government/publications/our-plan-to-rebuild-the-uk-governments-covid-19-recovery-strategy/our-plan-to-rebuild-the-uk-governments-covid-19-recovery-strategy. There is a note in the latter about the need to address underlying social, economic or political issues. Compare the document issued earlier by the Scottish government: 'the austerity driven response to the 2008 financial crash did not work and worsened the inequality that was part of its cause; we must not repeat those mistakes. Inequality is also worsening the outcomes for those people impacted by the coronavirus': Scottish Government, *Covid-19 – A Framework for Decision-Making* (Edinburgh: Scottish Government, April 2020), 22.

93 The 'red wall' seats are the parliamentary seats mainly in the north of England that traditionally returned a Labour MP but unusually returned a Conservative MP at the general election in 2019. In the vernacular, the voters in these seats 'lent' their votes to Johnson to 'Get Brexit Done'.

94 Phillip Inman, 'Rightwing Thinktanks Call Time on Age of Austerity', *Guardian*, 16 May 2020, https://www.theguardian.com/politics/2020/may/16/thatcherite-thinktanks-back-increase-public-spending-in-lockdown. There are, however, more recent signs of the government preparing for post-pandemic austerity measures, which will undermine its commitment to 'level up'. See 'The Guardian View on Austerity: A Grotesque Failure That Must Not Be Revived', *Guardian*, 22 July 2020,

https://www.theguardian.com/commentisfree/2020/jul/22/the-guardian-view-on-austerity-a-grotesque-failure-that-must-not-be-revived.

95 Sir William Beveridge is often credited with rebuilding the post-war British welfare state, though, as Fraser points out, his plan was not as revolutionary as sometimes portrayed: Fraser, *The Evolution of the British Welfare State*. William Beveridge, *Social Insurance and Allied Services*, Cmd 6404 (1942) ('the Beveridge Report') is nevertheless of great symbolic importance. Remarkably, the Beveridge Report was an inspiration for the managing director of the International Monetary Fund, Kristalina Georgieva, who 'urged global leaders to recognise the success of the 1942 Beveridge Report, which put forward reforms to raise welfare and health standards across Britain, and was ready to be implemented when the war was over': Phillip Inman, 'Pandemic Is Challenge to Reset Global Economy Says Prince Charles', *Guardian*, 3 June 2020, https://www.theguardian.com/uk-news/2020/jun/03/pandemic-is-chance-to-reset-global-economy-says-prince-charles.

96 Nancy Fraser, Susan Neiman, Chantal Mouffe, Saskia Sassen, Jan-Werner Muller, Dani Rodrik, Thomas Piketty, Gabrial Zucman, Ha-Joon Chang et al., 'Humans Are not a Resource. Coronavirus Shows Why We Must Democratise Work', *Guardian*, 15 May 2020, https://www.theguardian.com/commentisfree/2020/may/15/humans-resources-coronavirus-democratise-work-health-lives-market.

97 Daniel Boffey, 'Brexit Talks: Britain Accuses EU of Treating UK as "Unworthy" Partner', *Guardian*, 19 May 2020, https://www.theguardian.com/politics/2020/may/19/brexit-talks-eu-wants-us-to-obey-the-rules-of-their-club-says-gove. For further discussion of international trade agreements, labour rights and democracy, see Chapter 10 by Patricia Ranald in this volume.

98 HC Treasury Committee, Oral Evidence (HC 499, 2015–16, 23 March 2016). See further Nicola Countouris and K. D. Ewing, *Brexit and Workers' Rights* (Liverpool: Institute of Employment Rights, 2020), chapter 5.

NOTES ON CONTRIBUTORS

Iain Campbell is an honorary senior fellow attached to the Centre for Employment and Labour Relations Law at the University of Melbourne. He is currently engaged in research on temporary migrant labour, precarious work and labour regulation.

Keith Ewing has been a professor of public law at King's College London since 1989, having taught previously at the universities of Edinburgh and Cambridge. He is also the president of the Institute of Employment Rights. A frequent visitor to Australia, Ewing has held visiting positions at several Australian universities, including Melbourne, Monash, Queensland, Sydney and WA.

Anthony Forsyth is a professor at RMIT University Law School. He researches on collective bargaining, trade unions, labour hire and the gig economy. He is the vice president of Australian Labour Law Association; has chaired the Victorian Inquiry into Labour Hire and Insecure Work (2015-16); and runs the Labour Law Down Under Blog. His forthcoming book is *The Future of Unions and Worker Representation: The Digital Picket Line.*

Joanna Howe is an associate professor of law at the University of Adelaide, Australia, and a consultant with Harmers Workplace Lawyers. Her recent research has involved projects on labour challenges in the horticulture sector, the experience of international students in the labour market, the regulation of unpaid work experience and barriers to employment for refugee women.

Caroline Kelly is a PhD candidate at the Melbourne Law School. She researches in labour law and administrative law. She holds an LLM with distinction from University College London and a BA/LLB (Hons) from the University of Melbourne. Kelly has worked as a sessional academic, associate at the Federal Court of Australia, as well as a researcher at the NSW Court of Appeal and solicitor. She has published in the *Australian Journal of Labour Law.*

Jeremy Moss is a professor of political philosophy at the University of New South Wales, Sydney. His main research interests are in political philosophy and applied philosophy. Current research interests include projects on climate justice and climate transitions. He has published several books including *Reassessing Egalitarianism, Climate Justice Beyond the State*, and *Climate Change and Justice.*

David Peetz is a professor of employment relations at Griffith University and a co-researcher at the Inter-university Centre for Research on Globalisation and Work in Canada. He has undertaken work for unions, employers, the International Labor Organization, the OECD and governments at state and national levels in Australia and New Zealand. He is a fellow of the Academy of Social Sciences in Australia.

Patricia Ranald is an honorary research associate in the Department of Political economy at the University of Sydney, and was formerly a senior research fellow at the University of New South Wales. She has published widely on the social impacts of trade agreements and is the convener of the Australian Fair Trade and Investment Network (AFTINET).

Julian A. Sempill teaches law and legal philosophy at Melbourne Law School. He holds a DPhil from Oxford University and a BA/LLB (Hons) from the University of Melbourne. Sempill is a legal philosopher with a particular interest in the relationships between liberalism, capitalism, power and the law. He is currently writing a book entitled *Power and the Law.*

Joo-Cheong Tham is a professor at Melbourne Law School. His research spans the fields of labour law and public law with a focus on law and democracy, and the regulation of precarious work. Tham is also the director of the Electoral Regulation Research Network; deputy director of the Migrant Workers Centre; and the director of the Centre for Public Integrity.

INDEX

www.ingramcontent.com/pod-product-compliance
Ingram Content Group UK Ltd.
Pitfield, Milton Keynes, MK11 3LW, UK
UKHW041831100926
8556IPUK00002B/111

9 781785 277801